Pierre Vésinier, J.V Weber

History of the Commune of Paris

Pierre Vésinier, J.V Weber

History of the Commune of Paris

ISBN/EAN: 9783337428693

Printed in Europe, USA, Canada, Australia, Japan

Cover: Foto ©ninafisch / pixelio.de

More available books at **www.hansebooks.com**

HISTORY

OF THE

COMMUNE OF PARIS.

BY

P. VESINIER,

EX-MEMBER AND SECRETARY OF THE COMMUNE, AND REDACTEUR EN CHEF DU
"JOURNAL OFFICIEL."

TRANSLATED FROM THE FRENCH BY J. V. WEBER.

LONDON:
CHAPMAN AND HALL, 193, PICCADILLY.
1872.

CONTENTS.

PART FIRST.

THE REVOLUTION OF MARCH 18TH.

CHAP.		PAGE
I.	CAUSES OF THE REVOLUTION	1
II.	THE EIGHTEENTH DAY OF MARCH	14
III.	THE PRINCIPLES AND IDEAS OF THE PROLETARIAT DURING THE REVOLUTION OF MARCH 18TH . . .	47
IV.	RÔLE OF THE DEPUTIES, MAYORS, AND ADJUNCTS OF PARIS	70
V.	REACTIONARY ATTEMPTS	98
VI.	CONCILIATORY ATTEMPTS OF THE MAYORS AND ADJUNCTS OF PARIS WITH THE ASSEMBLY AT VERSAILLES .	105
VII.	ELECTION OF THE COMMUNE	124

PART SECOND.

THE PARIS COMMUNE.

I.	PROCLAMATION OF THE COMMUNE	133
II.	THE BATTLE	184
III.	THE POLICY OF THE COMMUNE	225
IV.	THE INVASION OF PARIS	272
V.	THE BATTLE IN THE CENTRE OF PARIS . . .	300
VI.	THE LAST ACT	317

TRANSLATOR'S PREFACE.

The Commune of Paris, the first Government erected by the working classes, may justly be considered as the beginning in earnest of the struggle between Capital and Labour.

The power of Capital is so great, and the belief in the sacredness of private property so old and so deeply rooted in the mind of man, that their abolition does not appear to be so near at hand as some predict. Labour cannot be entirely free until most of our political and social institutions and class distinctions, together with private property, the foundation of our social condition, have passed away.

We can see no other solution of this tremendous and most perplexing question, the great question of our age. All the remedies which have been proposed up to the present time are nothing but quack palliatives, and completely powerless to reconcile the opposite class interests to each other. Indeed, their reconciliation is a downright impossibility.

Education, true, complete education — for the education of the wealthy is likewise inadequate — can alone cure the social and political malady of modern society, and prevent and supersede Revolution. But we do not—as some reformers preach—expect from those in possession of wealth and power, who fear the enlightenment of the masses as much as, if not more so than, Revolution, such an education *as would make men wise and free*, without a struggle.

How easily liberty may be taken from an ignorant multitude France has proved, and may prove again; and how insufficient a semi-education, Germany has fully demonstrated; for after having enjoyed it for more than half a century, it still lies powerless at the feet of king, emperor, and priest.

It would scarcely be right to conclude these few timid remarks without a word in reference to this History of the Commune of Paris and its author.

This History is the result of study, experience, and close observation; it is instructive to those who agree with the principles it teaches, as well as to those opposed to them. In the face of the many misstatements which have been made, the truth, told by a man of M. Vésinier's integrity and worth, should be welcome to all.

J. V. WEBER.

AUTHOR'S PREFACE.

THE History of the Commune of Paris, the events of which are still fresh in the memory of everybody, and occupy the minds of all, will, we venture to hope, prove interesting and useful.

Our position as member and secretary of the Commune, and chief editor of the *Journal Officiel*, gave us an intimate knowledge of the men and things of the Commune.

Having preserved and procured a great number of documents relating to its history, and assisted by the recollection of recent events in which we took an active part, we possessed the necessary elements for writing this book with a perfect knowledge of the case.

We hope we have accomplished this task with that conscientiousness and sincerity which should characterise every true and honest man when describing events. We have never recoiled from the assertion of what we considered to be the truth, nor from the recital of events, whatever they may have been. Good and bad acts have been equally registered. In this book we have set down with impartiality facts we have seen, words we have heard, and deeds we have assisted in accomplishing.

Since the fall of the Commune, the press in the pay of the reactionary parties has engaged in a perfect orgie of calumnies, defamations, denunciations, injuries, and outrages against both it and its defenders. To refute all these infamies was out of the question, as many volumes would be insufficient for it.

We content ourselves with proving the falsity of the principal accusations, and exhibiting the acts and objects of the Commúne in their true light, without going too deeply into the senseless and calumnious accusations of which it has been the victim.

Concerning ourselves in particular, we have suffered the most odious calumnies and the coarsest outrages, so disgusting and unjust as seldom fall to the lot of man to endure. This disgraceful press has surpassed in cynicism against us anything ever heard of to this day.

It had been our first intention to refute all these false accusations and infamous calumnies, but after mature reflection we came to the conclusion that it would be more dignified and becoming not to lower ourselves by refuting accusations so false, and coming from a source so corrupted. We considered that these prostituted journalists and chartered scribblers, who were deeper in the mire than harlots, and so degraded and vile as to act the part of spies, denunciators, and purveyors for the bagnio and the fusillade, true assistants of the Paris executioners, were not worthy of an answer, and only deserved disdain and contempt.

Those acquainted with us know that we are incapable of committing a single one of the bad actions with which those miserable secret agents of a police press reproach us. Others will have no difficulty in informing and convincing themselves of the falseness of the accusations of these calumniators branded with infamy. Our life is no mystery. For more than twenty years we have occupied ourselves with politics. Our writings and our acts are sufficiently known to guide their judgment. Let them make their choice between the calumnies of tainted journalists, objects of universal contempt, and the protestations of a man who has nothing to reproach himself with, and who defies his enemies to bring forward a single fact tarnishing his honour. If any man has cause to complain of us, and is able to prove us guilty of an unjust deed against him, let him rise in accusation.

As one of its members, we have served the Commune with all the devotion of which we were capable. We fought to the very last moment; we were as zealous and courageous as possible; and we never used any but legitimate means against our enemies.

In our votes and acts we were inspired by a sense of justice and right, which was the basis of our convictions.

Not for a single moment did we depart from the obligations of duty imposed by morality and equity; and, in the midst of terrible and tragical events, we have neither to reproach ourselves with a bad proposition nor a bad deed.

We were guilty of no violence or injustice. We never made an attempt against the liberty, the produce of the labour, or the life of a single citizen.

We fought against the aggressors of Paris, the soldiers of Versailles, but we never struck an unarmed enemy.

We did our duty to the Commune, and we have written this history with a calm conscience, without fearing the judgment of our contemporaries or posterity.

P. VÉSINIER,
Ex-member and Secretary of the Commune,
Delegate to the *Journal Officiel*.

HISTORY OF THE COMMUNE.

PART FIRST.

THE REVOLUTION OF MARCH 18TH.

CHAPTER I.

CAUSES OF THE REVOLUTION.

THE Revolution of March 18th prepared the event of the Commune, and was, as it were, its prologue. We cannot, therefore, dispense with a brief sketch of it, in order to the better understanding of the history we are writing.

With this observation let us commence.

In searching for the material causes of the agitation which produced the Revolution of March 18th, we find that the preliminaries of peace, and the entrance of the Prussians into Paris, created this mighty popular rising. There were also other less direct and less obvious political and social causes at play.

All messages and newspapers from the capital during the last days of February prove the state of popular ebullition, and ascribe it to the two causes we have pointed out. The following very remarkable extract from the correspondence of an imperial newspaper inimical to the Revolution, which cannot be suspected of any partiality, gives an exact idea of the agitation by which the population of Paris were animated, and of the causes which created it :—

"Paris, February 28th, 1871, evening.

"The agitation, after having a little diminished throughout the day, seems to gain this evening near the boulevards in the northern and eastern suburbs (Montmartre, Belleville, La Chapelle, Ménilmontant).

"There are animated groups near the boulevards, sometimes growing into important meetings. At eight o'clock there was an assembly near the Porte Saint-Denis of more than two thousand persons.

"The northern and eastern suburbs have the appearance of the day before a battle. We meet armed men, and see solidly-built barricades, well armed with cannons and mitrailleuses. These pieces belonged to the artillery park taken from the Place Wagram. A formidable barricade, raised from the English workshops in the Rue Tredaine, and armed with fifteen mitrailleuses, bars the Boulevard Ornano. The construction of two others is going on by torchlight in the Rue Doudeauville at La Chapelle, and in the Chaussée Clignancourt at Montmartre. The inhabitants of these quarters will under no condition allow the enemy to enter. The proclamation of Thiers and the order of the day of Vinoy, announcing the preliminaries of peace and the entrance of the Prussians into Paris, and recommending quietness to the population, have had very little success. The placards of General Vinoy have been torn down in such a manner that no traces of them are left. . . . Till now everything indicates defensive intentions.

"In the central quarters calm and sadness replace the feverish emotion and lively agitation of the suburbs. Here the patriotic resentment is secured and tempered by cool reason, so that the feeling of resignation seems to predominate among the groups and at the meetings on the boulevards. Rage murmured in the very bottom of the heart just as much as, or perhaps more than, at Belleville. There the most moderate dream of a terrible revenge in the future.

"The quarters on the left bank are more calm, and those to be occupied by the enemy to-morrow look like a desert."

Another correspondent says :—

"Paris, February 28th.

"In consequence of the preliminaries of peace and the approaching entry of the Prussians, great agitation reigned yesterday at Paris. The National Guard, answering to the beat to arms, is marching to the Champs Elysées, and to other positions on the ramparts, to drive back the enemy. There was no disorder. . . .

"The popular emotion is this morning very great. All the quarters to be occupied by the Prussians will be surrounded by barricades.

"Sentinels will be placed so as to prevent the foreign soldiers going beyond the zone of occupation.

"The National Guards and the regulars are very discontented at the entry of the Prussians.

"At midnight a great crowd besieged the Café des Princes, Boulevard Montmartre, composed mostly of students of the Central School.

"The troops left their barracks in the Faubourg du Temple at one o'clock, and returned to the camp.

"The barracks of Prince Eugène had also been evacuated. At half-past one the Place du Château d'Eau was covered with National Guards, shouting, 'Vive la République!'

"The 17th battalion of the National Guards has determined to go to the Place Wagram with the view of taking the two hundred cannons, so as to prevent them falling into the hands of the Prussians. The 190th took its course to the Parc de Monceaux, headed by its commander and its vivandière. Stopping before the artillery park, after a parley of ten minutes, the 190th took two cannons, only ten artillerists having made any resistance.

"The Marseillaise Club, 51, Rue de Flandre, took some cannons, which, being levelled from the court, now defend its entrance.

"The Committee of Vigilance is permanently sitting in the hall of the Marseillaise. Every evening, and the greater part of the day and night, public meetings are held by this club.

"Vigilance Committees are being organised in all quarters, as also a Committee of the National Guard.

"On the 1st of March the cannons from the Place Wagram were transported to the Place des Voges.

"The 166th battalion of the National Guard last night transported eleven mitrailleuses to the top of the Buttes Montmartre, and refused to deliver them up to the authorities.

"Belleville and Montmartre are in a state of great exaltation. In these quarters barricades bristling with cannons and mitrailleuses are constructed. General Vinoy is impotent against the population, who possess more than two hundred cannons.

"All battalions refuse to surrender their cannons."

We have quoted all these despatches and correspondence of different newspapers to show that the preliminaries of peace and the entrance of the Prussians into Paris were the first causes of the deep agitations of February 26th, the prolongation of which led to the Revolution of the 18th of March, and created the Commune.

From the foregoing citations we see that the causes we have described were the very first to incite the National Guard of the old suburbs to barricade Paris and to take the guns. Those who maintain that the insurrectionary actions after the siege of Paris were the result of a conspiracy secretly organised are either grossly deceived or utter impudent falsehoods. The enmity, defiance, and insurrectionary resistance were spontaneous.

In addition to those already stated, other causes powerfully helped to force the people into insurrection.

The National Guard and the whole population of Paris had reason to accuse the Government of the National Defence of incapacity and treason, and to attribute to it the defeat, ruin, dismemberment, and shame of the nation.

The heroic National Guard of Paris had a deep conviction that if the Government of the National Defence had utilised its courage and its loyalty, as well as the forces and all the means of action possessed by Paris and the provinces, the enemy could have been beaten and driven back.

This belief, which will be hereafter justified by history, inspired the whole nation with the deepest contempt, and even more, with the profoundest hatred, against these incapable and traitorous men, the authors of all its evils.

The spirit of reaction of the Versailles Assembly; the royalist opinion of the majority; the openly-avowed projects for monarchical restoration; its Jesuitic, ultramontane, and Catholic tendencies; its reactionary voting; its liberty-killing leanings; its defiance and hostility against the population of Paris, refusing to hold its sittings in this town, and threatening its decapitalisation; everything contributed to the alienation of Paris from Versailles, and to enlarge the abyss which had already separated the people of Paris from the Government of M. Thiers and the majority of the National Assembly.

Incontestable symptoms of this deep rupture, this incurable disaffection, were manifest from the commencement of March. On the 4th of that month delegates from different battalions of the National Guard of Paris assembled, and decided by a vote that if the National Assembly should remain at Bordeaux, or in any other town than Paris, and the royalist majority of the Assembly wished to restore the monarchy, and put a Bourbon or an Orleanist on the throne, the National Guard would proclaim the liberty, independence, and autonomy of the capital and the Paris Republic.

A few days later, through the nomination of General d'Aurelle de Paladines to the command of the National Guard, the defiance of Paris was increased, and the population was more firm in its resolve to nominate all its own officers without exception, from the corporal to the general.

General d'Aurelle issued an order of the day which did much to increase the mistrust and rage of the National Guard, and to make them insist upon nominating their own commander-in-chief. In this official document the royalist general spoke of nothing but respect "of the discipline of order, which alone was capable of bringing back prosperity."

He declared "his unswerving determination to suppress with the greatest energy everything damaging to order and calmness," &c., &c.

In fine, he added: "It is necessary for labour to repair as soon as possible the misfortunes of war."

Now, in this precarious situation, in the face of danger, ruin, and disaster to the fatherland, to speak of the resumption of labour appeared to the working man a derision and a bitter irony. He understood as well as M. d'Aurelle de Paladines that for the moment there was no hope of the resumption of labour, and he feared that the commander of the National Guard wished to disarm and send him home without means of subsistence, under the pretence of the resumption of labour.

Citizen Brette, captain of the National Guard of Belleville, expressed in an energetic manner, in a proclamation to his company, the violent indignation which had taken possession of all hearts :—

"Citizens! we have arms, we have ammunition: who dares to take them away? Those who should try will have our bullets in their hearts."

Here is another proclamation from the same general to the National Guard, which leaves no doubt as to the hostility by which M. d'Aurelle de Paladines was animated against the great majority of the Paris National Guard, who had given their vote to the members of the Central Council :—

"*To the National Guard of the Seine.*

"The Government expects from you the defence of your capital, your family, and your property.

"Some misguided men, having put themselves beyond the pale of the law, obey secret chiefs, and level the cannons rescued from the power of the Prussians against Paris.

"They resist by force the army and the National Guard.

"Will you bear this?

"Will you act like them under the eyes of the enemy, ever ready to profit by our disorder?

"Will you abandon Paris to treason?

"If you do not strike at the root of the evil the Republic will be done for, and perhaps France also.

"Their fate is in your hands.

"The Government has decided that you shall keep possession of your arms.

"Use them with the resolution of re-establishing the reign of law, and of saving the Republic from anarchy, which would be its ruin.

"Stand by your chiefs; this is the only way to prevent ruin and the domination of the foreigner.

"The Commander-in-Chief of the National Guard,

"D'AURELLE.

"The Home Minister,

"ERNEST PICARD.

"Paris, March 18th, 1871."

The personality of M. d'Aurelle de Paladines was such as to justify pretty well all the fears, antipathies, and distrust of the people.

Here is his portrait by one of his biographers:—

"D'Aurelle de Paladines lost his command at Marseilles on account of his well-known royalist opinions.

"Brutal even to cruelty, he made himself detested by his soldiers.

"As a general he left his troops isolated, without orders, at Orleans. He abandoned those who, in their heroism, pushed in advance, and the marines he left alone to defend their field-pieces. He destroyed bridges filled with soldiers, whose corpses were found buried in the ice, and he retired at the moment when the defenders of Paris stretched out their hands from the plateau of Avron.

"As a deputy, he signalised himself by calling, in 'expediency,' a Republican deputy from Alsace to order, because he demanded for his country the help of France.

"This is the man who, by common consent, sends us the legitimist, the Orleanist, and especially the clerical reaction.

"This general marches with forty thousand men of the army of the Loire to subjugate the Republican National Guard of Paris.

"Fortunately, those men of the army of the Loire, which was lost by him, are more willing to give their hands to their brethren of Paris than to play the part of pretorians to this general, who was nowhere victorious but in the court-martial."

Such was the man on whom the profound wisdom of M. Thiers bestowed the command-in-chief of the National Guard.

The following is the report of a meeting of the chiefs of battalions and mayors of Paris, convened on March 8th by the same commander of the National Guard, and describes pretty perfectly the state of mind at that period, the fears and mistrust of the National Guard, the anguish of public opinion, and the sorrow of the Parisian population:—

"Yesterday, March 8th, at one o'clock, General d'Aurelle de Paladines convoked the staff-officers of the National Guard, the chiefs of battalions of four arrondissements, composed of the Fourth Section, and the mayors of these arrondissements.

"The mayor of the First Arrondissement, that of the Louvre, the most aristocratic of Paris, showed in very warm terms that the distrust of the National Assembly, which persists in its unwillingness to sit in the capital, was an injury to the population of Paris, and especially to the National Guard.

"He implored the general to make use of his influence, so that this state of uncertainty might cease.

"Afterwards, the mayor of the Ninth Arrondissement, likewise a reactionary quarter, said he feared that through the too sudden suppression of the allowance of 1 fr. 50 c. a day, granted to the citizens of the National Guard, who to a great extent have no means and no work, grave disorders would arise in the capital.

"He spoke also on the subject of rent; and he saw in the solution of this question difficulties which the sooner they were settled the better.

"General d'Aurelle replied that these questions were under consideration, and that the reorganisation of the National Guard, as to battalions and quarters, was being actively pushed forward.

"He added that the Home Minister had already named a Commission of competent men, and that their work would be done in three or four days.

"As to rent, the general advised the landlords to be very humane towards their tenants.

"The municipality of the Eighteenth Arrondissement having been attacked by a chief of battalion, the mayor, citizen Clémenceau, said that the official news from Paris received at Bordeaux made him fear great troubles in his arrondissement, and that on his arrival in Paris he was agreeably surprised to find all quiet, even round the famous cannons of Montmartre, which had so greatly frightened the quarters of the centre.

"With respect to these cannons, Commander Barberet gave an account to his colleagues, as well as to the general, of the culpable articles of the reactionary press, which for eight days had openly incited to civil war.

"Citizen Barberet called attention to the belief among the battalions of the centre that those of the outside quarters would come to plunder them, while in the outside quarters they imagined that those of the centre were trying to take their cannons for the military authorities.

"Everywhere the call to arms is sounded; all citizens are on the alert day and night, looking for an enemy who has no existence.

"Such a state of things cannot last much longer. Commander Barberet declared that it ought to be known that if the National Guard had taken some cannons now on the rising ground of Montmartre, it was first to prevent their falling into the hands of the Prussians, and then to serve as instruments for a pretorian army, the ambitious design of a tyrant trying to make another 2nd of December.

"He affirmed that these cannons were not levelled against the citizens of Paris; that a civil war was not wanted at Montmartre nor elsewhere; and that if they were confided to the National Guard, the citizens who actually had care of them would willingly give them up to the different battalions of the Paris National Guard.

"In concluding his observations, citizen Barberet begged of General d'Aurelle to contradict officially the vile projects against the Parisians which were laid at his door by unworthy newspapers.

"The general answered with all the commonplace talk usual on such occasions. He declared himself to be an honest man, who had thirty years' good and loyal service, &c., &c.

"At last a mayor said that calmness was not perfect because the people had no confidence in the Government nor in the National Assembly, and that in order to put an end to this uneasiness of spirit, the deputies must hold their sittings at Paris, and the Government and officers publicly declare that the *Republic* was not to be called in question."

All these laments and sensible observations, these just reclamations and reasonable conclusions, gave no satisfaction, and had no success. On the contrary, the situation became worse from day to day.

CHAPTER II.

THE EIGHTEENTH DAY OF MARCH.

The National Guard, greatly shocked and filled with disgust, seeing their fatherland given up to the stranger, notwithstanding all its efforts, goodwill, and heroism; the Republic betrayed, left in the hands of its most cruel enemies; and the royalists and the reaction every day making rapid progress, resolved at least to save the Republic, since it was impossible to secure the independence of France and the integrity of its territory. Then it came to the determination of organising itself independently of the Government, and of leaning and depending on its own resources.

It was this resolution which inspired the idea of forming its provisional Central Committee. This, in fact, took place. Each company of the National Guard elected two delegates, and as each battalion had twelve companies, the number of its delegates was twenty-four. The delegates of the battalions of an arrondissement nominated the members for an Initiative Commission of their arrondissement, which was to act in concert with the Republican Central Committee.

In addition, the delegates of each arrondissement elected four members, so as to form the Central

Committee of the National Guard; and Paris having twenty arrondissements, this Committee had eighty members.

This was effected on Wednesday, March 15th, at a meeting of the delegates of two hundred and fifteen battalions of the National Guard, which took place at Vauxhall, and at which nearly five thousand delegates were present.

This organisation, at once so simple and so mighty, since it had the support and co-operation of two hundred and fifteen out of two hundred and sixty-five battalions of the National Guard, greatly facilitated its acting, according to circumstances, with a promptitude, energy, decision, and force which would easily defy any attempt of the reaction to overthrow the Republic.

The Central Committee of the National Guard and the Committee of the Republican Confederation united a few days afterwards, and adopted the following statutes :—

"*Republican Federation of the National Guard.*

"STATUTES.

"Preliminary Declaration.

"The only possible government is the Republican; it admits of no dispute.

"The National Guard has the absolute right to choose all its chiefs, and to recall them as soon as they have lost the confidence of the electors, after a preliminary inquiry so as to insure justice.

"Art. I. The Confederation of the National Guard is organised as follows. It includes:

"1. The General Assembly of delegates;
"2. The circle of battalions;
"3. The Legion Council;
"4. The Central Committee.
"Art. II. The General Assembly is formed:
"1. Of a delegate elected, without distinction of grade, by every company;
"2. Of one officer for each battalion, elected by the officers;
"3. Of each chief of battalion;
"4. These delegates, whoever they may be, are always revocable by the electors.
"Art. III. The circle of battalions is formed:
"1. Of three delegates from each company, elected without distinction as to grade;
"2. Of the officer delegated to the General Assembly;
"3. Of the chief of the battalion.
"Art. IV. The Legion Council is formed:
"1. Of two delegates from the circle of battalions, elected without any distinction;
"2. Of the chiefs of the battalions of the arrondissement.
"Art. V. The Central Committee is formed:
"1. Of two delegates from each arrondissement, elected by the Legion Council, without distinction as to grade;
"2. Of one chief of battalion for each legion, elected by his brother-officers.
"Art. VI. The delegates of the circle of battalions, the Legion Council, and the Central Committee are the defenders of the rights of the National Guard. They have to watch over the maintenance of the armament of all special and other corps of

the said Guard, and to prevent any attempt to overthrow the Republic.

"Art. VII. The meetings of the General Assembly will be held on the first Sunday of each month, urgency excepted.

"The different fractions of the Federal Constitution have to fix, by an interior regulation, the time and place of their deliberations.

"Art. VIII. To supply funds for the administration, publication, and other matters of the Central Committee, a rate is to be levied on each company, which ought to produce at least a monthly payment of 5 fr., to be made from the 1st to the 5th of each month by the delegates, into the hands of the treasurer.

"Art. IX. To each delegate, member of the General Assembly, will be given an entrance card to the meetings.

"Art. X. All the National Guards are conjointly liable for the costs; and the delegates of the Federation are placed under the immediate protection of the whole National Guard."

(*The Signatures.*)

The National Guard of Paris, inspired by events and urged on by circumstances, became in this manner completely isolated from the Versailles Government, and created for itself a free and independent organisation, raising and disposing by itself of considerable forces.

From the day of its self-constituted organisation the National Guard was the only power in Paris before which the Government of M. Thiers, elected by the rural and reactionary Assembly of Versailles, should have vanished.

The Central Committee of the National Guard was the only and veritable Government of the capital.

Events soon verified this opinion.

On the 10th of March the following proclamation to the National Guard was posted upon the walls of Paris:—

"TO THE ARMY.

"*The Delegates of the Paris National Guard.*

"Soldiers, children of the people!

"Odious reports have been spread in the provinces.

// "There are 300,000 National Guards in Paris, and troops are still being sent there, and deceived as to the spirit of the Parisian population. The very men who have organised our defeat, dismembered France, and given up our treasure, are trying to escape from the responsibility to which they are liable for creating civil war, taking you for the instruments of their meditated crime. //

"Soldier-citizens, will you obey the impious order to shed the blood of your brethren? Will you tear out your own hearts? No, you will never consent to become parricides and fratricides!

"What is it that the people of Paris demand?

"To keep their arms, to elect their chiefs, and to recall them as soon as they have lost their confidence.

"That the army should be sent home, and the heart of the soldier be restored to his family, and his arms to labour.

"Soldiers, children of the people, let us unite to save the Republic. We have had enough of evil from emperor and king. You must not tarnish your life. Orders cannot free your conscience from responsibility. In the presence of those who, for a place and a king, try to make us annihilate each other, let us embrace.

"Long live the Republic!

"Voted on the 10th of March, at Vauxhall, 1871."

(*The Signatures.*)

This call was heard and understood by the National Guard and the army; and that the Central Committee of the Republican Confederation manifested their sympathy and their devotion we shall soon see.

After the preliminaries of peace the army and Mobile Guard, with the exception of one division, numbering an effective force of 12,000 men (afterwards, with the consent of the Prussians, raised to 40,000 men by the Versailles Government), were disarmed by the Prussians. This army of reserves was mostly composed of gendarmes, the old guardians of Paris, who were joined by a few regiments of the line. These troops were, according to the conditions imposed by the enemy, specially destined to keep order in Paris.

The National Guard, as well as these 40,000 men, had the privilege of keeping their arms. One of the greatest humiliations, and the most painful punishment to which they had been exposed, was the sorrowful spectacle of the regular army giving up their arms to the enemy. With tears in their eyes, with curses and sighs of indignation, did the National Guards witness the defiling of 1,800 splendid cannons and mitrailleuses, and 200,000 chassepots from the regular army, to be given up to the Prussians, and assist at the heart-rending and no less painful spectacle of the re-entrance of our soldiers and Mobile Guards with downcast heads and without arms.

In the presence of these misfortunes and this disgrace, the National Guards, pressing their arms convulsively, resolved never to part with them, nor to forget that incapable and cowardly men were the cause of all this misery.

The National Guards had not only saved their guns, but their cannons also, the product of their own subscriptions.

A great number of those adorning and defending the ramparts were, as required by the preliminaries of peace, dismounted and thrown under their carriages; others were formed into parks. After the entrance of the Prussians all were abandoned and left without guards.

Inspired by a sentiment of preservation, and a very natural love for these arms, on which they reckoned for defence against the foreigner, the National Guards gathered with much pains the cannons so carelessly abandoned by the so-called National Defence. Having placed them on their carriages, they put the horses to, and guided them to the Buttes Montmartre, La Villette, or Batignolles, to be parked or put in batteries, watching carefully so that they should not fall into the hands of the Prussians or of the police, old sergents de ville, gendarmes, or guardians of Paris.

As we said before, these cannons mostly belonged to the National Guard, being bought with their own subscriptions. We need not, therefore, be astonished at their anxiety for their property. Alas! who would believe that this very sentiment for their preservation, so natural and so legitimate, could have served M. Thiers and his Government as a pretext to provoke civil war, and to incite the people to insurrection?

M. Ernest Picard, the Home Minister, published in the *Journal Officiel*, and posted on the walls of Paris, a proclamation in which the conduct of the National Guard was incriminated.

"Facts much to be regretted," he said, "have been consummated, which greatly menace the peace of this city. Armed National Guards, disobeying the orders of their legitimate chiefs, and yielding to an anonymous Central Committee, which can give no orders without committing a crime punishable by the law, have taken a great number of arms and war ammunition, under the pretext of keeping them from the Prussians, by whom they feared an invasion. Such acts should cease after the Prussian invasion. . . .

"Those who provoke these disorders undertake a terrible responsibility," &c.

The National Guards did not care much for this proclamation, and peaceably guarded the cannons, round which they quietly made their tour.

The greatest tranquillity prevailed in the capital, the inquisitive going to visit the artillery parks at Montmartre, La Villette, Batignolles, and the Place des Voges. These visits were very agreeable, and nobody, the Government excepted, had his mind much absorbed on account of the cannons of the National Guard, for none had a doubt as to the use the citizen soldiers would make of them.

The authorities made a few attempts to take these cannons by surprise, but they failed. Thus, for example, on March 17th the gendarmes marched to the Place Wagram, where a park of artillery of the National Guard was posted, with the intention of taking those cannons; but they were driven back by the battalion on guard. The call to arms was heard in the whole quarter of Saint-Antoine. The National Guards, being immediately on the alert, surrounded the gendarmes, and carried the cannons to the park at the Place des Voges, and thence to Montmartre.

All this was done without violence or collision, and the public tranquillity was in no way disturbed. But on March 18th great were the astonishment and consternation in Paris when, on its awaking, the population read the following threatening proclamation of M. Thiers and his Government, which was posted on every wall:—

"Inhabitants of Paris,

"We address ourselves again to you, to your reason and your patriotism, hoping to find a hearing.

"Your great city, which can only live by order, is in some quarters much troubled, and though the disaffection does not spread to others, it is sufficient to hinder the return of labour and freedom.

"Under the pretext of resisting the Prussians, who left your city some time ago, evil-intentioned men have taken possession of some quarters, erecting strongholds, mounting guard, and forcing you to do the same by order of an occult Committee, pretending to command a part of the National

Guard, setting aside the authority of General d'Aurelle (who is so worthy to be at your head), and intending to constitute a government in opposition to your legal Government elected by universal suffrage.

"These men, who have already caused you so much evil, and whom you dispersed on the 31st of October, pretend to defend you against the Prussians, who, on account of these disorders, retard their definite departure; they level cannons, which being fired would only destroy your houses, your children, and yourselves; and, lastly, instead of defending the Republic, they compromise it, for if the opinion be established in France that the Republic is the battle-field for disorder, then it is doomed: Do not believe them, but hear the truth, which we speak sincerely!

"The Government, which is instituted by the whole nation, could have taken these cannons, and destroyed these ridiculous entrenchments, which hinder nothing but trade, and given over to the hands of justice the criminals who are not afraid of transforming the war with the foreigner into a civil war; but we will give these misguided men time to separate from the seducer.

"But the time given to honest men to separate from the dishonest is taken from your peace, your well-being, and the welfare of all France. It must not be prolonged indefinitely. So long as this state of things exists, commerce will be arrested, the workshops deserted, orders suspended, you will remain without work, credit will not revive, and the money of which the Government is in want to free our country from the presence of the foreigner will not be forthcoming. In your own interest, in the interest of your city and of France, the Government has resolved to act. The guilty, who have pretended to establish a government of their own, will be given up to regular justice. The stolen cannons will be again put into the arsenals, and the Government reckons on your help to execute this act of urgent justice and reason. Let the good citizens separate from the bad; let them help the public power instead of resisting it. The return of plenty will be hastened, as well as a great service done to the Republic itself.

"Parisians, we speak to you in this manner, knowing your good sense, your prudence, and your patriotism; but after this advice you will approve of our returning to force, since not a day must be delayed in reviving order, the only condition for our entire, immediate, and unalterable welfare.

"THIERS, President of the Council, Chief of the Executive of the Republic.
"DUFAURE, Minister of Justice.
"E. PICARD, Home Minister.
"POUYER-QUERTIER, Minister of Finance.
"JULES FAVRE, Foreign Minister.
"General LE FLÔ, Minister of War.
"Admiral POTHUAU, Minister of Marine.
"JULES SIMON, Minister of Public Instruction.
"DE LARCY, Minister of Public Works.
"LAMBRECHT, Minister of Commerce.

"Paris, March 17th, 1871."

It will be easily seen that this proclamation was a challenge to the National Guard and to public opinion, a true provocation to civil war, and it was followed by the most serious consequences.

Nobody knew better than M. Thiers that the cannons claimed by him belonged rightfully to the National Guard; and if there had been any embezzlement of them, the battalions of the National Guard, which were able to show clearly that they were their property, would have had the right to reclaim them.

The Government could not be ignorant of the fact that the National Guard of Montmartre had bills posted, and articles published in the newspapers, offering the cannons to those battalions which should come to claim them as their property.

Nor could M. Thiers ignore the inoffensive manner in which they had been parked and watched over, or the peaceable intentions of their possessors. And he knew also that if his Government had possessed the patience and sagacity to wait a few days, so that the irritation brought about by the preliminaries of peace and the entrance of the Prussians might have calmed a little, the National Guards would most probably not have insisted upon watching over these cannons, but, as many had already done, would have been disposed to give them up to an artillery corps of the National Guard as soon as it was formed.

It was not difficult to find a peaceable solution as to the conflict about the cannons of La Villette, Batignolles, and Montmartre; and if M. Thiers had only been willing to do so, it is certain that, with his compliant temper, he might have terminated this misunderstanding to the satisfaction of all concerned, without any violence, and without the spilling of a single drop of blood.

But such a pacific solution did not enter into the view of the Chief of the Executive. He wanted a pretext not only for taking the cannons, but also for the disarmament of the National Guard, and especially for the dissolution of the Central Committee.

M. Thiers desired the dissolution and disarmament of the working men, in order that he might easily and securely work out his plan of monarchical restoration, with which idea he had been busy from the beginning of the war. The old minister of Louis Philippe had his plan, which he followed up with tenacity and perseverance; and the hour was approaching, as he said in his proclamation, "for having recourse to force, for order must be at once reinstated—entire, immediate, and unalterable order at any price." Now let us see how events answered the expectations of the Chief of the Government.

During the night of the 17th to the 18th of March troops of different arms marched on Montmartre with the view of taking the cannons of the National Guard.

At four o'clock in the morning the exterior boulevards were taken possession of, from Batignolles to the Rue Puebla, as also the Boulevards la Chapelle, Rochechouart, Pigalle, &c. A double cordon of sentinels was posted in the entrance of the Rue de Clignancourt.

Cannons and mitrailleuses were placed on the Boulevard de la Chapelle, levelled in the direction of La Villette and Batignolles.

Another mitrailleuse at the entrance of the Rue

Virginie menaced Montmartre; others were levelled against the entrance of the Rue Biot, facing the Rue de Clichy, and in different other thoroughfares.

Artillery and detachments of the line were posted at these mitrailleuses. At the Place de Clichy there was a station of different companies of the line, a squadron of Republican Guards, horse gendarmes, and two or three pieces of horse artillery.

All the streets from the boulevards upwards were guarded by companies of the line belonging to the 137th, 38th, 121st, 136th, 35th, 109th, and 88th regiments of the army of the Loire. On the Place de Clichy were three cannons, placed so as to thread the Avenue de Clichy and the Rue Biot. The Rues des Martyrs, Dancourt, and others were occupied by mitrailleuses.

The Paris Guard was in battle array at the Boulevard de la Villette.

In the streets leading upwards all circulation was suspended, and parks of artillery with armed forces were posted there.

Some Republican Guards (the old Municipal and Paris Guards) and detachments of ex-sergents de ville, transformed into guardians of the peace, and armed with chassepots, received orders to take the cannons under the care of a picket of the 159th battalion of the National Guard, numbering forty men all told.

The commander of the Republican Guards demanded from the National Guard the surrender of the cannons and arms, which was refused.

After exchanging a few gun-shots the National Guards retreated, and the attacking party, far superior in numbers, took the position, which was occupied by strong detachments of the 129th of the line, and by chasseurs de Vincennes, under the command of Lecomte, General of Division.

All over Montmartre the call to arms was heard during the time of taking possession of the heights by the troops, so as to assemble the National Guard, and to retake the position thus easily lost by surprise. The 166th, 129th, and 158th battalions of the National Guard, which were rapidly concentrated, in a short time surrounded the Republican Guards, the sergents de ville, and the other soldiers occupying the Buttes.

The artillery, who had yoked their horses to ten cannons, conveyed the latter to the corner of the Rue Lepic and the Rue des Abbesses, where they were stopped by a crowd of about four hundred people, mostly composed of women and young men.

A detachment of infantry, sent to the assistance and liberation of the artillery, was surrounded, circumvented, and disarmed by the crowd. The conductors of the cannons, finding themselves incapable of fulfilling their mission, imitated the example of the other soldiers by giving way to the solicitations of the people, and restoring the cannons to the National Guards, who took them at a quick pace to the mairie of Montmartre.

In a short time the greater part of the soldiers of the line, the artillery, and also some Republican Guards, imitated the example of their comrades, and fraternised with the people, turning their rifles downwards, and refusing to fire. The 88th of the line was remarkable for its Republican sentiments and its sympathy with the National Guard, fraternising the first instant. Raising butt-ends *en masse* in the air, loud cries of " Vive la ligne !" " Vive la Garde Nationale !" " Vive la République !" were uttered by the National Guard and the populace.

General Lecomte, who had four times commanded the troops to fire on the people, which they flatly refused to do, was abandoned by them, arrested, and taken as a prisoner to the Château-Rouge.

The mitrailleuses and cannons belonging to the regulars were at the same time, with good grace, given to the National Guards.

Everywhere, and particularly on the boulevards, might be seen crowds of soldiers of all arms fraternising with the National Guard, vociferating " Vive la République !" and singing the Marseillaise and the Hymne des Girondins.

At eight o'clock in the morning the victory of the people was complete.

The friendly attitude of the troops had secured the triumph of the Revolution and prevented the shedding of blood. But a few conflicts, much to be regretted, had been provoked by some of the higher officers, and seven or eight lives were lost. This was certainly a great misfortune. But we may congratulate ourselves that the insensate provocation of M. Thiers and his colleagues did not entail more serious consequences, and that on this day rivers of blood were not shed.

During the whole day many workmen, of their own free will, laboured on the fortifications of the Buttes Montmartre, digging trenches and solidifying the redoubts.

A great number of barricades were erected in the suburbs, especially at Montmartre.

Citizens, protected by a line of National Guards, erected a strong barricade at the top of the Rue des Martyrs, at the corner of the Boulevards Rochechouart and Clichy. This barricade was then armed with a cannon, levelled in such a way as to sweep the Rue des Martyrs.

The Rue Germain Pilon was likewise barricaded, and defended by a cannon. The square formed by the meeting of the Rues Lepic, des Abbesses, and des Dames was defended by an enormous barricade, furnished with four pieces of artillery, sweeping the Rue Lepic and the Place Blanche. The latter was similarly barricaded at the entrance of the Rue Blanche and the Rue de la Fontaine.

The Eleventh Arrondissement followed the example of Montmartre. The Rues Saint-Sébastien, Saint-Sabin, Sedaine, and Chemin Vert were covered with solid, well-constructed barricades of paving-stones.

At Belleville, where the insurrection had also triumphed, the Rue de Paris, between the exterior boulevard and that of Puebla, was swept by the cannons of five barricades. The side streets were likewise barricaded, as well as the Rue du Faubourg du Temple and the Rue Saint-Maur. The same was the case with most of the suburbs of Paris and the quarters of Saint-Antoine and the Bastille.

At four o'clock in the afternoon General Clément Thomas, in the dress of a citizen, was discovered on the Boulevard Rochechouart, at the corner of the Rue Marie-Antoinette, taking the plan of the barricades of the defenders of Montmartre. Arrested

as a spy by the National Guard, he was marched
off to the Château-Rouge, near General Lecomte,
who had been previously arrested. At a quarter-
past four o'clock these two generals were removed to
the Rue des Rosiers, near the Buttes Montmartre,
where a great number of National Guards, Gari-
baldians, and soldiers of the line were assembled.

The execution of the two generals, Clément
Thomas and Lecomte, is narrated with circum-
stantial details by a fellow-prisoner, Captain
Beugnot, who was an eye-witness of the dismal
scene. We shall allow him to speak, because, as
he belonged to the army of Versailles, the adversaries of the Commune will have no reason to doubt
his veracity.

The following is his narrative:—

"At nine o'olock in the morning I was made a
prisoner by the insurgents near the Boulevard
Magenta. I was on horseback, followed by an
escort of two troopers, with orders from General Le
Flô, the Minister of War, to explore the quarters
of Belleville and Montmartre, and to report on the
projected operation for taking the cannons.

"Notwithstanding the advice of numerous passers-
by, who feared for the security of an officer in
uniform proceeding towards these much-agitated
quarters, I passed by the Gare du Nord, advancing
to the heights; but, as soon as I arrived at the
junction of the Boulevard Magenta and the old
exterior boulevard, I was surrounded by a crowd of
thirty or forty armed National Guards, who emerged
from a neighbouring guard-house, and, taking
my horse by the bridle, threw it down into the

middle of the pavement. In a few minutes I was surrounded by four hundred madmen, yelling and gesticulating with their guns in a manner anything but reassuring, 'They have come to shoot us; they have come to kill our brothers! You are giving orders to the troops! Down! down with him!' My horse, taking fright at their yells, reared, and, profiting by its movements, a foot was passed beneath the saddle, and I was thrown on the ground. My two troopers had been also surrounded by the crowd, so that help was impossible. I was marched off by a line of a hundred or a hundred and fifty National Guards to the Central Committee, which they said was sitting at the Château-Rouge, an establishment for public balls, in the Rue Clignancourt. During this journey, which took about half an hour, they excited each other, and loaded me with insults and menaces.

"At length we arrived at the Château-Rouge, and after traversing the yard, I was led into the pavilion, where I should have to give a report to the said Committee as to my conduct. I had to stand before the door more than half an hour, the National Guards constantly around me growing all the more menacing because no one gave any orders.

"It was then about ten o'clock. Some proposed to leave me in the garden, while others wanted to lead me into the house before the Committee. The latter prevailed, and after a violent dispute with their comrades, I was taken to the first floor of the house. There I was shown into a room, where a captain of the 79th battalion of the National Guard received me, I admit, in a most polite manner, but without any explanation as to the authority which caused me to appear before him, or as to the right of arresting me. He contented himself by saying, in an evasive but always polite manner, that his party must have guarantees, and that we were considered as hostages. The grand word was spoken, and I was open to all possible reprisals.

"I asked the captain for his name: he said it was M. Mayer; that he was a journalist, having a son in the service, a prisoner of the Prussians, and would be always willing to mitigate the severity of my position as far as lay in his power. He told me that General Lecomte had been made prisoner by a furious crowd, that he was abandoned by his troops, and that a young captain of the 18th battalion of foot chasseurs, M. Franck, tried to follow and liberate the general up to the very last moment. I perceived, in fact, that Captain Franck, whom I had at first taken for an officer of the National Guard, was present.

"Two armed National Guards never lost sight of us, and communication with General Lecomte was impossible. In the meanwhile other prisoners taken by the insurgents arrived: M. de Poursargues, chief of battalion of the 18th regiment of foot chasseurs, under the orders of General Lecomte, who, having heard of the arrest of the general and inquiring about his fate, was arrested; also a chief of battalion of the 89th infantry; two captains of the 115th of the line, abandoned by their men at the Gare du Nord; and a captain of the 84th in private clothes, returning from his German captivity, arrested as a *mouchard* on his arrival at the railway. I remained in company with these gentlemen till half-past three. Captain Mayer, whom we much questioned about the Committee of which everybody spoke, was very kind to us, but greatly embarrassed for an answer.

"At this moment I walked to the window, and saw a movement of bad omen in the garden: National Guards formed a line with fixed bayonets. All seemed to me the announcement of a departure. It was evident that we were to leave the Château-Rouge. Indeed, Captain Mayer came to inform us that he had orders to march us to the Buttes Montmartre, where the Committee, after being sought the whole morning, was holding its sittings. I then saw that this Committee either had no existence, or that it would have nothing to do with us; and from this I came to the conclusion that we were doomed—that we were destined for another act in the tragedy of General Bréa and his aide-de-camp, cowardly assassinated on the 24th of June, 1848, at the Barrière Fontainebleau.

"We descended, and then, for the first time, I saw General Lecomte, who had been guarded in secret in a separate room: he was calm and resolute. We saluted him, and the officers of the National Guard did the same; but the men who formed the line abused us, and threatened us with a speedy end. This I was well prepared for.

"On arriving at the Buttes we were led into a small house in the Rue des Rosiers. I took notice of the name of this street. This house had a carriage entrance, a covered yard, a ground-floor, and two stories.

"We were pushed into a narrow and dark hall on the ground-floor, and an old Knight of the Legion of Honour of July, with a white beard, told us that the Committee was deciding our fate. General Lecomte demanded to see the Committee immediately, frequently repeating that we had been arrested since morning without cause and without judgment. The answer was that he would be called. Captain Mayer, our protector against the brutality of the armed men at the Château-Rouge, did not come up with us to the Rue des Rosiers. But, in his absence, we had much cause to praise Lieutenant Meyer, of the 79th battalion, who frequently made his body a rampart to us, and a young National Guard, whose name I have unfortunately forgotten, and who defended me twenty times against the attacks of the crowd.

"The Committee did not arrive. The crowd outside, tired of waiting for it and its decision, broke the window-panes, and every moment levelled a gun at us; but the officers of the National Guard, seeing the gravity of our position, and finding too late that it was gross carelessness to make us leave the Château-Rouge, and expose us to the rage of a populace who believed that each of us had killed at least ten men with his own hands in the morning,—these officers thrust back the arms that were directed against our breasts, and spoke to the crowd, who yelled, 'To death!' and did everything to gain time, promising to defend our lives with their own.

"But all this only irritated the crowd the more, who loudly and unceasingly demanded our death.

"The window-frame was broken by the efforts of those outside, and gave passage to the most furious of them. Must I say that the very first who laid their hands on the general were a corporal of the

3rd battalion of foot chasseurs, a soldier of the 88th infantry, and two Mobile Guards? One of the two last-named miserable men, striking his face with his fist, cried out, 'You once put me in prison for thirty days: it is I who will give you the first shot.' This was a horrible scene, enough to make us mad, although we were ready to sacrifice our lives. It was five o'clock, an immense clamour drowned everything else, a horrible disturbance took place in the yard, and all at once an old man, whom I did not know, was thrown into the midst of us, who evidently had only a few instants to live. Lieutenant Meyer told me that he was Clément Thomas, who had been arrested in the Rue Pigalle, while going for a walk as a spectator; that he had been recognised by National Guards, and dragged to the Buttes Montmartre to share our fate.

"At this time the rage of the National Guards knew no bounds: it was a wonder their courageous officers, who defended us with energy and desperation, were not murdered, but they foresaw their inability to protect us much longer. In vain an individual in a red shirt climbed upon a wall and adjured the crowd to elect a court-martial to judge the prisoners; in vain he told them that they were about to commit a cowardly murder, and contaminate the Republic they so much cherished. All was useless. The unexpected arrival of the unfortunate General Thomas, so much detested by these battalions of Montmartre and Belleville on account of his just severity during the siege, had ruined us all. The crowd, like unchained and furious beasts, wanted blood.

That of Clément Thomas was shed first. Notwithstanding the resistance of Lieutenant Meyer and a few other courageous citizens, who were compelled to fall back exhausted, he was grasped by the neck, while we, being constantly watched and every instant aimed at, could not move.

"The old captain of the Legion of Honour of July was one of the most ardent in inveighing against the unfortunate general, who, disappearing from our sight, was dragged a few steps aside, and killed by ten or a dozen shots, which echoed dismally in our hearts. It was not a platoon fire, but isolated, one shot after another, like that of tirailleurs.

"A few moments later, the unfortunate General Lecomte had to submit to a like fate in the same manner. It was half-past five.

"Then came our turn. We were well prepared for death, and each of us expected to commence the funeral march. But our defenders of the National Guard, after half an hour's last effort, partly succeeded in appeasing the crowd, who, enlightened after the murder of the two generals, consented to our being led back to prison at the Château-Rouge, to be once more at the disposal of the Committee.

"It was now six o'clock. We quitted this house of blood, where we had been for two mortal hours, and from which none of us expected to go forth alive. The line of National Guards who escorted us seemed to have recovered from their odious instincts of the morning. The abominable crime which had been committed lay heavily on their consciences and oppressed their hearts. Scarcely had we advanced a few steps in the descent of the Buttes when we saw running a very pale, wild-looking man dressed in black, and wearing crosswise a tricoloured scarf.

"'Where are you leading these officers?' cried he. He thought we were being marched to execution, and the misunderstanding which arose between him and our escort, by stirring up the mob once more, caused us to lose time, and very nearly proved fatal to us. On inquiring who this man was, we were informed that he was M. Clémenceau, the mayor of the Eighteenth Arrondissement, and the deputy for Paris. M. Clémenceau afterwards gave an explanation of his conduct from the tribune of the National Assembly. We can only say that he did not make his appearance during these shameful and sanguinary scenes, which he might perhaps have prevented, till six o'clock in the evening, after the murder of the two generals.

"At last we reached the Château-Rouge. At the moment of our entrance we met Captain Mayer, bearing a paper, which he said was an order of release for all the prisoners, the unfortunate generals included. He said that the many journeys he had been obliged to make to get this order from the Committee had cost him so much time that he did not arrive till after the perpetration of the crime.

"We were reinstated in the pavilion of the Château-Rouge, and, constantly watched by National Guards, were told to wait for the decision of the invisible Committee.

"Lieutenant Meyer returned at seven o'clock with an order from the Committee. This order was for me to appear immediately before the Central Committee. Was it a new sentence of death or a glimpse of hope? I was perfectly ignorant. But after the emotions of this terrible day I feared nothing, and I was conveyed to a house in the Rue de Clignancourt, near the Château-Rouge, where my fate was to be decided.

"At the *entresol* of this house two rooms had been converted into bureaux, where two men were writing; and in a very narrow place at the back I was presented to a chief of battalion of the National Guard, a M. Jaclard, who seemed much confused in his questions and ill versed in his mandate. He contented himself with listening to the recital of the events of the day, and seemed to attach great importance to my words, which he partly wrote down. At the end of this examination I was liberated; but this was a dangerous step for my security, the streets being full of National Guards and people excessively excited.

"But, thanks to the night, and especially to the presence of Lieutenant Meyer and the young National Guard of whom I have spoken before, I made my escape, and reached home safe and sound. An hour later Captain Franck left the Château-Rouge; but the other prisoners, of whom Commander Poursargues was one, did not escape before the next morning, as the National Guards in possession of them would not acknowledge the orders emanating from the bureau by which I was liberated.

"Such is a truly exact account of the 18th day of March as regards the assassination of the two generals and the deeds at Montmartre and

Château-Rouge. The officers of the National Guard, the chiefs of the movement in the morning, comprehended at noon the dreadful consequences of their acts, and, to speak the truth, did all in their power to save the two victims and the other prisoners, whose doom for two long hours seemed sealed.

"What was most to be lamented was that French soldiers were the first, at such a moment, to fire on their general, alone and disarmed; that the authorities of Montmartre, as well as that famous Committee which every instant was spoken of, did not show themselves at the Château-Rouge, nor at the house in the Rue des Rosiers; and that throughout the day they did not make a single visible effort to save even appearances.

"Signed: Captain BEUGNOT,
"Ordnance Officer of the Minister of War.

"Versailles, March 23rd, 1871."

This statement is an evident proof that the execution of Generals Clément Thomas and Lecomte was the result of popular irritation—of the exasperation of an infatuated crowd of people, accusing the former of being a spy and making plans for the erection of barricades for their massacre, and the latter of having four times given orders to fire on the people.

This document shows also that the officers and many National Guards did all in their power to save the two unfortunate generals.

Their death, therefore, can only be attributed to the exasperation of the masses, and it is notoriously unjust to lay the responsibility of it on the Central Committee.

On the same day, General Chanzy and M. Edmond Turquet, deputy of the Aisne and formerly Imperial Procureur, were arrested, and, on arriving at six o'clock in the evening in the train from Tours, placed at the disposal of the Central Committee. The same evening the Belleville and Montmartre battalions occupied the Staff Office at the Place Vendôme.

Such was the 18th day of March, which resulted in the triumph of the Central Committee of the National Guard, and prepared the advent of the Commune.

The following are the terms in which the *Journal Officiel* gave an account of this day:—

"Citizens,

"The 18th day of March, interestedly disguised in an odious manner, will be called in history the day of the people's justice!

"The fallen Government, always unskilful, sought to provoke a conflict, without having taken into account either its unpopularity or the fraternity of the different troops. The whole army, commanded by a fratricide, General Vinoy, responded to the order for the massacre of the people with the cry: 'Vive la République! Vive la Garde Nationale!' Only two men, who had made themselves unpopular by acts which to-day we call iniquitous, were smitten by the crowd in a moment of indignation.

"The Committee of the Confederation of the National Guard is doing justice to the truth by declaring itself unconnected with these two executions.

"To-day the ministries are constituted, the purified Prefecture of Police enters on its functions, the different administrations commence their work, and we invite all citizens to maintain calmness and keep perfect order.

"Citizens, you have seen the work of the federation of the National Guard under the greatest difficulties. By what we have already done, you may judge of the work we should have been able to do for the national defence, and what will be our future exertions for the salvation of the Republic.

"For the Central Committee,

"VÉSINIER, Delegate of the *Journal Officiel.*"

In addition to this, the Central Committee published the following proclamations, informing the people and the National Guard of the victory of March 18th:—

"*To the People.*

"Citizens,

"The people of Paris have thrown off the yoke which was sought to be imposed upon them.

"Calm and unmoved in their power, without fear and without provocation, they awaited the shameless fools who sought to lay hands on the Republic.

"This time our brethren of the army did not lay their hands on the holy ark of our liberty.

"Thanks to all, and may Paris and France in common lay the foundation of a Republic, joyfully welcomed, with all its consequences, the only government which will close for ever the era of invasions and civil war!

"The state of siege is raised.

"The people of Paris have been convoked in their sections to make their communal elections.

"The security of all citizens is secured by the co-operation of the National Guard.

"The Central Committee of the National Guard.

"Signed: ANT. ARNAUD, ASSY, BILLORAY, FERRAT, BABICK, ED. MOREAU, DUPONT, VARLIN, BOURSIER, MORTIER, GOUHIER, LAVALETTE, FR. JOURDE, ROUSSEAU, CH. LUILLER, HENRI FORTUNÉ, G. ARNOLD, VIARD, BLANCHET, J. GROLLARD, BARROUD, H. GERESME, FABRE, BERGERET, BOUIT.

" Hôtel-de-Ville, Paris, March 19th, 1871."

"*To the National Guards of Paris.*

"Citizens,

"You have entrusted us with organising the defence of Paris and of your rights.

"We are confident of having fulfilled this mission. Assisted by your generous courage and admirable coolness, we have overturned the Government which betrayed us.

"Our mandate has now expired, and we return it to you, having no desire to usurp the places of those whom the popular will has overthrown.

"Prepare and proceed to your communal elections in order, and give us the only recompense hoped for, the establishment of a true Republic.

"In the meantime we keep possession of the Hôtel-de-Ville in the name of the people.

"The Central Committee of the National Guard.

(*The signatures of the Central Committee.*)

"Hôtel-de-Ville, Paris, March 19th, 1871."

These two brief and simple documents need no comment. Have more modest, more moderate, and more honest victors ever been seen? The victory of the 18th of March had placed them in power, and the very next day, the 19th, they laid it down by convoking the electors in their several districts, and asking for successors.

Let any one compare the conduct of these men with that of members of the Government of the so-called National Defence, who, after perpetuating themselves for seven months, refused to dissolve when the people of Paris, after the summons of October 31st and January 21st, gave them for the third time, on March 18th, the most formal dismissal, and we may frankly ask on which side were moderation, propriety, and justice?

The following is the proclamation in which the Central Committee convoked the electors for the nomination of the members of the Commune:—

"FRENCH REPUBLIC.

"*Liberty, Equality, Fraternity.*

"The Central Committee, considering the immediate creation of a Communal administration of Paris urgent,

"Decrees:

"Art. I. That the elections of the Communal Council of Paris shall take place on Wednesday next, March 22nd.

"Art. II. That the voting shall be by ballot in each arrondissement. Each arrondissement shall nominate a councillor for every twenty thousand inhabitants, or fraction exceeding ten thousand.

"Art. III. That the balloting shall take place from eight o'clock in the morning till six in the evening, when the inspection will be immediately proceeded with.

"Art. IV. That the municipalities of twenty arrondissements shall be charged, each in its own district, with the execution of the present decree.

"A subsequent placard will announce the number of councillors to be elected in each arrondissement.

"The Central Committee of the National Guard.
(Signatures.)

"Hôtel-de-Ville, Paris, March 19th, 1871."

The members of the Central Committee of the National Guard, after having honestly and courageously accomplished their mandate, addressed the following affecting adieu to the electors of the Commune:—

"FRENCH REPUBLIC.

"*Liberty, Equality, Fraternity.*

"CENTRAL COMMITTEE.—ELECTORS OF THE COMMUNE.

"Citizens,

"Our mission has terminated: we return our places in the Hôtel-de-Ville to your newly-elected representatives, your regular mandataries.

"By the help of your patriotism and devotedness we have been able to perform the difficult task undertaken in your name. Thanks for your persevering help; solidarity is no empty phrase; the welfare of the Republic is secured.

"If our advice is of any value in your resolutions, permit your most zealous servants to make known to you, before the elections, what we expect to-day.

"Citizens,

"Do not lose sight of the fact that the men who will best serve your cause are those whom you elect from your own order, those who live your own life, and who bear in common with you the same evils.

"Mistrust the ambitious and the upstart; both only consult their own interests, and end by regarding themselves as indispensable.

"Suspect also mere talkers incapable of action, who sacrifice everything for a speech, an oratorical effect, or a witty saying.

"Shun likewise those too much favoured by fortune, since the possessor of wealth is ill disposed to look on workmen as his brethren.

"Lastly, seek out men with sincere convictions, men of the people, resolute, active, just, and of acknowledged probity. Give preference to those who do not court your votes. True worth is modest, and it is the duty of electors to know their men.

"We are convinced that if you take these observations into account you will at last inaugurate a popular Assembly, and find representatives who will never consider themselves your masters.

"The Central Committee of the National Guard."

(Signatures.)

CHAPTER III.

THE PRINCIPLES AND IDEAS OF THE PROLÉTARIAT DURING THE REVOLUTION OF MARCH 18TH.

AFTER the modest and honest conduct of the Central Committee, it was natural to expect the approval of the political world and the press. Alas! such was not to be the case. On receiving the news of the convocation of the electors, all the members of the Government and of the Assembly of Versailles uttered loud cries of usurpation, anarchy, demagogism! The newspapers protested against the conduct of the Central Council of the National Guard, which, according to their view, had no right to convoke the electors, and which in doing so usurped the sovereignty of the people. And immediately putting into practice their reactionary and Jesuitical theories, twenty-two journals published the following protest:—

"Considering the convocation of the electors as an act of national sovereignty, only to be accomplished by the power emanating from universal suffrage;

"Considering that the Committee established at the Hôtel-de-Ville has consequently no right nor quality to make such a convocation;

"The representatives of the newspapers consider the convocation fixed for the 22nd of this month as the day for election as null and void, and request the electors to take no notice of it.

"Signed:

"*Le Journal des Débats, Le Constitutionnel, L'Electeur - Libre, La Petite Presse, La Vérité, Le Figaro, Le Gaulois, Paris-journal, Le Petit-journal, Le National, L'Univers, La Cloche, La Patrie, Le Français, Le Bien-Public, Le Journal des Villes et des Campagnes, Le Journal de Paris, Le Moniteur Universel, La France-Nouvelle, La Gazette de France, La Monde.*"

This open call to disobedience and resistance against the decree of the Central Committee of the National Guard was a positive instigation to civil war, and, as such, should have been suppressed by the Committee.

This Committee was, as we have said, the product of a free election by two hundred and fifteen out of two hundred and sixty-five battalions of the National Guard, incontestably representing the great majority of the National Guard and citizens.

Under the empire of universal suffrage and the government of majorities, nobody could seriously contest its right. No body ever did better represent the sovereignty of the people of Paris than the Central Council. It had also the incontestable right to convoke the electors for the nomination of a Communal Assembly, and it was besides its strictest duty to do so. The whole argument of the reactionary press against this right and this duty was worthless.

The Central Council had not merely the right, but it had also the power at its disposal, because the army had not only refused to act against it, but had made common cause with the National Guard to serve the Central Council.

The Central Council might have severely punished the editors of the twenty-two newspapers who dared to publish this protest, as an undoubted provocation to civil war. Well, it did nothing of the kind. It preferred mansuetude and forbearance, and refrained from prosecuting this culpable press, which was accustomed to every reaction and violence. It contented itself with the publication of the following warning in the *Journal Officiel:*—

"After the incitement to civil war, the gross abuse and odious calumnies, it may be assumed that open provocation to contempt and disobedience against the government at the Hôtel-de-Ville will follow.

"Several newspapers published to-day a provocation to disobedience against the decree of the Central Committee of the National Guard, convoking the electors for the 22nd of this month, for the nomination of the Communal Assembly of Paris.

"This act, committed by the editors of the reactionary press, is an undoubted attempt against the sovereignty of the people of Paris.

"The Central Committee of the National Guard, sitting at the Hôtel-de-Ville, respects the liberty of the press, as it has already declared; that is to say, the right possessed by all citizens to control, discuss, and criticise its acts by all means of publicity. But it will exact respect for the decisions of the representatives of the sovereignty of the people of Paris, and it will not any longer permit with impunity the committal of such an offence as the incitement to disobedience against its decisions and decrees.

"A stringent suppression will be the consequence of such attempts if continued.

"P. Vésinier,
"Delegate of the *Journal Officiel.*"

The Central Committee of the National Guard published the following remarkable declaration, which we commend to our readers:—

"Republican Federation of the National Guard.

"*Organ of the Central Committee.*

"If the Central Committee of the National Guard were a government, it might easily, for the dignity of the electors, disclaim to vindicate itself. But, as its first affirmation was to declare 'that it did not pretend to' take the place of those who were overturned by the popular breath, resolving, in simple honesty, to preserve the exact limits of the mandate which had been confided to it, it is, nevertheless, a compound of personalities, having the right of defence.

"Offspring of the Republic, having for its device the grand word Fraternity, it forgives its calumniators, but desires to open the eyes of honest but ignorant men who have accepted the calumny.

"It is not occult: every document is signed by its members; and if their names are obscure, they have never eluded their great responsibility.

"It was not unknown, for it was the issue of the free expression of the suffrages of two hundred and fifteen battalions of the National Guard.

"It is no abetter of disorder, for no excesses nor reprisals have been committed by the National Guard, who honoured it with its leadership. It is strong by its sagacity and moderation.

"But, for all this, provocations have not been wanting; whilst the Government of Versailles has adopted the most shameless means for the perpetration of the foulest crime—civil war.

"It has calumniated Paris, and excited the provinces to sedition against it.

"It has armed against us our brethren of the army, who have died of cold in our streets, whilst their homes had the greatest need of them.

"It wanted to impose a general-in-chief upon us.

"It has, by nocturnal efforts, tried to take our cannons, after we had prevented the delivering of them up to the Prussians.

"It has, lastly, with the aid of its scared accomplices from Bordeaux, said to Paris, 'You are about to show yourself heroic! We fear you, and we will take away your crown, the capital!'

"What was the answer of the Central Committee to these attacks? It founded the Federation; it preached moderation; let us say, generosity. At the commencement of the armed attack it said to all, 'No aggression, and only reply at the very last extremity!'

"It has called together all intelligences and all

capacities; it has solicited the help of the officers; it has opened its doors to all comers for the sake of the Republic.

"On which side were right and justice? on which side wrong and injustice?

"This history is too short and too near us to have passed from the memory of any one. If we write on the eve of our retirement, we do so for the sake of honest men who lightly believed calumnies worthy only of those who hurled them.

"One of the greatest causes of their rage is the obscurity of our names. Alas! many names were known, well known, and their notoriety has been fatal to us.

"Shall we make known to you one of the last means they have used against us? They have refused bread to the troops who preferred to be disarmed rather than fire on the people. And yet we are called assassins by men who punished with hunger those who refused to assassinate!

"Well, we say it indignantly, the attempt to tarnish our honour by hurling sanguinary mire at us is a vile infamy. Not one death warrant has been signed by us; the National Guards have never taken part in the perpetration of a crime.

"What interest could they have in it? and what had we?

"It is as absurd as it is infamous.

"Moreover, it is almost a disgrace to defend ourselves. Our conduct plainly shows what we are. Have we solicited salary and honours? If we were unknown, and could still get the confidence of two hundred and fifteen battalions, which in fact was the case, was it not because we scorned to form ourselves into a propaganda? Notoriety is cheap: a few empty phrases or a little cowardice are sufficient, as a recent event has proved.

"The mandate with which we have been entrusted lies heavily on our hearts; we have accomplished it without hesitation, without fear; and, having now reached our goal, we say to the people, 'Take back the mandate confided to us: our duty ends where personal interests begin; do as you please. Being masters, you are free to do so. Having been obscure yesterday, we return obscure into your ranks, showing how easily we can descend, with head erect, from the Hôtel-de-Ville, with the certainty of feeling the clasp of your true and vigorous hand.'

"The members of the Central Committee:
"ANT. ARNAUD, ASSY, BILLORAY, FERRAT, BABICK, ED. MOREAU, C. DUPONT, VARLIN, BOURSIER, MORTIER, GOUHIER, LAVALETTE, FR. JOURDE, ROUSSEAU, CH. LULLIER, HENRI FORTUNÉ, G. ARNOLD, VIARD, BLANCHET, J. GROLLARD, BARROUD, H. GERESME, FABRE, BERGERET, BOUIT."

The *Journal Officiel* contained, besides, a reasonable and moderate address to the departments, stating events at the capital with as much simplicity as truth. The publication of the following document produced the greatest effect in the provinces:—

" *To the Departments.*

"The people of Paris, having given, since September 4th, an incontestable proof of their patriotism and their devotion to the Republic, after bearing with praiseworthy resignation and courage the sufferings and strife of a long and painful siege, keep pace with the present circumstances by the courage and devotedness which our country justly demands.

"By their calm, imposing, and vigorous attitude, and their Republican spirit of order, they were enabled to rally an immense majority of the National Guard, to engage the sympathy and active help of the army, to maintain public tranquillity, to prevent the effusion of blood, to reorganise the public services, and to respect international agreements and the preliminaries of peace.

"They hope that the whole press will acknowledge and verify their moderation and honesty, their courage and devotion, and that the ridiculous and odious calumnies spread in the provinces will cease.

"The enlightened and disabused departments will do justice to the people of the capital, and will comprehend that the union of the whole nation is indispensable for the common weal.

"Since the elections of 1869 and the Plébiscite, the great towns have shown that they were animated by the same Republican spirit as Paris. The new Republican authorities hope, under the present circumstances, for serious and energetic co-operation, and expect a helping hand in the work of regeneration and salvation which they undertake amidst the greatest dangers.

"The peasantry should be jealous to imitate the towns. After our disasters the whole of France has but one object in view—to secure the common welfare.

"This is a great task, worthy of the French people, and it will not fail.

"The provinces, uniting with the capital, will prove to Europe and to the whole world that France wishes to avoid all intestine division and the shedding of blood.

"The present powers are essentially provisional, and will be replaced by a Communal Council, to be elected on Wednesday next, the 22nd instant.

"Let the provinces hasten to imitate the example of the capital in organising themselves in a Republican style, and put themselves as soon as possible in relation with the capital by delegates.

"The same spirit of concord, union, and Republican love must inspire us all. Let us have one hope only—our country's welfare, and the triumph of the democratic, social, the one and indivisible Republic.

"The Delegate of the *Journal Officiel*."

The chief editor of the official organ of the Central Committee also published an article on the prolétariat and bourgeoisie, in which the *rôle* to be played by the former in the coming Revolution was explained.

We subjoin this article, with the reflections of the Bonapartist writer by whom it was reproduced. In our opinion it is interesting to read the judgment passed on the Commune by defenders of the Empire; and their estimate is all the more curious as it is addressed to the chief editor of the *Journal Officiel*, who is one of the most implacable enemies of the Empire. He fought desperately against the *coup d'Etat* of September 2nd, 1851, and was condemned in consequence to transportation. The author of the reflections on this article in the *Journal Officiel* was ignorant of this circumstance.

Here is the document in question, preceded and followed by the estimate of the imperial journalist :—

" Shall we to-day accord our attention to the infamous Government whose first care, after basely and clumsily provoking Paris, was to proclaim, through its prefects, the necessity of placing itself in safety at Versailles ?

" Others besides the defunct claim our attention at the present moment.

" Shall we accord it to those journalists who, after having applauded the 4th of September, pitilessly condemn the 18th of March, without appearing to have any idea of the direct solidarity between these two dates ?

" Other matters besides impotent venality and audacious cynicism demand our consideration at this moment.

" Shall we give our attention to those deputies of Paris who, seized with dismay at their misdeeds, disown them at Versailles, and abandon the people they have misguided, through fear of having to place themselves to-morrow between their breast and the bullets cast by order of M. Thiers ?

" Others far more than hypocrites and cowards claim it at this moment.

" It is to the victors of the Government ; to the logical opponents of a usurping Assembly ; to the instinctive lovers of justice towards a condemned press ; to the instruments, freed at last, of thirty political leaders, unmasked by their own victory, that we shall to-day give our attention," says the Bonapartist writer.

"We consider it necessary to republish the remarkable reply of the Central Committee, in the *Moniteur* of last Monday, to its accusers :—

"'The reactionary journals continue to mislead public opinion, and to distort with premeditation and dishonesty the political events of which the capital has for three days been the theatre. The grossest calumnies, the most false and outrageous accusations are published against the courageous and unselfish men who, amidst the greatest perils, assumed the heavy responsiblity of the welfare of the Republic.

"'Impartial history will surely do them the justice they deserve, and prove that the Revolution of March 18th was another step in the march of progress.

"'But yesterday obscure prolétaires, whose names will soon be spread all over the world; animated by a profound love of justice and right, and an unlimited devotion to France; inspired by these generous sentiments, and by a courage proof against everything, they have resolved to save their invaded country and their imperilled liberty. This will be their merit before their contemporaries and before posterity.

"'The prolétaires of the capital, amidst exhaustion and the treason of the governing classes, have comprehended that the hour has come for them to save the situation and to take in hand the direction of public affairs.

"'They have used their powers with a moderation and wisdom which cannot be too highly praised.

"'They have remained calm under the provocations of their enemies, and prudent in presence of the foreigner.

"'They have given proof of the greatest disinterestedness and the strictest abnegation. Scarcely come to power, they hastened to convoke the people of Paris to their *comitia*, in order to immediately nominate a Communal Municipality, into whose hands they might abdicate their authority of one day.

"'In all history there is not an instance of a provisional government more eager to lay down its mandate in the hands of those elected by universal suffrage.

"'In presence of such disinterested, honest, and democratic conduct, we ask with amazement how such an unjust, dishonest, and shameless press dares to exist, and to cast calumny, injury, and outrage on respectable citizens, whose acts are worthy of all praise and admiration.

"'Shall the friends of humanity, the defenders of right, be again defeated, and for ever be the victims of falsehood and calumny?

"'Are the workers, who produce everything and enjoy nothing, who suffer accumulated misery, the fruit of their labour and their sweat, for ever to be exposed to outrage?

"'Are they never to be allowed to work unmolested at their emancipation, without raising a concert of maledictions?

"'Will the bourgeoisie, their elder brothers, having accomplished, nearly a century ago, their emancipation, and preceded them in the track of Revolution, never comprehend that the turn for the emancipation of the prolétariat has arrived?

"'The public disasters and calamities into which its political incapacity and its moral and intellectual decrepitude have plunged France should be taken as proof that its time has passed, that the task imposed in the year '89 is accomplished, and that if not forced to give place to the workers, it at least must not hinder them accomplishing in turn their social emancipation.

"'In presence of real catastrophes, the concurrence of all is requisite for our preservation.

"'Why, in fatal blindness and with an unheard-of persistency, refuse to the prolétariat their legitimate share of emancipation?

"'Why deny them for ever the common right; why oppose with all its power and means the free development of the working classes?

"'If, since the 4th of last September, the governing class had given free scope to the aspirations and needs of the people; if it had frankly accorded to the working classes common justice and the exercise of all their liberties; if it had permitted them to develop all their faculties, to practise all their rights, and to satisfy their necessities; if it had not preferred the ruin of the nation to the certain triumph of the Republic in Europe, we should not be where we now are, and our disasters would not have come to pass.

"'The prolétariat, in spite of the permanent menacing of their rights, the absolute denial of all their legitimate aspirations, the ruin of their country, and of all their hopes, have comprehended their imperative duty and absolute right to be masters of their own destiny, and to secure their triumph by taking the power into their own hands.

"'For this reason they have replied by Revolution to the mad and criminal provocations of a blind and culpable Government who did not fear, in the presence of invasion and occupation by the foreigner, to provoke civil war.

"'The army, which had orders from the Government to march against the people, refused to turn its arms against them, and joined its brethren.

"'May the blood spilt, if ever so little, and always to be lamented, fall on the heads of the instigators of civil war, and of the people's enemies, who for more than half a century have been the authors of our intestine strifes and national ruin!

"'The march of progress, interrupted for the moment, is beginning anew, and the prolétariat, in spite of everything, will accomplish their emancipation.

"'VÉSINIER, Delegate of the *Journal Officiel.*'

"Does not this language contrast most favourably to its author with that of the men of the 4th of September, which the Government of M. Thiers used yesterday, and which the deputies of Paris would surely have given to the workmen, if they had had the courage to accept the direction of a Revolution which owed its still unknown proportions to their but too evident cowardice?

"There is a great distance between these precise declarations, these modest pretensions, these disinterested and patriotic sentiments, and the lies imposed by telegraph, the ambitious boasting, the dictatorial demands, and the egotistical sentiments of MM. Favre, Thiers, and Floquet.

"We yesterday gratuitously dishonoured the

author of this article by placing him in the same rank as these men. The lines we have reprinted compel us to declare that we were in the wrong. The delegate of the *Journal Officicl* is an honest man. MM. Thiers, Favre, and Floquet are not honest men."

The Central Committee of twenty arrondissements of Paris also published a very remarkable programme of reforms, in the form of a manifesto, to be accomplished by the Commune.

Here is this document :—

"*Manifesto of the Committee of Twenty Arrondissements.*

" By its Revolution of the 18th of March, and the spontaneous and courageous efforts of the National Guard, Paris has regained its autonomy; that is to say, the right to organise its public force, its police, and its financial administration.

"On the eve of the sanguinary and disastrous defeat suffered by France as the punishment it had to undergo for the seventy years of the Empire, and the monarchical, clerical, parliamentary, legal, and conciliatory reaction, our country again rises, revives, begins a new life, and retakes the tradition of the Communes of old and of the French Revolution. This tradition, which gave victory to France, and earned the respect and sympathy of past generations, will bring independence, wealth, peaceful glory, and brotherly love among nations in the future.

" Never was there so solemn an hour. The

Revolution which our fathers commenced and we are finishing — pursued through centuries with such an abnegation and heroism by the artisans of the middle ages, by the citizens of the *renaissance*, by the combatants of 1789, and which cost the lives of so many glorious and obscure heroes—is going on without bloodshed, by the might of the popular will, speaking supremely by depositing its votes in the urn.

"To secure the triumph of the Communal idea, which we are pursuing to its peaceable accomplishment, it is necessary to determine its general principles, and to draw up in due form the programme to be realised and defended by your mandataries.

"The Commune is the foundation of all political states, exactly as the family is the embryo of human society.

"It must have its autonomy; that is to say, self-administration and self-government, agreeing with its particular genius, traditions, and wants; preserving, in its political, moral, national, and special group, its entire liberty, its own character, and its complete sovereignty, like a citizen of a free town.

"To secure the greatest economic development, the national and territorial independence and security, association is indispensable; that is to say, a federation of all communes, constituting a united nation. It will find its organisation in the affinity of races, language, geographical situation, historical community, relations, and interests.

"The autonomy of the Commune guarantees liberty to its citizens; and the federation of all the communes increases, by the reciprocity, power, wealth, markets, and resources of each member, the profit of all.

"It was the Communal idea, pursued from the twelfth century, confirmed by morality, right, and science, which triumphed on the 18th of March, 1871.

"It implies, as a political form, the Republic, which is alone compatible with liberty and popular sovereignty.

"The most complete liberty to speak, to write, to meet, and to associate.

"Respect to the individual, and the inviolability of opinion.

"The sovereignty of universal suffrage, being for ever its own master, and constantly able to convoke and manifest itself.

"The electoral principle for every functionary and magistrate.

"The responsibility of mandataries, and consequently their permanent revocability.

"The imperative mandate, that is to say, the precise statement and limitation of the power and mission of those elected.

"As to Paris, the mandate could be determined as follows :—

"Immediate organisation of the districts according to the industrial and commercial situation of each quarter.

"Autonomy of the National Guard, formed of all electors, nominating all its chiefs and its general staff-officers, and preserving the civil and federal organisation of the Central Committee, to which the triumph of the 18th of March is due.

"Suppression of the Prefecture of Police. Surveillance of the city by the National Guard, under the direct command of the Commune.

"Suppression of the standing army, so dangerous to liberty, and so burdensome to social economy.

"Financial organisation, which will permit Paris to dispose internally and freely of its budget, subject, however, to its share of contributions towards the general expenditure for the public service, and to distribute according to the right of equity the losses and charges in proportion to services received.

"Suppression of all subsidies to creeds, theatres, and the press.

"The spread of entirely secular education, conciliating the liberty of conscience, the interests and rights of children, with the rights and liberty of the head of the family.

"The immediate opening of an inquiry to fix the responsibility on public men guilty of the disasters suffered by France; to state precisely the financial, commercial, industrial, and social situation of the city; the capital and the force at its disposal; and to furnish the means and elements for a general and amicable liquidation requisite for the paying up of arrears and the recovery of credit.

"Organisation of a Communal assurance system against all social risks, crises, and failures.

"Constant and assiduous researches to find out the best means of furnishing the producer with capital, tools, markets, and credit, so as to settle for ever the question of wages and horrible pauperism, and to prevent the return of their fatal consequences, sanguinary revenge and civil war.

"Such is the mandate which we propose, and which we demand of you, citizens, to give to those whom you elect. If they discharge it as they ought to do, with intelligence and fidelity, Paris will, by the glorious and brotherly Revolution of the 18th of March, be the freest and most fortunate of all cities—not only the capital of France, but of the world.

"It depends upon you, citizens, to complete peaceably, with the pride and calmness of sovereignty, the greatest act of our century and of all history by recording your vote, by which means your capacity, your idea, and your power will be asserted.

"In the name of the Delegation of the Committee of Twenty Arrondissements,

"PIERRE DENIS, DUPAS, LEFRANCAIS, EDOUARD ROULLIER, JULES VALLÈS."

A peep at the documents we have quoted will be sufficient to convince us that, besides the material causes, the accidents of war, and the political phenomena which gave rise to the Revolution of the 18th of March, there were others of a philosophical, economical, and social order still more grave and urgent, the solution of which would prove far more beneficial, and which, indeed, was imperatively demanded.

First, we must say that philosophical and religious teachings are no longer in harmony with the wants of our time; that the progress of human intellect, as well as the light of reason, rejects the antiquated philosophical theories, the absurd superstitions and dogmas of modern systems of religion.

Without going more deeply into this subject, and turning to economical and social matters, we say, that whether the privileged and governing classes comprehend it or not, the great question of our time is the prolétariat, the solution of which must be found and applied.

It is absolutely necessary, under pain of decadence or death, that this question should be resolutely broached. It is indispensable that the prolétariat should be transformed, and the salariat abolished. This social problem must be solved.

The present society cannot act, cannot any longer be endured, and cannot live. It must either die or be transformed. But since it cannot die, it must be transformed.

The progress of the arts and sciences, by its development, expands the horizon, the wants, and the appetites of the disinherited classes; enlightens them, and also increases the knowledge of their rights; gives them an earnest and rational conscience; and incites them, whether they will or not, to the acquisition of these rights and the satisfaction of their wants, which are indispensable to the intellectual development of the individual.

Another reason for this transformation is the growing difficulty which workmen-prolétaires experience in procuring the necessaries of life.

The equilibrium between production and consumption becomes day by day more disturbed. The difference between wages and the wants of material life is constantly increasing; that is to say, the price for work falls more and more, while the cost of maintenance is considerably augmented. The disparity between the producing and the selling price becomes greater, and misery follows in the same proportion. The workmen are unable to procure sufficient sustenance, on account of the constant decrease in their wages; they suffer, they are on the rack, in misery, and rapidly sink into pauperism.

Our society, it is sad to say, has arrived at this point, this terrible situation; but it must be stated. The misery of the workmen-prolétaires increases in direct and proportional ratio to the progress of labour, industry, arts, trades, sciences, and wealth. The latter is accumulated in the hands of a few, a scheming minority, who alone profit by it, and in this manner gain the means and power of oppression against the great majority of workmen, whose misery they unceasingly augment. A social organism which has arrived at this point, which produces such disastrous effects, growing worse from day to day, is a bad order of things, and doomed to perish, for its days are numbered.

Societies, like individuals, can only exist under certain normal conditions; when these fail, and the elements indispensable to their life are wanting, they lie at the point of death, and speedily succumb.

These are precisely the phenomena of to-day. Blind are those who do not see them, and culpable are those who, from personal interests, will not yield to evidence, but seek in empirical means for remedies which can only be found by the aid of social science.

Because the governing classes have not appreciated all this, because they closed their eyes against the light, because they stopped up their ears so as not to hear, because they persistently refused to comprehend, we have been brought to the crisis into which we are plunged to-day, and which produced the Revolution of the 18th of March.

The men in power, their satellites, associates, co-partners, accomplices, and domestics, who dare to insult, slander, and calumniate us every day in the most infamous manner, should study the causes of this evil, and seek for the natural remedies which science teaches; and surely this would be of more value than their outrage upon us. Let them read us; let them inquire into our past and present conduct, our ideas and principles, our tendencies and aims, and they will see that those whom they so readily treat as barbarians; as rude, stupid, and ignorant; as incapable and culpable; as dishonest; as the rabble; as miscreants, scoundrels, and robbers—are honest and earnest men, skilful and intelligent, who ought to be heard and studied rather than insulted.

To seek to dishonour opponents in social economy, adversaries in philosophy, and political enemies; to imprison, proscribe, and shoot them; to massacre them *en masse;* to frighten and terrify a population; to depopulate a city like Paris;—this is no solution of the vexatious social questions we propound: only to do such things rather aggravates instead of healing them.

All the mistakes, all the crimes of individuals, of parties, and of society, are deviations from natural laws, errors of the human intellect, outrages against common sense, reason, and justice; and if the governing classes are guilty thereof, grave accidents, profound commotions, catastrophes, and revolutions will be the result. The 18th of March ought, in our humble opinion, to have opened the eyes of the least clear-sighted. This tremendous social commotion should have persuaded and convinced them that the great and most difficult problem of the prolétariat demanded solution.

Alas! it was unfortunately otherwise. The terrible events which have happened since the 18th of March—the inexorable, sanguinary, and foolish reaction—have proved to us that the emigrants of Versailles, like those of Coblentz, have forgotten nothing and learnt nothing; they are deaf, blind, and pitiless.

They inexorably and fatally lead us on to the most tremendous misfortunes, the most terrible catastrophes, and into the deepest abysses. But, in spite of them, and whether it is agreeable or not, the solution they most dread, on account of their triple exploitation—religious, political, and economical—will be accomplished. The present prolétariat will be abolished in the same manner as slavery and modern bondage.

CHAPTER IV.

RÔLE OF THE DEPUTIES, MAYORS, AND ADJUNCTS OF PARIS.

Now let us see what was the part played by the mayors, adjuncts, and deputies of Paris during the events we are narrating.

On March 19th the municipal magistrates of Paris held meetings at two and six o'clock in the afternoon, in the mairies of the Third and Second Arrondissements, under the presidency of M. Tirard. These gentlemen decided, at both meetings, to send a deputation to the Government at Versailles, to obtain the revocation of the Bonapartist general, Vinoy, one of the men most compromised at the time of the *coup d'Etat* of the 2nd of December, 1851, as well as of the royalist general, D'Aurelle de Paladines, whom the Government of the Assembly at Versailles had the unlucky idea to nominate as commander-in-chief of the National Guard of the Seine.

The meeting of the mayors and adjuncts of Paris demanded, in addition, that these two superior officers should be replaced by General Billaut and Lieutenant-colonel Langlois.

The revocation of the prefect of police, Valentin, commander of gendarmes, and of the mayor of Paris,

Jules Ferry, was also demanded, and that MM. Edmond Adam and Dorian should take their places.

After many proceedings and a great number of preliminary conversations, the Government decided to give way as to the replacement of General d'Aurelle de Paladines by M. Langlois, and M. Ferry gave in his resignation as mayor of Paris.

The new commander of the National Guard then repaired to the Hôtel-de-Ville to inform the Central Council of his nomination.

He was asked by Commander Brunet, who received him, if he acknowledged the power of the Central Committee of the National Guard.

"No!" was the arrogant answer of Lieutenant-colonel Langlois.

"Then," replied citizen Brunet, "we can neither acknowledge you nor accept you as commander of the National Guard of Paris;" and M. Langlois retired.

The mayors and adjuncts of the capital, who were soon joined by the deputies, continued negotiations with the Government of Versailles, without arriving at any satisfactory solution.

The deputies of Paris, in concurrence with the mayors and adjuncts, resolved to bring the question, before the Assembly of Versailles, in order, if possible, to hasten its solution.

The following is the proclamation published in Paris, in which the electors were informed of their intentions and resolutions:—

"Citizens,

"Feeling the absolute necessity of saving Paris and the Republic, and of avoiding all cause of collision, and convinced that the best means for realising this supreme result is to give satisfaction to the legitimate wishes of the people, we have to-day resolved to induce the National Assembly to adopt two measures, which we hope will not be rejected, and which will contribute to re-establish calmness in your minds.

"These two measures are the election of all the chiefs of the National Guard, and the formation of a Municipal Council nominated by all the citizens.

"What we desire, and what, under present circumstances, is necessary for the common welfare, is order in and by liberty. 'Vive la France!' 'Vive la République!'

"Signed: LOUIS BLANC, SCHOELCHER, PEYRAT, ADAM, FLOQUET, BERNARD, LANGLOIS, LOCKROY, FARCY, BRISSON, GREPPO, MILLIÈRE."

The following is Paschal Grousset's opinion on the proclamation and the conduct of the deputies of Paris:—

"It was with no astonishment, but with veritable pain, that we read this morning, on the walls, the manifesto of the deputies and mayors of Paris.

"Certainly we do homage to the eagerness with which those elected by the people have accepted, on their personal account, the two principal points of the popular programme—the Communal election and the independence of the National Guard. We willingly acknowledge the good grace they have shown in attesting publicly, and by means of placards, their adhesion to a movement which was accomplished without their assistance.

"To those who know the littleness and the miseries of politics, this sacrifice—for it is a veritable sacrifice—has its value: it would be unjust not to appreciate it.

"But making these reservations, where are we, in what a degree of political decadence is France, if those elected by Paris believe themselves bound to subordinate the programme of the 18th of March to the approbation of the Assembly of Versailles?

"What! citizen Louis Blanc, citizen Lockroy, citizen Greppo, and citizen Millière, do you seriously think that the people of Paris are in want of the authorisation of the worthy peasants to lay the foundation of their municipal liberty?

"What! do you think that such an authorisation could be of any value whatever?

"Seriously, we cannot believe it.

"The right of Paris not to submit any longer to the oppression of the provinces—not to allow the spirit to be stifled by matter, or science obscured by stupidity—is too evident not to be seen by every one, and especially by the representatives of Paris.

"In point of fact, of what value at the present moment can be the opinion of a rural Assembly, which has not even one bayonet remaining in its small towns, against a population of three hundred thousand men armed to the very teeth, united in one idea, and masters of the position? As far as facts are concerned, we say, it must be patent in itself, and cannot be judged in two ways.

"What, then, can be the reason for this proposition, which the deputies of Paris persist in dragging before the Assembly at Versailles?

"Is it a fine project to give an appearance of 'legality' to the act of taking possession of their sovereignty by the people of Paris?

"Are they of opinion that this politeness will touch the hearts of the provincials, and settle the act of union which they think necessary between Paris and the provinces?

"If this be the case, poor policy, like all parliamentary policy, and as little as possible adapted to the spirit of the present Revolution!

"Go on, we have no need to take these mittens! The departments as well know that they cannot do without Paris, as Paris knows that it can do very well without them.

"And if it were otherwise, what would they do? We have power, which they have not. We have right, which they cannot contest, because they were the first to repudiate us, and to put us under the ban of the nation.

"The present situation is stronger than the reasoning of the whole world.

"We wish to organise ourselves and govern ourselves. We have the power to do this. We have the will. We are going to do it.

"The departments have only to bow down their heads; and it is already too much to condescend to give them this advice."

In order to afford a still more exact idea of the negotiations commenced by the deputies of Paris, we will give an impartial *résumé* of the discussions on this subject in the Assembly of Versailles.

In the sitting of March 20th M. Clémenceau laid a proposition before the Assembly relative to the municipality of Paris in these terms:—

"Under the grave circumstances through which we are passing, I lay this bill, signed by different members of this Assembly, on the table:—

"Art. I. To proceed as speedily as possible with the municipal elections of Paris.

"Art. II. The Municipal Council of Paris shall be composed of eighty members.

"Art. III. The Council shall nominate its president, who shall have the same powers as the mayor of Paris.

"Art. IV. There shall be incompatibility between the functions of the mayor and adjuncts of the different arrondissements and those of the Municipal Council.

"Signed: LOUIS BLANC, LANGLOIS, LOCKROY, MARTIN-BERNARD, TIRARD, CLÉMENCEAU."

The depositor of the bill added, "We demand urgency."

"*The President.*—But since bureaux meetings are to be held, urgency cannot be demanded.

"*M. Clémenceau.*—We did not come to provoke a debate, and it is on this account that we do not wish to develop our reasons for urgency. ('Speak, speak.')

"There is at the present moment no other power in Paris but that of the municipalities. The Government has left its post. (Protestations from the Government benches.)

"The post of the Government was where danger lay. It is certain, then, that in Paris no other power exists but the authority of the municipalities.

"*M. Picard.*—That authority is disputed.

"*M. Clémenceau.*—All the more reason to demand urgency; but, as I have already twice said, there is no other authority in Paris.

"*The President.*—You have no right to say that there is no authority in France.

"*M. Clémenceau.*—I did not say so. I should not be here if I did not recognise the supreme power of this Assembly. If you wish to get out of this fearful situation, organise a municipal authority in Paris at once, so that all those who desire order may draw around that authority.

"That authority can only emanate from the vote of Paris. You will find no other point of support which you could offer to all who are willing to return to legality.

"*M. Picard.*—If a municipality were the only question, I should not contradict the honourable member who has just spoken. But in the face of an insurrection which does not recognise certain municipalities, and to-morrow will not recognise any, is it possible to make true, that is to say, free elections? No. We demand that the Chamber shall pronounce itself against urgency.

"*M. Tirard.*—We do not contest this point. Yes, it is indispensable that the elections should be free. But believe me, we only demand urgency because we feel its absolute necessity. We have done all in our power; we have for two days faced the greatest danger.

"*M. Thiers.*—And so have we.

"*M. Tirard.*—But Paris has been abandoned by the Government.

"*M. Thiers.*—No!

"*M. Picard.*—The ministers have been expelled by force.

"*M. Tirard.*—I will only prove one fact; we blame nobody. . . .

"I return to the question. We met at our mairies, without power to intervene even in trifles. I was yesterday with two of my colleagues at the Home Office. The National Guard came to take possession of it, and we had to retire. In a word, we remained in our mairies, and only to-night has the Home Minister sent us power to act in an administrative sense. We received delegates from the Hôtel-de-Ville, to whom we declared that we were the only persons elected by universal suffrage, and that we would not allow our mandate to be endangered.

"Amongst the causes which have placed us in this situation, some have strongly impressed all minds. At first astonishment was expressed that the National Guard did not respond to the call of the Government. The law on bills of exchange had a little to do with it. Besides, Paris has no municipal administration. I guarantee the end of the civil war as soon as the honest men of Paris are appealed to by placards inviting them to elect mandataries.

"*M. Picard.*—But the electors have already been convoked.

"*M. Tirard.*—To the objection of the Home Minister I reply that there are placards inviting them to the elections on the 22nd. We have declared that we will oppose them. And you tell us that we make common cause with the rioters! Be assured that the population will be with us if you only do what we ask of you.

"*M. Picard.*—The Chamber has heard the explanations of some members. What difference is there between them and us? A shade. In the present circumstances we must not be stopped by shades. It appears to me that the proposition for urgency should not be rejected by the Chamber. Besides, several of our colleagues know that we have for some time been disposed to propose a bill for the municipal elections. . . .

" Urgency was then put to the vote and adopted."

In the sitting of March 21st a member of the Assembly again spoke on the subject of the municipal elections in the following terms :—

"We have this morning examined the question of the Municipal Council of Paris. This question affects the elections for the whole of France. The Assembly should at the present moment know how to accept its mandate. Time presses on you to decide that the commissioners named by the bureaux shall at once commence. Ought we to remain here all night?

"While we are here doing nothing, the insurgents are at work. Activity is wanted. We cannot call this being active, retiring at two o'clock when the whole day is before us.

* * * * *

"*M. Clémenceau.*—I have already declared that we recognise no other authority than yours, and that I only demand the re-establishment of this authority in Paris. This may be attained either by force or by peace. I believe that we can accomplish it by peace.

"We have said that we wish to intervene between Paris and the Central Committee. But in order to intervene, a basis is requisite. This basis is the municipal election. If we make these elections, the struggle will be a peaceable one. You will re-establish calmness in Paris without shedding a drop of blood. (Loud cries on the Right.) But you cannot make the siege of Paris! The chiefs of battalions are there, but their men do not obey them. Believe me, there is only one means of saving order, and that is the municipal elections of Paris; but let us make haste.

"*M. Langlois.*—I am of the same opinion as M. Clémenceau. But I wish the Assembly to declare, since the elections to be made to-morrow will be void, that the municipal elections shall take place soon. Give from this day to Paris the common right of municipal elections—that is the practical solution. By this means you will diminish the number of those who vote under the compulsion of the Central Committee. Do this, I implore you.

"*M. Brisson.*—We all acknowledge that the proposition of citizen Langlois is of extreme urgency. But we declare that this municipal assembly will have no right over France. If the report of the Commission on the elections cannot be got ready in time, let the Assembly place Paris under the common right by a law made by an order of the day.

* * * * * *

"*The President.*—It is deplorable that all the bureaux have not nominated commissioners. Here is the order of the day laid on my bureau:—

"'Considering that a free Government has replaced the arbitrary Government which has fallen;

"'The National Assembly decrees:

"'The city of Paris shall return to its common right respecting its municipal administration.'

"*M. Thiers.*—It is true this question is of enormous importance; we comprehend the interest which it exercises. Will you say to Paris that it shall be treated like the rest of France? Yes. But France cannot bear the yoke of Paris, know that. (Applause on the Right.)

"The common right cannot be accepted as it has been explained. Under the last *régime* Paris was not represented; it was governed by a Commission nominated by the prefect of the Seine. If you mean by common right that Paris shall be governed by its representatives, I am of your opinion.

"But if you say that Paris shall be governed by three hundred thousand men, no! We must contrive measures so as to organise a system agreeable to Paris before voting a law.

"If Paris requires this guarantee that it shall have a Municipal Council like all other towns, we will give it; but if Paris will be the slave of sections, we love Paris too well to do so. Give us a few days, and before long Paris shall govern itself. We ask only for time to vote a law.

"*M. Louis Blanc.*—We join with all our heart in the words of the Chief of the Executive power. But in order to give all good citizens a centre around which to rally, we must hasten to grant Paris a Municipal Council.

"*On the Right.*—Yes, yes!

"*M. Louis Blanc.*—Let the Assembly declare it immediately.

"*M. Clémenceau.*—I thank the Chief of the Executive for his declaration; but he demands time, and time is just the thing that we cannot spare. It is true that we cannot make a law in a hurry. But could we not proceed with the municipal elections, and vote the law afterwards?

"*On the Right.*—Come then, nonsense!

"*M. Clémenceau.*—If I spoke in that manner, gentlemen of the Commission, I did so because I did not wish to give my country up to civil war. You are afraid, it seems to me, of appearing to make common cause with the riot.

"But if the government of the Hôtel-de-Ville is obeyed, the elections will be made to-morrow in Paris.

"I free myself from all responsibility for the misfortunes that may follow. If you do not pass this law speedily, we shall go down into the abyss —know this.

"*On the Right.*—Close, close!

"*A Member.*—Has Paris regular electoral lists? ('Yes,' on the Left.) We shall allow Paris to come under the common law as soon as it returns to itself.

"*Admiral Saisset.*—I was called to the chief command of the National Guard of the Seine, and immediately wrote to the mayors that if they would assist me with their authority I could draw around my flag all good citizens.

"After this I wrote to a commune to send me two battalions in order to take the Elysée and the Home Office; but they would not come. There was danger in delay. Requisitions were made at one's own house. Citizens were arrested. General Allain was made prisoner, and kept as a hostage; and, as I have been assured, his wife also.

"I was told in Paris that after having been abandoned by the Assembly (murmurs), nobody knew whom to follow. I found three hundred men at my disposal; but these were not enough to master the situation. Yes, the position is terrible; the insurrection is capable of anything. I speak as a man who knows the state of affairs. Listen to me: give every facility to Paris for making the municipal elections. Let the elections take place the day after to-morrow. (Uproar.)

"For two days have I been in the midst of all this, and blush to have been obliged to be there. I am ready to fight against the insurgents, but we must remember that five hundred thousand women and innocent children are there.

"*M. Tolain.*—After these explanations it appears to me that all your delusions ought to vanish. If you desire to avoid civil war, give to the deputies and mayors of Paris the means of acting. You must bow down if you wish to save Paris and the Republic. ('Oh, oh! the Republic!')

"I do not argue whether, justly or unjustly, the insurrection is in the wrong. Yes, if I believed the insurrection to be just, I should be at the Hôtel-de-Ville.

"I have done all I could to re-establish order in Paris—I who am not, as you know, a declared partisan of order. (Uproar.) My name is not precisely identical with conservative opinions, but for all that, it does not prevent me wishing for order in the hearts and in the streets. If you would save the population of Paris, that population which for six months has suffered so much misery, and which at this moment is so sad, allow us to carry the news to Paris that in a few days it can hold its municipal elections.

"One member thinks the proposition out of place. (' Oh, oh!')

"*M. Thiers.*—Paris complains of not being represented like other towns of France. It is right. But we only ask it to recognise the absolute impossibility, at this hour, of gratifying its wishes. We must combine a system; we will do so as soon as possible. How can you make so important a law in twenty-four hours? Do you believe that the men in possession of Paris, who have killed Thomas, the soul of the Republic. . . . .

"*M. Jules Favre.*—Outlaw of December! It was the Bonapartists who killed him.

"*M. Thiers.* — Who have taken Chanzy as a hostage—for if we make a mistake, it is he who is responsible—do you believe that these men will listen to you—you, Lockroy; you, Clémenceau? And if you are not Republicans, who then is? We have heard that Admiral Saisset had an ovation on the boulevards; we nominate him General-in-Chief.

"*Admiral Saisset.*—I have been condemned to death.

"*M. Thiers.*—Let us clear up the situation. What have we done in Paris? You have been told that the cannons would be given up. I was not of that opinion. I consented to wait. After this you said to us, 'What! you support the spectacle of a hundred cannons levelled at Paris, menacing affairs, and keeping the Prussians on the soil of France!'

"We agree with you (to the Left), you said to us, 'They will be given up to you.' But they were not surrendered. I resolved to take them, and I prefer being beaten rather than to refuse to fight. If we have been beaten, it is because of the confusion. The troops were surrounded by women and children, and did not fire.

"In the year 1848, the Government, dear to me, fell for the same reason. On that occasion I at once raised the troops out of that chaos; I sent them to the other side of the Seine; and there they made the law and the national sovereignty respected. General d'Aurelle certainly demanded ten thousand National Guards to fight by the side of the active army; but they made no appearance. As Paris did not wish to save itself, we have resolved to save France and you.

"It is on account of this Revolution that we have saved the army, and found for our meetings a place protected by the faithful army and the whole of France. (Bravos.)

"We know that Paris has saved the honour of France, but we must not sacrifice its right.

"Paris did not help us to deliver it from the insurgents. Paris has given us the right to prefer France to itself. But, for all that, we shall come to the aid of Paris as soon as we can. (Murmurs on the Left.)

"No, I defy your ability to make a law which will be accepted by these men. If assassination could not open the eyes of Paris, a bill never will.

"*M. Tolain.*—We protested on the same day against assassinations; we told them so.

"*M. Thiers.*—Yes, Paris shall be represented; we shall make a law—perhaps not after our own ideas, but we shall make it hopelessly—so that these men may have no further excuse for their blindness. They are not to be disarmed by reason. The firm attitude of this Assembly and of France will alone disarm them. In an instant they will find themselves isolated, and then we hope that Paris will save itself; but the offer of three hundred men to Admiral Saisset seems to prove that they are little disposed to do so.

"We do not wish to attack Paris. Let it open its arms to us, and we shall do the same. Paris has rights; we shall not refuse them recognition. But let there be no illusions; for if the law be made, I defy you to put it in execution.

"*M. Clémenceau.*—The Chief of the Executive has explained to you how he was led to become the principal cause of the events which have taken place. (General rumours.)

"*M. Jules Favre.*—That is an act of accusation.

"*M. Clémenceau.*—I believe that the Government has made mistakes; but those mistakes are nothing compared with the crimes committed. ('Ah, ah!')

"The mayors had promised to do all in their power towards a peaceable solution. I told the Home Minister that had it not been for the removal of the National Assembly to Versailles and the suppression of the five journals, all would have been ended ten days ago.

"The Chief of the Executive power said to us, 'You will never satisfy these men with your law;

but I do not care to satisfy them. I wish to give a support to the men of order in Paris. They are in the majority. Without this you will be obliged to use force; you will have to bear all the responsibility of your acts.'

"*M. Jules Favre.*—Just now the President of the Council said, 'Let Paris give a sign, and we shall be with it.' We have never ceased to be with it. But time presses; the evil must be crushed by energetic acts. The citizens of Paris bear the shameful yoke with trembling. Some journals have set a noble example. Under the knife of the assassins they have published the following protest.

"(He read the protest of the journals and the signatures.)

"You see that the press of Paris has almost unanimously protested against the culpable attempt of which Paris is the victim. And concerning the question we are debating, I say, Yes, Paris shall have its representation. We have, in concert with the Home Minister, prepared a bill with this view. If the only question was to give to Paris the liberty of election, the majority of this Assembly would before now have accorded to Paris the rights we are debating. But these questions are not the same as those which are debated in Paris.

"There are some fatal doctrines which in philosophy are called individualism, and in politics materialism: the Republic above universal suffrage. With that Paris may be made to believe that it can have its own individuality, that it can live upon its autonomy; and it is sad, after so many centuries, to find ourselves facing a sedition which might be compared to the fable of the members and the stomach.

"How then! Would Paris separate itself from the provinces, the 'rurals,' as they call them? How could Paris stand this political and social error after that siege which it has sustained with so much heroism? It should have comprehended that separation from the provinces would be its death. A free Commune is direct servitude.

"It appeared to me that during such an extraordinary movement it was not unreasonable to point out the error which has led simple-minded men astray. How is it that we should hesitate to take energetic steps for destroying such an opprobrium? (Bravos on the Right.)

"Is not this situation of Paris that of civil war? Requisitions have commenced. We shall see that the mistake of those who did not understand taking up arms for their defence caused the whole of society to give way. If the Government quitted Paris, it did so to save the army. But let the *émeute* thoroughly understand that though the Government is now at Versailles, it hopes to return.

"The *émeute*, doubting whether we have the right to suppress it, appeals to a foreign army. How can we give security for our solvency after such shocks? They came to ask if we would not continue to negotiate with the Prussians. (Laughter.)

"You must not laugh over such serious things, and, in my opinion, men who seek to ruin you deserve no pity. To give you an idea of their morality, I will read the following article from their official journal.

"(M. Jules Favre read the article in the *Officiel*

relative to the assassination of Generals Lecomte and Clément Thomas, accompanying it with some commentaries.)

"However, what have we done?

"The Prussians wanted to disarm the National Guard. With considerable efforts we saved their arms. Let France know that, come what may, we shall be with her.

"*Admiral Saisset.*—Well, call on the provinces, and let us march to Paris.

"*M. Tolain.*—We are not paid with words; we want a vote.

"*M. Tirard.*—I come from Paris. All the mayors are assembled at the mairie of the Second Arrondissement. A great number of mairies are occupied by the real mayors. (Murmurs.) We are in front of men from the Hôtel-de-Ville; we keep them at bay. I pass my days at the mairie. I am going to return after the sitting. I know better than any one what is passing in Paris.

"I tell you, in all sincerity, that Paris may be saved by measures of preservation. It is a measure of preservation which we have proposed. The measure was announced, and the result was immediately felt. I called the chiefs of battalions together, and said to them, 'This must come to an end,' and they signed the proclamation which is placarded at this very hour in my arrondissement.

"I am not in the secret of the means at the disposal of the minister, but a great portion of the battalions of the National Guard are armed with chassepots. There are red trousers in the ranks of the insurgent National Guards. I do not believe you to be strong enough. (Uproar.)

"One word in conclusion. One thing in the speech of the Foreign Minister has greatly impressed me—the division sought to be created between Paris and the provinces. Well, facts are transpiring in Paris which I have no wish to make known. ('Speak, speak!' 'No, no!') I announce to you that our work is going on well: do not prevent us following it up. . . . .

"*On the Right.*—And Chanzy?

"Chanzy! We have been looking out for him.

"If you will adopt our project, tranquillity will return. In three days we shall be masters of the Hôtel-de-Ville. If we return to Paris this evening with empty hands, I do not know what may happen. I leave you to say.

"*M. Thiers.*—The graver the circumstances, the longer the discussions. I thank M. Tirard for his courage under these difficult circumstances.

"Let it be well understood that we do not intend to march upon Paris; we expect that Paris will come to reason. We will grant Paris its rights, with one single restriction : we shall take measures to prevent such infamies in the future.

"*The President.*—I have received several voted orders of the day.

"MM. Picard and Jules Favre declare that the Government accepts the orders of the day without distinction.

"A member having demanded the order of the day, pure and simple, M. Favre replied that the adoption of this proposition would be regarded as hostile to the Government.

"The following order of the day is adopted :—

"'The National Assembly, in concert with the

Executive, declaring that the municipal administration of Paris and the departments shall be constructed upon the principle of elected councils, passes to the order of the day.'"

After this vote, which afforded no guarantee to the population of Paris, because it neither named the time, nor by whom, nor how the Municipal Councils were to be elected, the deputies of the Left, and the mayors and adjuncts of Paris, published the following protest against the elections of the Communal Council, to be held on the next day, March 22nd:—

"Citizens,

"Your wishes have been laid before the National Assembly: the Assembly has satisfied them by a unanimous vote, guaranteeing the municipal elections in Paris and in all the communes of France.

"Pending these elections, which are *the only legal and regular ones, and conformable to true Republican principles*, it is the duty of good citizens to pay no attention to a call addressed to them without title or authority.

"We, your municipal representatives and deputies, declare that we shall keep entirely aloof from the elections announced for to-morrow, and protest against their *illegality*.

"Citizens, let us unite to respect the law, and the country and the Republic will be saved.

"Vive la France! Vive la République!"

(*Signatures.*)

We see, by this proclamation, that the mayors,

adjuncts, and deputies of Paris denied the electors of the capital the right of proceeding with the elections of the Communal Assembly without the sanction of the majority at Versailles.

This protest of the municipal magistrates and deputies, which had no foundation in equity, was productive, in a moral sense, of the most fatal consequences.

The secession of the magistrates and deputies from the Central Committee of the National Guard on so grave a question as the communal elections was fatal not only to the cause of the Commune, but also to that of the Republic.

If on March 21st, three days after the triumph of the Revolution of the 18th, the adjuncts, mayors, and deputies of Paris had united themselves with the cause of the Revolution, recognised by the electors of the 22nd, it would have been victorious in public opinion, and the Assembly of Versailles and the Government of M. Thiers would have been powerless any longer to oppose its definite triumph. But unfortunately such was not the case. The deputies of the Left, the mayors, and the adjuncts, in supporting the Assembly of Versailles, gave a fatal blow to the Revolution and the triumph of the Communal cause, and created civil war, massacres, and transportations. The representatives and magistrates may justly be considered as responsible for the bloodshed and the reaction which followed.

If one day the Republic succumbs, they may with justice accuse themselves of having been the principal authors of its ruin.

The difficulties and opposition which the deputies,

mayors, and adjuncts of Paris put in the way of the communal elections, which were to have been held on March 22nd, compelled the Central Committee of the National Guard to adjourn them till the following Sunday, the 26th.

The subjoined proclamation of March 22nd, placarded on the walls of Paris, will give an exact idea of the arbitrary and reactionary spirit of the mayors and adjuncts of Paris, and will leave no doubt on the minds of our readers :—

"FRENCH REPUBLIC.

"*Liberty, Equality, Fraternity.*

"The assembly of the mayors and adjuncts of Paris, by virtue of the powers conferred upon it;

"In the name of universal suffrage, of which it is the issue, and the principles of which it intends to make respected;

"Pending the promulgation of the law which will confer the right of election on the National Guard of Paris;

"Urgency considered, nominates provisionally:

"Admiral Saisset, representative of the Seine, superior commander of the National Guard of Paris;

"Colonel Langlois, representative of the Seine, staff-general-in-chief;

"Colonel Schoelcher, representative of the Seine, commander-in-chief of the artillery of the National Guard.

"The mayors and adjuncts of Paris."

(*The Signatures.*)

The people of Paris, on reading this proclamation, asked with surprise how long it was since the municipal magistrates, mayors, and adjuncts elected for the administration of the mairies had received the mandate to nominate to military commands of the first order, and where they had borrowed the right to usurp the sovereignty of the people, and to take away their imprescriptible right to elect the chiefs of the National Guard, from the corporal to the general-in-chief.

This pretension of the municipal magistrates, so ridiculous, presumptuous, and arbitrary, after the people's Revolution of the 18th of March to acquire the selfsame right to nominate the commanders-in-chief of the National Guard and the Communal Assembly, did much towards inspiring the profoundest contempt and raising the general indignation.

In consequence of this step, the mayors, adjuncts, and representatives of Paris were estimated at their just value; that is to say, as reactionary allies of Versailles, and enemies of the people, their rights, and their political and social emancipation.

Admiral Saisset, who had exclaimed, in the Assembly of Versailles, "Let us at once march on Paris!" anxiously strove to mitigate the bad effect which his nomination had produced.

With this object he published the following proclamation:—

"Dear Fellow-Citizens,

"I hasten to inform you that, in common with the deputies of the Seine and the mayors of Paris, we have obtained from the Government of the

National Assembly the complete recognition of your municipal franchise, and your right to elect all officers of the National Guard, the commander-in-chief included; a modification of the law concerning bills of exchange; and a bill in favour of all occupiers paying not more than 1,200 francs rent.

"Till you have either confirmed my nomination or I am replaced, I shall keep at my post, in order to insure the execution of the laws of conciliation which we had the good fortune to obtain, and through them to contribute to the consolidation of the Republic.

"Signed : SAISSET.

"Paris, March 24th, 1871."

To find a more cunningly lying proclamation would be a rather hard problem.

It is sufficient to read the debates on the subject of the elections of the Communal Council to see that the Assembly of Versailles never expressed its willingness to accord "the complete recognition of the municipal franchise, and the right to elect all the officers of the National Guard, including the commander-in-chief," &c.

It was more for the sake of form, and under the express reserves of M. Thiers and his colleagues, that the Assembly of Versailles voted an order of the day declaring that "the municipal administration of Paris and of the departments shall be constituted on the principle of *elected councils*," without saying by whom or how these councils should be elected, or what were to be their attributes and their rights. This vote bound the Assembly to absolutely nothing, and was no more than juggling hypocrisy.

The project of a municipal law, which was subsequently voted, was an indubitable proof of the reactionary spirit of the Assembly as to election and other matters.

The following are its principal articles :—

" Art. I. The municipal elections shall be held in the whole of France ; the powers conferred by the electors shall not extend beyond three years.

" Art. II. The municipal commissions shall give up their functions, &c.

" Art. III. The law of July 3rd, 1849, for the choice of mayors, is provisionally reinstituted.

" Art. IV. Of the twenty arrondissements of Paris each shall nominate three members to the Municipal Council, elected from eligible dwellers in the arrondissement in which their business is carried on, and who are of at least *three years' standing*.

" Art. VIII. To each department of the twenty arrondissements there shall be one mayor and three adjuncts, selected by the *Chief of the Executive power*. . . .

" Art. IX. The prefect of the Seine and the prefect of the police shall assist at the sittings of the Municipal Council, with the right of discussion.

" Art. X. The Municipal Council *can only be convoked by the prefect of the Seine*. . . .

" Art. XII. Every year a special meeting shall be held for the presentation and discussion of the budget. This sitting must not last more than a month.

"Art. XIII. The Municipal Council shall vote the budget, and deliberate on objects of municipal administration only," &c.

The whole economy of this law is contained in these reactionary provisions:—The Municipal Council of three members, selected from those who have dwelt three years in the arrondissement, convoked and assembled under the superintendence of the mayor and the prefect of police, and the control of the Government, which has the right of dissolving it. It has no other right but that of voting on the budget which is presented to it: it is a voting machine for the Government. And by its side are the twenty mayors and ninety adjuncts nominated by the Government. This municipal law is a bitter irony, a mystification, an outrage on the population of Paris, which it puts under tutelage, and whose rights it confiscates.

As to the nomination of the commander-in-chief of the National Guard, the staff general-in-chief, the commander-in-chief of artillery, and the chiefs of legions, not even a word was spoken during the discussions of the Assembly.

Admiral Saisset was not ignorant of the opinion of the Government and Assembly of Versailles upon this subject. He well knew that the Chief of the Executive power, the ministers, and the whole Assembly, without exception, comprising amongst it himself, Admiral Saisset, MM. Schoelcher, Louis Blanc, Langlois, and all the deputies of the Left, were positively opposed to the nomination of the superior officers of the National Guard by the latter.

Was not the nomination of Commanders Saisset, Langlois, and Schoelcher, by the mayors and adjuncts of Paris, to such high functions the most absolute negation of the rights of the National Guard?

After that, and after having accepted the benefits of this illegal nomination, was Admiral Saisset a fit man for the promise to respect the rights of the National Guard?

Nobody could have had the least doubt as to the secret aim pursued by the mayors, adjuncts, and deputies of Paris attached to the Assembly at Versailles. All they wanted was to stifle the Revolution of March 18th in its cradle.

CHAPTER V.

REACTIONARY ATTEMPTS.

ADMIRAL SAISSET tried, by means of a second conciliatory proclamation and a feigned respect for the Republic, to rally around him the National Guards of the party of *order*, in the hope of destroying the Central Council of the National Guard, and restoring the power of the tottering Government of Versailles.

The following is this second document:—

"Paris, March 25th.

"By the consent of the elected mayors I enter to-day upon the functions of commander-in-chief of the National Guard. I have no other title to the honour of commanding you than the wish to share in your heroic resistance in defending the forts and the positions under my command against the enemy. I hope, by persuasion and good advice, to effect the reconciliation of all Republicans; but I am firmly resolved to lay down my life for the *defence of order*, and to exact respect for person and property, as my only son has given his in the defence of his country. Rally around me! Give me your confidence, and the Republic will be saved.

"My device is, Honour and Country!"

What Admiral Saisset, as well as all the Versailles men, desired was to rally around his name, and those of MM. Schoelcher and Langlois, all the friends of order and all honest and moderate Republicans, so as to form a mighty reactionary nucleus, capable of neutralising the power of the Central Council of the National Guard, until a favourable opportunity presented itself of destroying it altogether.

The debates of the Assembly of Versailles superabundantly prove the intention of the mayors, adjuncts, and deputies of Paris.

All the reactionary journals made no secret of it, and openly confessed it, saying, "Admiral Saisset, commander-in-chief of the National Guard, M. Langlois, and M. Schoelcher, are occupied in concentrating the battalions which do not recognise the authority of the Commune.

"Admiral Saisset is at this moment at the head of twenty thousand well-armed men, composed of zouaves, marines, mobiles, pupils of the Polytechnic School, and a battalion formed entirely from the army. The National Guards, *friends of order*, will receive their pay every day at the Bourse.

"Admiral Saisset hopes, by this means, to get a greater number of followers.

"Admiral Saisset has received cannons and ammunition by the Northern Railway.

"Cannons and mitrailleuses were brought into Paris in flour bags, and transported by the National Guards, the friends of order, at ten o'clock this morning, to the Place de la Bourse.

"A great number of the Mobile Guards unite

with the friends of order. The chassepots taken from the National Guard will be given to them. A battalion will be formed for the special defence of the Bourse. Many zouaves have placed themselves under the orders of the legitimate authorities.

"The Bourse is guarded by the 8th, 11th, and 228th battalions.

"An artillery corps, armed with mitrailleuses, has rallied round the cause of order, and taken the Grand-Hôtel, where Admiral Saisset has established his head-quarters.

"Battalions of order occupy the Marché Saint-Honoré, the Palais-Royal, the Rue Montmartre, the Grand-Hôtel, and the Saint-Lazare Station.

"The attitude of the Sixteenth Arrondissement is firm.

"The 32nd battalion of Montmartre has refused to obey the Central Committee, &c., &c. . . . . ."

But the National Guards of the reactionary quarters, enrolled under the flag of order by MM. Saisset, Langlois, Schoelcher, the mayors, and adjuncts, soon had occasion to act openly against their brethren who were devoted to the socialist-democratic Republic, the Revolution of the 18th of March, and the Central Committee.

The following extracts from an official report prove this in the most incontestable manner:—

"The friends of order, determining, on March 22nd, to commence the fight and bloodshed, and to provoke civil war, organised numerous meetings and demonstrations, so as, if possible, to attempt a surprise in the name of order.

"At half-past one, the manifestation, which since

noon had been massing on the Place du Nouvel Opéra, began the engagement in the Rue de la Paix. The National Guard recognised in the first ranks, amongst a much-excited group, MM. Heckeren, De Coetlogon, and H. de Pène, old friends of the Empire, violently brandishing a flag without any inscription. Arrived at the top of the Rue Neuve Saint-Augustin, the mob surrounded two detached sentinels of the National Guard, and disarmed and maltreated them. They were only saved by flight, till, without guns and with torn garments, they found refuge at the Place Vendôme.

"The National Guards, seizing their arms, immediately marched in battle array to the top of the Rue Neuve des Petits-Champs.

"If broken, the first line was ordered to raise butt-ends in the air, and to fall behind the third; the second to act in the same way; and the third only was to cross bayonets, but was recommended not to fire.

"The first rank of the crowd, numbering from about eight hundred to a thousand persons, soon found themselves face to face with the National Guards. The character of the manifestation quickly assumed a distinct form. From the ranks of the so-called men of order arose the cries, 'Down with the assassins!' 'Down with the Central Committee of the National Guard!' The Republican National Guards were subjected to the rudest insults. They were called 'Assassins! brigands! cowards!'

"Some enraged men seized the muskets of some National Guards and the sword of an officer. The cries increased. The demonstration was transformed into a riot. A revolver was fired by one of this band of furious savages, styling themselves *defenders of order*, which wounded citizen Majournal, staff-lieutenant, and member of the Central Committee, in the thigh.

"General Bergeret, who commanded the place, immediately hurried up to the first line, and summoned the rioters to retire.

"Ten summonses were made, and the beat of the drums lasted for more than five minutes, as prescribed by law. The defenders of order replied by cries, insults, and shots. Two National Guards fell badly wounded. Still their comrades hesitated to fire on the rioters, and discharged their guns in the air.

"The reactionary insurgents, growing bold, fell upon their too-indulgent adversaries, and attempted to disarm them and break their lines.

"But at last the Republican National Guards lost their patience and forbearance, and, forced either to defend themselves or be slaughtered, used their arms. With the first salvo at the insurgents they dispersed in all directions, and escaped.

"General Bergeret immediately ordered the discontinuance of the firing. All the officers united their efforts to those of the general, and precipitated themselves in front of their men to prevent bloodshed.

"In the meantime some shots still resounded from the pretended defenders of order, concealed and lying in ambush in houses, cowardly assassinating some National Guards who had left off firing at them and their accomplices."

Two defenders of order, in the truest sense of the

word, citizens Wahlin and François, belonging to the 7th and 215th battalions of the Republicans, were killed; and nine, namely, citizens Majournal, Cochet, Miche, Antelot, Legat, Reyer, Pingamot, Train, and Laborde, badly wounded.

The pretended men of order, who were guilty of this bloodshed, likewise had some killed and wounded. The first who was deadly wounded and carried to the ambulance was Vicomte de Molinet, who, in the first rank of the insurgents, was struck in the head from behind. He fell at the corner of the Rue de la Paix and the Rue Neuve des Petits-Champs, near the Place Vendôme. Vicomte de Molinet must have been killed by the insurgents; for if he had been struck in flight his body would have fallen in the direction of the Nouvel Grand Opéra. A poniard fixed to his girdle by a little chain was found upon him.

A great number of revolvers and sword-sticks belonging to the rioters were collected in the Rue de la Paix, and carried to the staff-office of the place.

Dr. Ramlow, surgeon-major of the Toulouse camp, residing at 32, Rue de la Victoire, and Drs. Nolé, Pannard, Dolle, Trélat, and Leclerc, came to give their help to the wounded, and signed the *procès-verbaux*.

The property found on the rioters was put under seal, and deposited at the staff-office.

It is to the coolness and firmness of General Bergeret, who knew how to curb the just indignation of the National Guards, that we are indebted for the prevention of greater misfortunes.

The American General Sheridan witnessed these

sad events from a window in the Rue de la Paix, and testified that the first shots were fired by men of the manifestation, falsely calling themselves the friends of order.

On the next day, March 23rd, whilst a certain number of National Guards, partisans of the Central Committee, were peaceably crossing the Rue de Valois, drawing two waggons filled with muskets, the men of order, far superior in numbers and without warning, surrounded and fired shots at them, wounding three, taking twenty-two prisoners, disarming fifty, and carrying off the two waggons laden with arms. This culpable aggression caused great panic in the quarter; the shops were immediately shut up, and the streets deserted.

As on the 18th of March and always, so on the 22nd and 23rd the pretended defenders of order were the aggressors: it was they who were the first to provoke civil war and shed blood.

CHAPTER VI.

CONCILIATORY ATTEMPTS OF THE MAYORS AND ADJUNCTS OF PARIS WITH THE ASSEMBLY AT VERSAILLES.

THE violent aggressions, attempts at insurrection, and rash enterprise at the Place Vendôme, far from being beneficial to the party of order, only served to show its cruelty, weakness, and powerlessness. The rioters were dispersed, and obliged to take to ignominious flight. The deputies, mayors, and adjuncts of Paris saw, with the greatest anxiety, their authority disappear, while every day the influence and power of the Central Committee of the National Guard increased. Above all, they dreaded the approaching elections of the Communal Council. To avert the danger by means of a Municipal Council with fixed powers, created by a vote of the Assembly, the municipal magistrates of the capital proceeded to Versailles, and used all their power and influence to induce the deputies to resolve to convoke the electors of Paris without delay, in order to nominate the Municipal Council, and to hinder the communal elections.

We give the following extract of the sitting of the Assembly on March 23rd, which will thoroughly enlighten our readers concerning the spirit by which the mayors and adjuncts of Paris were animated, and which, at the same time, will clearly prove the sort of reception the Paris magistrates met with from the majority of the Assembly :—

"*M. Arnaud* (of the Ariége).—In view of the gravity of circumstances, all my brother-magistrates came from Paris to Versailles with the object of putting themselves in communication with the National Assembly. They knew that, according to the general rule of the house, members only were allowed to enter its hall; but they believed that an exception would be made in their favour. (Protests on the Right.)

"Be assured that a brother-deputy will be charged with this communication, so that all thought of disorder may be dismissed. The Assembly will decide as it thinks proper and convenient.

"I was charged with this communication. I have conscientiously made it. Since some of the mayors of Paris are likewise deputies, one of them will read from the tribune the proposed communication. I may observe, however, that as all of them came in a body as delegates charged with this communication . . . .

"*On the Right.*—Delegated by whom? (Clamour.)

"*Some voices.*—Is it by authority?

"*M. Floquet.*—You desire, then, the continuance of the civil war?

"*M. Arnaud* (of the Ariége).—In speaking of the delegation, I do not think there is any necessity to give an explanation, since we only acknowledge the power issuing from universal suffrage. If it had been a question of convenience, we could have easily settled it.

"But what I have to state is, that we all came here to make known the results of our common efforts, and I may add that we hope to be triumphant. We desire to be strengthened by the opinion and co-operation of the Assembly.

"I leave it in the hands of the President to choose the best means of conciliating everybody.

"I ask at least that a tribune may be granted to my brother-magistrates of Paris.

"*The President.*—There is nothing more simple than to conciliate the rights, prerogatives, and interests of the Assembly, which ought never to be sacrificed, with the regard we owe to the mayors of Paris.

"M. Arnaud (of the Ariége) has said that the mayors of Paris had to make a communication to this Assembly. Among them are found several of our colleagues. As the mayors have no idea of alternately occupying the tribune, it will be sufficient that one of them, being our colleague, should be the organ of their communication.

"As far as regards the deference due to the mayors of Paris, it is easy to give them satisfaction. A tribune shall be placed at their disposal; and I may as well add that the questors have already taken steps in the matter.

"*M. Baze.*—I have put the most conspicuous places at the disposal of the mayors. (A laugh.)

"It was six o'clock. Fourteen members of the Paris municipality entered a tribune of the first class. Each mayor and adjunct wore a scarf across his shoulder. They remained standing. On their entry into the hall, the Assembly rose and applauded loudly. The Left uttered [loud cries of 'Vive la France!' and 'Vive la République!' On the Right they only cried 'Vive la France!'

"The mayors answered with, 'Vive la France! Vive la République!'

"Scarcely were these cries uttered by the Parisian municipality when fifty or sixty members of the extreme Right, pointing to the mayors, vociferated, 'Order, order! The Assembly is not respected! Clear the tribune! They have no right to stand up in this manner! They are on a level with the public!' These exclamations of the extreme Right, seconded by another part of the Right, were intermixed with protestations from the Left in favour of the mayors.

"At this moment the tumult was so great that it was impossible to understand the divers exclamations crossing and recrossing from Right to Left.

"About thirty deputies of the extreme Right put on their hats, although the President remained uncovered in his arm-chair, and had neither announced the suspension nor the breaking up of the sitting.

"Loud cries were heard on the Left, 'Hats off! Respect your President! Respect yourselves! Uncover!'

"*M. Floquet*, addressing the Right.—You insult Paris!

"*A voice on the Right.*—And you insult France!

"Far from becoming appeased, the agitation grew stronger instead of weaker. The deputies of the Left kept their seats. A great number of the

Right, on the contrary, left their places and prepared to go away.

"The President, unable to control this profound emotion, announced that the sitting was closed, that the meetings in the bureaux would immediately take place, and that another sitting would be held in the evening.

"The sitting closed at half-past six."

By this more than malignant reception the unfortunate municipal magistrates of the capital perceived the spirit of hostility, intolerance, animosity, and hatred with which the royalist majority of the Assembly at Versailles were animated against the capital. If they had failed to gain an insight into it before, it wanted but the experience of that day to convince them that this refractory and inexorable majority desired no accommodation with the Parisian population, whom it regarded with the greatest horror. The spirit and ideas of the National Guard of Paris were to them an abomination, only worthy of being covered with their wrath and foul anathemas, and then exterminated, in order that the Republic might be thoroughly overthrown, and the monarchy, their dream and ideal, restored.

As had been already agreed upon, the sitting of the Assembly was resumed at ten o'clock at night. The mayors of Paris were no longer there. The tribune was reserved for them, but it remained empty. They had set out again for the capital.

The President tried with all his might to mitigate the bad effect which the thoughtless insult of the deputies of the Right produced on public opinion, and especially on the minds of the municipal magistrates of Paris.

"The incident which closed our last sitting," said he, "revealed an emotion which appears to me to be the result of a deplorable misunderstanding.

"The President of this Assembly regrets that it should have led to the closing of its sitting during the reception of the mayors of Paris, who gave such laudable examples of courage, and of devotedness to liberty and order."

But this parliamentary holy water failed to efface the disastrous impression caused by the outrageous insult on the mayors of Paris. After the affront to which they had been subjected, they should have renounced, at least for the present, every species of conciliation between the right of the Versailles Assembly and the Parisian population. But such was not the case. Before leaving Versailles they instructed their brother-magistrate, M. Arnaud, to communicate to the Assembly the petition of the Parisian electors.

This deputy acquitted himself of his charge in the following terms :—

"*M. Arnaud.*—In the name of the magistrates of Paris, I come to lay a communication of the greatest importance before the Assembly.

"Paris is on the eve not only of an insurrection, but of a most horrible civil war. Under such circumstances the mayors of Paris think that measures should be promptly taken.

"We consider the resolutions we propose to you to be calculated to prevent greater bloodshed.

"We are convinced that the re-establishment of order and the welfare of the Republic demand the following measures :—

"'1. The Assembly shall in future put itself in more direct and intimate communication with the municipalities of Paris.

"'2. That the mayors shall be authorised to take measures according to circumstances.

"'3. That the elections of the National Guard shall be held before the 28th of this month.

"'4. That the elections of the Municipal Council shall, if possible, take place before the 3rd of April. That the domicile clause shall be reduced to six months, and the mayors and adjuncts be eligible for election.'

"This communication," continued M. Arnaud, "was drawn up before the departure of the mayors of Paris, and nothing has since been altered. The event alluded to by the President had no influence whatever on the terms of our communication. Allow me to make a fresh appeal for conciliation. There was some misunderstanding.

"*A voice.*—That was all.

"*M. Arnaud.*—Nothing of this sad incident should remain either on one side or the other. (Prolonged applause.)

"*The President.*—This proposition can only emanate from a member of the Assembly. I invite M. Arnaud to sign it.

"M. Arnaud having complied with the request of the President, a resolution of urgency was unanimously adopted."

Before the close of the sitting the Assembly

decided on holding a public meeting at ten o'clock in the evening.

After numerous negotiations and difficulties the Commission nominated for this object decided on making its report on the proposition of M. Arnaud. M. de Peyramont expressed himself on this subject as follows:—

" Gentlemen, we understand the restlessness of the Assembly: it is very legitimate; but your Commission demands permission to affirm that not a single minute was lost in fulfilling the mission confided to it.

"It was nominated at two o'clock. During the course of our sitting it constituted itself, and immediately began its deliberations. It has heard the mayors of Paris, or at least one of them. It has listened to them with the sentiment which their attitude under the present circumstances commands.

" After having heard the mayors, it felt the necessity of hearing the President of the Executive also. It desired to know his opinion on the said proposition, the importance of which assuredly demanded it, as well as on the state of affairs in Paris.

" Your Commission has this instant come from the President of the Council. It received his words with the religious attention due to them, and, after mature reflection, it is unanimously convinced that the proposition of the honourable M. Arnaud would, under present circumstances, only involve a discussion fraught with danger, and without the least advantage. (Assent from several benches.)

"An imprudent word would cause great bloodshed, and in this situation, which it thoroughly appreciates, your Commission has unanimously charged me to point out to you the dangers of such a discussion; and it adjures the honourable member, my brother-magistrate, to withdraw his proposition. (Exclamation on the Left.)

"He has presented it under the influence of the noblest sentiments, in a spirit of pacification; but the end which he proposes would be far more surely attained by withdrawing it than by yielding it up to our debates. ('Very good, very good.')

"*M. Ducuing.*—I demand to speak.

"*Some members.*—Let the authors of the proposition speak.

"M. Arnaud conversed with some of his brother-magistrates under the tribune.

"*The President.*—The authors of the proposition should lay their heads together, and give us their resolutions to-morrow. ('Yes, yes.' 'No, no.')

"*M. Clémenceau.*—Oh no, it is impossible!

"*The President.*—If the authors of the proposition are agreed now, they might let us know their decision.

"*Many voices.*—To-morrow, to-morrow.

"M. Tirard ascended the tribune, and descended a moment afterwards in consequence of the agitation.

"M. Arnaud immediately occupied his place.

"*M. Arnaud.*—Gentlemen, I cannot understand the impatience of the Assembly. There is no doubt about the gravity of the circumstances. Events hurry on, not hourly, but momentarily. We have news from Paris. Well, we have just been told that a single word in the discussion might have the effect of a spark falling into inflammable matter, and become a sufficient provocation to make blood flow in streams. (Interruption.)

"It is necessary, then, that I, and those of my colleagues who have signed the proposition, should at least be allowed a hearing. ('Yes, yes.') There is joint liability between us.

"Consequently, whatever may be the impatience of the Assembly. . . .

"*Some members.*—It is not impatient.

"*M. Arnaud.*—You must understand that an act made in haste would be unpardonable. The circumstances are so grave that this very evening we should know what ought to be done. Let us, then, understand each other. ('Yes, yes.' 'To-morrow.')

"*M. Paris.*—I demand that the sitting shall be suspended for a quarter of an hour, in order to give the authors of the proposition time to agree upon this question. ('No, no.' 'Yes, yes.' Confusion.)

"M. Thiers, Chief of the Executive power, ascended the tribune, and silence was restored.

"*The President.*—The Chief of the Executive power wishes to speak.

"*M. Thiers.*—I beseech all the members of this Assembly, of whatever opinion they may be, to ponder well their words and their acts.

"In the presence of such immense events every one here has a grave responsibility. Return to yourselves; stifle your passions; think only of the public interest; and, if you do this, you will undoubtedly arrive at a right solution. ('Very good, very good.')

"As to us who are members of the Government, were a debate to take place, we should have nothing to fear from publicity. It is not on our account, then, that I now demand of you to keep silence, but for the sake of our country. Great events may result from explanations in a public sitting. It is possible that a single thoughtless word, spoken without bad intention, may cause torrents of blood to flow.

"Well, allow me to speak frankly. In the midst of great events we feel an inward agitation which can only find satisfaction in discussion. This is the temptation to be resisted. (Approbation.) I adjure you, if you are a truly political Assembly, to vote for the proposal of the Commission, and not to ask for explanations which, at the present moment, would be so very dangerous. ('You are right.' 'Very good.')

"I say again that if a discussion should take place, to the misfortune of our country, you would find out that we had no interest in remaining silent. (Commotion. 'To-morrow, to-morrow!')

"*The President.*—Under no condition can this discussion take place. The deliberation cannot be opened, since no report has been made by the Commission. The president of the Commission has contented himself with adjuring one of the authors of the proposition to withdraw it. He has not yet received an answer: the situation is still the same. Before the report of the Commission discussion is impossible. ('That is just.' 'Very good.')"

M. Thiers well knew that he told a falsehood in

order to frighten the Assembly when he declared that a single word, though without any evil intention, might cause "torrents of blood to flow," and that he grossly exaggerated imaginary dangers which had no existence at that moment.

M. Thiers also knew but too well that the men of the Central Committee did everything in their power to prevent civil war and bloodshed. He had a convincing proof of this in the prudent, moderate, and conciliatory manner in which they acted against the reactionary party of the National Guard of the First and Second Arrondissements, who occupied the mairies of the Louvre, the Grand-Hôtel, the Banque, the Bourse, &c. The more than moderate repression of the culpable act of aggression against the National Guards, partisans of the Central Committee, by the friends of order, near the Place Vendôme, on the 22nd of March, proved in the most striking manner the spirit of moderation and humanity by which the former were animated.

The leaders of the National Guard had, since the 18th of March, such considerable forces at their disposal that it would have been a very easy matter to silence the opposition of their adversaries.

Out of two hundred and sixty-five battalions, which composed the entire strength of the National Guard, two hundred and fifteen belonged to the Central Committee; forty battalions did not participate in the election; and many remained neutral or indifferent. There were only about five or six battalions openly hostile, and even these contained a Republican element. The friends of order could never give to Admiral Saisset more than two thousand National Guards, notwithstanding all their efforts, manœuvres, and means of action and influence. The admiral himself declared that he had only three hundred, but this number was greatly underrated.

One thing is but too positive—that if the Central Committee of the National Guard had only desired to make an end of the reactionary leaders and their *seïdes*, it would have been very easy to accomplish their object. If it did not do so, it was because it was animated by the most peaceable intentions, looked upon civil war with horror, and wished to employ all possible means of preventing bloodshed.

M. Thiers knowingly outraged truth by affirming that one imprudent word spoken in the Assembly might be the cause of torrents of blood.

The very day on which M. Thiers uttered these deplorably exaggerated fears, the Assembly, by its dishonest, offensive, and rude reception of the mayors of Paris, had surely done all it could to excite civil war, had that been possible; and after the imprudent and provocative scene which transpired on the entrance of the mayors into their tribune, it cannot be supposed that a population which had endured the rudest outrage against their magistrates without a murmur would be disposed to "shed torrents of blood" on account of a single word from the tribune. M. Thiers, however subtle, acute, and profligate he may be, will never succeed in making an intelligent, true man believe in his terrible hypothesis.

The Chief of the Executive power had a secret aim in conjuring up the sanguinary phantom of civil war before the Assembly. He wished to prevent all compromise, all means of conciliation between the Assembly and the population of Paris. He desired to let events which he plainly foresaw be accomplished; to let the Commune, which he sought to destroy, be installed, so as to gain time for the organisation of an armed force capable of stifling the Revolution of the 18th of March; to annihilate the Commune; and to drown both in torrents of blood. He was resolved not to draw back before the sanguinary deluge which, at the same time, he pretended to fear. Clever, cold, and cruel in policy, he prepared the ground and the elements necessary for his sanguinary triumph.

The adhesion of the Assembly to the communal elections, or the acceptance of the proposition of the mayors detailed by M. Arnaud, would have had a chance of leading, if not to a reconciliation, certainly to a compromise, between Paris and Versailles, and would have destroyed M. Thiers' plan, which was precisely what he did not want. This was the real motive of his burying the Arnaud proposition beneath the flowers of his perfidious rhetoric.

As with Cæsar, the die of this fatal man had been cast; the realisation of his plan and his political projects must be accomplished, even if a Rubicon of blood had to be crossed.

While M. Thiers was planning his parliamentary intrigues and succeeding in repelling M. Arnaud's proposition, the Central Committee was not idle. It made laudable efforts to secure the free success of the elections which were to be held on March 26th, and decided upon energetic means capable of compelling the inimical municipalities to allow the elections to go on. There was no time to be lost, for they were to take place the next day. On the 25th of this month, at three o'clock, a column of three thousand National Guards, with three cannons and preceded by some horsemen, quitted the Place de l'Hôtel-de-Ville for this purpose. It proceeded along the Rue de Rivoli to the mairie of the First Arrondissement, where it halted. Delegates of the Central Committee presented themselves to the adjuncts, who, in the absence of the mayors, received them. The negotiations lasted nearly an hour. The crowd was enormous, and the anxiety general. A conflict was feared.

The propositions of the Committee were at length accepted. It was decided by common consent that next day, the 26th, the elections for the Communal Council by direct universal suffrage, and the nomination of the commander-in-chief of the National Guard, should take place.

After the Second Arrondissement had also been induced to approve of these conditions, the battalions of the Federation continued their march through the Rue de Rivoli, traversing the Place du Palais-National, and following the Rue de Richelieu to the Rue Neuve des Petits-Champs, which they entered, so as to gain the Rue Vivienne, where a halt was made.

The delegates then made their way to the Bourse, where twelve or fifteen mayors and adjuncts received them.

There again great difficulties arose. On one side the municipal magistrates opposed the proposed ultimatum, and refused to accede to propositions made by an armed force and manifestation;

on the other, the delegates of the Central Council declared that delay was dangerous, that the elections could no longer be adjourned, that they should be held at any price, and that, whatever might be decided upon, they should take place the next day.

At last, after a stormy debate of an hour and a half, the propositions of the Committee were also accepted, and the municipalities of the arrondissements, which had till then refused, consented to give their assistance at the elections on the morrow.

At the termination of the meeting the delegates announced to the National Guards, drawn up in battle array before the Bourse, the fortunate result at which they had arrived. On hearing this excellent news the countenances of the citizen soldiers glowed with joy, their brows became smooth, and they raised the butt-ends of their muskets in the air and defiled before their brethren of the aristocratic quarters, who in their turn imitated this good example, lifted butt-ends into the air, and received them with cries a thousand times reiterated of " Vive la République!" The drums beat a salute, and the greatest enthusiasm prevailed among all the inhabitants.

The ladies at the windows participated in the general joy, mingled their cheers with those of the National Guards, and applauded the Republic.

The population of the central quarters crowded *en masse* to the boulevards, and made friends and united with those of the suburbs; hands were pressed, hearts were gladdened, and faces were radiant with joy. Every one felt, in presence of the complicated situation which a quarter of an hour before seemed without a solution, an oppressive weight removed.

A rendezvous was agreed upon for the evening at the Bourse, so that the mayors who were absent might have an opportunity of adopting the conventions already agreed upon by their brother-magistrates.

The reconciliation was general, and the deputies of Paris agreed to the electoral conditions made by the mayors and adjuncts.

As a public consecration of this treaty the following proclamation was placarded all over Paris:—

"Paris, March 25th, six o'clock in the evening.

"Citizens,

"The deputies of Paris, the mayors, and the adjuncts, reinstated in the mairies of their arrondissements, and the members of the Federal Central Committee of the National Guard, convinced that the only means of preventing civil war and bloodshed in Paris, and at the same time of strengthening the Republic, is to proceed to immediate elections, consequently convoke all citizens in their electoral districts for to-morrow (Sunday).

"The bureaux will be open from eight o'clock in the morning until midnight.

"The inhabitants of Paris must understand that under the present circumstances their patriotism demands that all of them should come and take part in the voting, in order that the elections may have the serious character which alone can secure the public peace of our city."

(*The Signatures.*)

Admiral Saisset and the so-called battalions of order, who occupied the Grand-Hôtel, the Saint-Lazare Terminus, the Boulevard des Capucines, the First and Second Arrondissements, &c., gave up these posts to the battalions of the Central Committee.

M. Louis Blanc, in the name of the deputies of Paris, announced to the Assembly at Versailles that placards signed by the mayors and adjuncts of Paris called the Parisian electors together for to-morrow to nominate a Municipal Council. He added that to retard the elections would seriously endanger the position of affairs. He consequently conjured the Assembly, in the name of the deputies of Paris, to recognise the decision imposed by circumstances, and to make a declaration to the effect that the mayors and adjuncts of Paris had acted as good citizens.

The proposition of M. Louis Blanc was sent to the Initiative Committee, which was instructed to bury it in good and due form.

On the next day, the reporter of the Parliamentary Initiative Committee declared from the tribune that this Commission, " in continuing to adhere to the wisdom and firmness of the Government, was of opinion that the proposition of M. Louis Blanc and his co-deputies could not be taken into consideration."

These conclusions were immediately adopted by the Assembly.

A deputy, whose name, I am sorry to say, is unknown to me, deposited, on behalf of eight of his colleagues, a resolution couched in the following terms :—

"The National Assembly declares the municipal elections to be held in Paris null and void." (Exclamations on the Left, applause on the Right.)

This proposition, signed by eight deputies, and applauded by the Right, was a proof of the scorn of the majority against the sovereignty of the people and universal suffrage, which they invoked daily when it was their interest to do so.

Nevertheless, from a feeling of fear inspired by the victorious Revolution of Paris, and also that it might not furnish a flagrant proof of its antipathy to universal suffrage, it repelled the urgency of this proposition.

The Assembly of capitulators, elected only to make peace, implicitly recognised that its power was gone, and that *there were no more orders of the day*, as the report of one of its last sittings so well observed.

But the rural Assembly at Versailles, notwithstanding all the serious reasons which ought to have constrained it to limit its mission to the tacit mandate which it had received to conclude peace with the Prussians, persisted none the less in the liberticide work which it had pursued from its first meeting. It continued, against all right, to hold its sittings, and persisted in its pretension to erect itself into a sovereign Assembly, and to impose itself by might on the population of the capital, who repudiated it. We shall see it make another siege of Paris, bombard that city, cover it with ruin and dead bodies, shed rivers of blood, and depopulate it.

CHAPTER VII.

ELECTION OF THE COMMUNE.

WITHOUT taking into account the ill-will, hostility, hatred, ridiculous propositions, and odious, sinister, and senseless projects of the Assembly of Versailles, the electors of Paris proceeded, on March 26th, with calmness, good order, and complete liberty, to the election of the Commune.

On that day the weather was beautiful; an immense crowd promenaded the streets; all was quiet, and the most perfect order reigned everywhere. So said all the journals, without distinction as to political creed.

The ballot boxes for the election of the Communal Council were opened at eight o'clock in the morning. The electors went peaceably to the different polling-places of the twenty arrondissements, so as to fulfil their electoral duty as citizens; and each of them voted with the fullest liberty. Never was freedom of voting so scrupulously observed.

The Central Committee of the National Guard had, from first to last, given proof of its liberal spirit and impartiality, its respect for the sovereignty of the people and universal suffrage. Its loyalty was equal to its modesty and disinterestedness.

To give another proof of its moderation, it liberated General Chanzy the same day.

The Central Committee, had it been less inclined to exercise clemency, might have kept this superior officer of the army, and condemned him; for it had proof that he came with his army to organise resistance to it, and to conspire against it in company with Thiers, Jules Favre, Saisset, Schoelcher, Langlois, and all the renegades of the 4th of September.

But the Central Committee appeared to have forgotten or ignored this crime. Clemency, always the best counsellor, swayed its spirit, and we most sincerely applaud it. This was a generous as well as an intelligent manner of doing honour to the elections of the 26th, and of preparing under the best auspices the advent of the new power.

The elections gave satisfaction to the partisans of the Commune; its devoted candidates, in fact, triumphed in all the arrondissements, except the First, Second, Ninth, and Sixteenth, where the Conservatives carried the day.

In the First Arrondissement, that of the Louvre, one of the most aristocratic of Paris, the candidates of the Commune, citizens Vésinier, Miot, and Pillot, had more votes than they anticipated: the first-named had 3,500 votes. The same phenomenon was repeated in the Second Arrondissement.

A great number of influential members of the Central Committee of the National Guard were elected as members of the Commune, and the Workmen's International Association met with the same success.

The communal elections of March 26th were a

great and peaceable victory gained by the social and democratic Revolution.

Nearly all those elected were prolétaires; the bourgeois element was in a small minority. The greatest number of them were workmen; all, except the candidates of the First, Second, Ninth, and Sixteenth Arrondissements, were men labouring either with the hand or head. Some, it is true, belonged to the so-called liberal professions, but they were none the less devoted to the cause of the social and democratic Revolution, and to the emancipation of the prolétaires. Amongst these were the names of Félix Pyat, Delescluze, Blanqui, Flourens, and Miot, whose Republican principles are sufficiently known.

Some other less celebrated citizens were not working men, but all of them served the Republican cause with devotedness and courage. Among them we may mention:—

Citizen Tridon, advocate, who had only exercised his profession in defending himself against the tribunals of the Empire, by which he was condemned to many years of imprisonment, and finally to transportation.

Citizen Rigault, student, late editor of *La Marseillaise, La Patrie en Danger*, and several other Republican, socialist, and free-thinking journals. Rigault gave proofs of his capacity under the Empire by fighting courageously for the cause of the people and of the Revolution. He had braved and submitted to numerous condemnations in the defence and vindication of his political, philosophical, and social ideas. Rigault was one of the most devoted, courageous, and intelligent members of the Commune.

Citizen Protot, a very distinguished young advocate, one of the accused of the so-called Renaissance, whose admirable pleadings before the Sixth Chamber had been much taken notice of. Though very young, citizen Protot had already worked hard for the deliverance of the prolétariat.

Citizen Vermorel, advocate, journalist, and publicist, author of several volumes of history, who always attracted attention by his vigorous attacks against the men of the Opposition, whom he rightly accused of having ruined the Republic, and compromised all liberty by their culpable conduct, reactionary measures, and liberticide decrees.

Citizen Paschal Grousset, late editor of *La Marseillaise*, an original, revolutionary, daring, and devoted writer, condemned by the Court of Blois.

Citizen Vaillant, a learned student, very intelligent, and with deep convictions, who placed his knowledge at the service of the social Revolution.

Citizen Jules Vallès, a talented writer and popular journalist, who took part in a great number of social and democratic publications, and was one of the most esteemed pamphleteers of the Parisians.

Citizen Cournet, chief editor of the *Réveil*, a militant Republican, well known for his zeal and devotion.

Citizen Arthur Arnould, formerly editor of the *Rappel* and *La Marseillaise*.

Citizens Régère, doctor; Lefrançais, ex-schoolmaster; Goupil, doctor; Parisel, doctor; Jules Allix, economist; Eudes, student; Verdure, ex-tutor, editor of *La Marseillaise;* Léo Meillet, advocate; J. B. Clément, journalist; Bergeret, officer, &c., did not belong to the working classes properly so called, but all of them had precisely the same aspirations and needs, and pursued similar objects in politics, philosophy, and social economy.

The other members of the Commune were working men in the strictest sense. There was another member, M. Beslay, who was not a working man, but a rich, independent gentleman.

The following is an authentic list of the communal elections of March 26th:—

First Arrondissement (*Louvre*).

(Complete Result.—Four Councillors to be elected.)

Adam	7,272
Méline	7,251
Rochard	6,629
Barré	6,294
(These four candidates were returned.)	
Vésinier	3,565
Grandjean	3,458
Dr. Pillot	3,309
Jules Miot	3,219

Second Arrondissement (*Bourse*).

(Complete.—Four Councillors to be elected.)

Brelay	7,025
Loiseau-Pinson	6,922
Tirard	6,386
Cheron	6,068
(These four candidates were returned.)	
Pothier	4,422
Serraillet	3,711
Durand	3,656
Johannard	3,639

Third Arrondissement (*Temple*).

(Seven Sections.—Five Councillors.)

A. Arnaud	8,679
Demay	8,736
Pindy	7,816
Cléray	6,115
Clovis Dupont	5,661
(These five candidates were returned.)	

FOURTH ARRONDISSEMENT.

(Eleven Sections.—Five Councillors.)

Lefrançais	8,705
Arthur Arnould	8,584
Clémence	8,173
Gérardin	8,104
Amouroux	7,906
(These five candidates were returned.)	
Louis Blanc	5,232

FIFTH ARRONDISSEMENT.

(Five Sections.—Five Councillors.)

Régère	4,026
Jourde	3,949
Tridon	3,948
Blanché	3,271
Ledroit	3,236

SIXTH ARRONDISSEMENT (*Saint-Sulpice*).

Albert Leroy	5,800
Goupil	5,111
Varlin	3,602
Beslay	3,714
Dr. Robinet	3,904
(These five candidates were returned.)	
G. Courbet	1,172
Laccord	1,146
Hérisson	956

SEVENTH ARRONDISSEMENT.

(Twelve Sections out of Nineteen.)

Dr. Parisel	3,367
Ernest Lefèvre	2,859
Urbain	2,803
Brunel	1,947
(These four candidates were returned.)	
Ribeaucourt	968
Arnaud (de l'Ariége)	653
Toussaint	627

EIGHTH ARRONDISSEMENT.

Raoul Rigault	2,175
Vaillant	2,145
Arthur Arnould	2,114
Allix	2,028
(These four candidates were returned.)	

Carnot	1,922
Aubry	1,840
Denormandie	1,804
Belliard	1,618

NINTH ARRONDISSEMENT.

(Six Sections out of Nine.—Five Councillors.)

Ranc	8,950
Desmarest	4,232
Ulysse Parent	4,770
E. Ferry	3,732
Nast	3,691

(These five candidates were returned.)

Dupont de Bussac	2,005
George Avenel	1,449
Dr. Sémerie	1,382
Briosne	1,085

TENTH ARRONDISSEMENT.

(Complete result.—Five Councillors.)

Fortuné (Henri)	11,042
Pyat (Félix)	11,813
Gambon	11,734
Rastoul	10,325
Babick	10,738
Olive	3,985

ELEVENTH ARRONDISSEMENT.

Mortier	19,397
Delescluze	18,379
Protot	18,062
Assi	18,041
Eudes	17,392
Avrial	16,193
Verdure	15,577

TWELFTH ARRONDISSEMENT (*Bercy-Reuilly*).

(Eighth and Eleventh Sections.)

Varlin	2,312
Geresme	2,194
Fruneau	2,173
Theisz	2,150

(In the First, Second, and Third Sections the same candidates were returned by a very large majority.)

THIRTEENTH ARRONDISSEMENT.

Léo Meillet	6,531
General E. Duval	6,482
Chardon	4,663
Frankel	4,480

FOURTEENTH ARRONDISSEMENT (*Montrouge*).

(Three Councillors.—Complete result, except one Section.)

Billoray	6,100
Martelet	5,927
Descamps	5,830

(These three candidates were returned.)

FIFTEENTH ARRONDISSEMENT (*Grenelle*).

Parisel	2,773
Lefèvre	2,370
Urbain	2,304
Brunel	1,528
Ribeaucourt	1,247

SIXTEENTH ARRONDISSEMENT (*Passy-Auteuil*).

(Two Councillors.)

Dr. Marmottan	2,036
De Bouteiller	1,909
Félix Pyat	1,332
Victor Hugo	1,274

(The first two were returned.)

SEVENTEENTH ARRONDISSEMENT (*Batignolles*).

Varlin	9,356
Clément	7,121
Gérardin	6,142
Chalin	4,547
Malon	4,199

(These candidates were returned.)

EIGHTEENTH ARRONDISSEMENT (*Montmartre*).

(Six Sections out of Twelve.—Seven Councillors.)

Dereure
Theisz
Blanqui
J.-B. Clément
Th. Ferré
Vermorel
Paschal Grousset

(These candidates were returned with about 14,000 votes.)

NINETEENTH ARRONDISSEMENT.
(Ten Sections out of Sixteen.)

Paget	9,547
Oudet	10,060
Delescluze	5,840
Jules Miot	5,520
Cournet	5,540
Ostyn	4,100

(These six candidates were returned.)

TWENTIETH ARRONDISSEMENT.
(*Belleville and Charonne*).

Ranvier	14,127
Bergeret	14,003
Blanqui	13,498
Flourens	13,333

The *Nouvelle République* gives the following summary as the definitive result of the elections :—

"Number of voters, more than 250,000.

"The average number of votes received by the elected candidates exceeded a fourth of the inscribed electors. It was far above the ordinary average majority in the municipal elections.

"Out of twenty arrondissements the Revolutionary list triumphed in sixteen, namely, the Third, Fourth, Fifth, Sixth, Seventh, Eighth, Tenth, Eleventh, Twelfth, Thirteenth, Fourteenth, Fifteenth, Seventeenth, Eighteenth, Nineteenth, and Twentieth, and obtained a half-success in the Ninth.

"Only the First, Second, Ninth, and Sixteenth Arrondissements voted for the reaction, as represented by the mayors and adjuncts."

PART SECOND.

THE PARIS COMMUNE.

CHAPTER I.

PROCLAMATION OF THE COMMUNE.

The proclamation of the result of the communal election was made with affecting and imposing solemnity, at four o'clock in the evening of March 28th, in the Place de l'Hôtel-de-Ville.

At two o'clock the battalions of the National Guard began to arrive from all directions; over the bridges, from the quays, the squares, and out of all the leading streets; joyous, sprightly, full of animation and enthusiasm, with a martial step, to the beat of drums, the sound of clarions, the singing of the Marseillaise, and with flags flying, being everywhere received with a hearty welcome and with sympathising acclamations, to which they responded with enthusiastic *vivats* in favour of the Republic and the Commune.

The whole of the National Guard of Paris took part in this imposing filing off. Towards evening the flowing tide of battalions overran the place, and broke into the Rue de Rivoli, the squares, the quays, the Avenue Victoria, and the Boulevard Sebastopol, which were all inundated by it.

The crowd of spectators was immense. Everywhere they squeezed and packed themselves together upon the footpaths, in the warehouses, and in the lanes; the apartments of houses were crammed; all the windows were lined with spectators; while the barricades served as stages, on which men, women, and children were so closely packed as to cause some of them to give way.

The equestrian statue of Henri IV., which decorates the façade of the Hôtel-de-Ville, was veiled with red tapestry, on the top of which, overshadowed with red flags, and with a Phrygian cap on its head, was raised the bust of the Republic. Before the central door, under the popular goddess, and communicating with the inside of the Hôtel-de-Ville through a passage, arose a large stage covered tightly with red, and furnished with seats and a table, serving as a bureau.

The people's red flags floated on the summit of the Hôtel-de-Ville, as also on the Tuileries and all other public monuments. The flag of the Commune was in front of the Communal monument, and those of the battalions of the National Guard had been piled before the platform.

The members of the Central Committee and of the Commune made their appearance on the platform at four o'clock, and took their places around the bureau. They were welcomed with the greatest enthusiasm and most lively applause, and with innumerable cries of "Vive la Commune!" "Vive la République!"

All Paris was with them.

The greater part of the newly-elected members were in private clothes, while others were in the uniform of officers of the National Guard; but all wore a red scarf fringed with gold, and had ribbons of the same colour, with similar fringes, in their button-holes.

As soon as the members of the Commune and the Central Committee had taken their places the President of the latter rang a bell, and the thunder of the cannons from the Quai de Grève was heard, and was answered by other detonations from all parts.

At this moment the Place de l'Hôtel-de-Ville presented the most grand, solemn, and exciting spectacle. The flags of the battalions; the standards of the companies floating in the breeze; the forest of muskets and bayonets glittering in the sun; the innumerable uniforms everywhere displayed; the bronzed and martial figures of the National Guard, animated and sparkling with enthusiasm, and their eyes glistening with hope;—all seemed as if a regenerating breath had passed over this immense multitude, who had been weighed down for more than twenty years beneath the shameful despotism of a monomaniac tyrant—who, by his stupid ambition, had delivered it over to the foreigner—and who all at once uplifted themselves by the revivifying breath of liberty.

In presence of the inauguration of this Commune, which was a personification of all their wishes and all their hopes, the end of their misery and their evils, a future of reparation, liberty, and justice, the people recovered their native pride, their unaffected goodness, their courage, their dignity, their greatness, their conscience—all their good qualities and virtues. They wanted to be great, strong, and generous. For the first time in twenty years they felt themselves to be really supreme, worthy of themselves, and of the great cause—the deliverance of the prolétaires. At this moment of sublime enthusiasm their joy and delirium burst out at the sound of the cannons, and manifested themselves again and again with the cries, a hundred thousand times repeated, "Vive la Commune!" "Vive la République!"

As if with an electric, magnetic, and irresistible movement, all the National Guards swung their arms, put their képis on the points of their bayonets, lifted up and brandished their muskets, and uttered frantic hurrahs.

The President of the Central Committee rose and rang the bell again. The cannons were silent, the cries ceased, and the crowd stood still. The silence was now as profound as the roaring of the artillery, the flourish of the cavalry trumpets, and the cries of the people a few minutes ago had been great. The President then read, in a powerful voice, the names of the newly-elected members of the Commune.

We give this list just as it was published at the Place de l'Hôtel-de-Ville:—

First Arrondissement (four councillors to be elected).—Adam, Méline, Rochart, Barré.

Second Arrondissement (four councillors.)—Brelay, Loiseau-Pinson, Tirard, Chéron.

Third Arrondissement (Temple; five councillors).—Demay, Arnaud, Pindy, Cléray, Dupont.

Fourth Arrondissement (five councillors). — Lefrançais, Arthur Arnould, Gérardin, Amouroux, Clémence.

Fifth Arrondissement (five councillors).—Jourde, Régère, Tridon, Blanchet, Ledroit.

Sixth Arrondissement (Saint-Sulpice).— Albert Leroy, Goupil, Dr. Robinet, Beslay, Varlin.

Seventh Arrondissement. — Dr. Parisel, Ernest Lefèvre, Urbain, Brunel.

Eighth Arrondissement (Faubourg Saint-Honoré; four councillors).—Raoul-Rigault, Vaillant, Arthur Arnould, Jules Allix.

Ninth Arrondissement (five councillors).—Ranc, Ulysse Parent, Desmarest, E. Ferry, Nast.

Tenth Arrondissement (five councillors).—Gambon, Félix Pyat, Henri Fortuné, Champy, Babick.

Eleventh Arrondissement.—Eudes, Mortier, Protot, Assi, Avrial, Verdure.

Twelfth Arrondissement—(Bercy-Reuilly).—Varlin, Fruneau, Geresme, Theisz.

Thirteenth Arrondissement (Gobelins).—Léo Meillet, Duval, Chardon, Frankel.

Fourteenth Arrondissement — (Montrouge; three councillors).—Billoray, Martelet, Decamp.

Fifteenth Arrondissement (Vaugirard - Grenelle). —Clément, Jules Vallès, Langevin.

Sixteenth Arrondissement (Passy-Auteuil; two councillors).—Dr. Marmoteau, De Bouteiller.

Seventeenth Arrondissement (Batignolles).—Varlin, Clément, Gérardin, Chalain, Malon.

Eighteenth Arrondissement (Montmartre; seven councillors).—Blanqui, Theisz, Dereure, J.-B. Clément, Th. Ferré, Vermorel, Paschal Grousset.

Nineteenth Arrondissement.—Oudet, Puget, Delescluze, Cournet, J. Miot, Ostyn.

Twentieth Arrondissement (Belleville).—Ranvier, Bergeret, Flourens, Blanqui.

The reading of the names was twenty times interrupted by applause, which again burst forth after the proclamation of the names for each arrondissement; and when it was ended numberless *vivats* succeeded. The bands of the National Guard then played the Marseillaise, the Chant du Départ, and other Republican airs.

Several speeches, alternately followed by music and patriotic songs, were made by citizens Lavalette, Assi, Ranvier, and Beslay, and very loudly applauded.

The following is the speech of citizen Beslay, the oldest member of the Commune, and the only one taken down in shorthand:—

"Citizens,

"Our presence here attests to Paris and to France that we have no doubt that the Commune of Paris is the enfranchisement of all the communes of the Republic.

"For fifty years mere practitioners of the old politics tossed us about with the grand words of decentralisation, and the government of the country by the country; fine phrases, which cost us much and have given us nothing.

"More valiant than your ancestors, you have acted like the philosopher who marched about in order to prove the nature of movement. You have marched, and we are satisfied that the Republic will march with you.

"This is, in fact, the crowning of your peaceable victory. Your adversaries said that you would strike the Republic. We answer, that if we did strike it, it was only as we should a pile which we strove to bury deeper in the earth.

"Yes, it is on account of the complete liberty of the Commune that the Republic takes root with us. The Republic of to-day is no longer what it was in the days of our great Revolution. The Republic of '93 was a soldier, who, in order that he might be able to fight both at home and abroad, had need to concentrate all the power of our country in his hand. The Republic of 1871 is a labourer, who requires liberty for the fertilisation of peace.

"*Peace and labour!* This is our future—the certitude of our revenge and social regeneration; and in this sense the Republic is able to make France the supporter of the weak, the protector of the worker, the hope of all the oppressed, and the foundation of the universal Republic.

"The enfranchisement of the Commune is therefore, I repeat, the enfranchisement of the Republic itself. Each of the social groups will recover its simple independence and its full liberty of action.

"The Commune will occupy itself with local matters.

"The departments will look after their transactions.

"The Government will employ itself in national affairs.

"And let us say it boldly, the Commune which we have founded will be a model Commune. Whoever says 'work,' proclaims order, economy, honesty, and strict control; and it is not under the Commune that Paris will find frauds of four hundred millions.

"On its side, the Government, reduced by half, will be nothing more than the docile mandatary of universal suffrage and the guardian of the Republic.

"This, citizens, is, in my opinion, the path to be followed. Let us enter upon it boldly and resolutely. Let us not overstep the limits fixed by our programme, and the country and the Government will be happy and proud at having assisted in this great day's work, which to us is the day of salvation. My age will not permit me to take part in your work as a member of the Commune of Paris; my strength would too often betray my courage, and you are in want of vigorous athletes. In the interest of the propaganda I am compelled to give in my resignation; but be assured that as far as lies in my power I shall afford you my most devoted help, and, like yourselves, serve the holy cause of labour and the Republic.

"Vive la République! Vive la Commune!"

As soon as the speeches came to an end the President closed this inauguration, and once more the cannons resounded, and the battalions began to file off. The drummers beat a salute, the trumpets sounded, the exclamations redoubled, and during two hours more than two hundred and fifty thousand National Guards defiled before their elected members, with the cries, a million times repeated, "Vive la Commune!" "Vive la République!"

The enthusiasm was general; it prevailed among

all. Everywhere, in all the streets, on all the quays and boulevards, the crowd—men, women, and children, prolétaires and bourgeois—greeted the National Guard on its passage with the most sympathising manifestations and acclamations.

The windows were crowded with joyous spectators, the houses adorned with red flags, and nobody was at all alarmed by them.

In the evening, the Hôtel-de-Ville, the Tuileries, the Louvre, and a great number of other public monuments and private houses were illuminated. Paris and its suburbs made holiday.

The Commune was proclaimed under the best auspices.

The following are the terms in which the Central Committee announced the happy advent of the Commune, and made its adieux to the people and the National Guard:—

"Citizens,

"We have to-day (March 28th) had the pleasure of assisting at the most magnificent popular spectacle we have ever witnessed. Our hearts are gladdened. Paris has saluted and applauded the Revolution. Paris has opened a new leaf of its history, on which it has inscribed its name.

"Two hundred thousand free men have presented themselves to affirm their liberty and proclaim the new Constitution with the thunder of artillery. The Versailles spies prowling around our walls may tell their masters what it was that made the voice of a whole population heard; how this voice not only filled the city, but re-echoed beyond its walls. Let these spies, who glided into our ranks, give them a faithful picture of this admirable spectacle of a people regaining their sovereignty, crying with all their might, and in a manner truly sublime, 'We will die for our country!'

"Citizens,

"We return into your hands the work with which you entrusted us. At the last moment of our ephemeral power, and before finally quitting our places in the Committee of the National Guard, from which events recall us, we wish to express our gratitude to you.

"By the help of your admirable patriotism and wisdom, we have, without violence, but also without weakness, performed our task. Bound in our proceedings by a loyalty which forbade our setting ourselves up as a government, we have, supported by you, at least prepared a radical Revolution in the short space of eight days. You know all we have done, and with pride we submit our actions to your judgment. But, before undergoing your examination, we are happy to say that everything which has been done has been done by you.

"We also wish to proclaim aloud that, in your quality of absolute and legitimate masters, your power was principally established by your generosity. If you have prosecuted your rights and made demands, you have never used reprisals.

"France, for twenty years guilty of weakness, now comprehends the necessity of its regeneration, of redeeming itself from the tyranny and indolence of the past by means of peaceable liberty and labour. Your liberties will be energetically defended by those whom you have elected to-day. They will devote themselves to it for ever. The work depends upon you, and carries with it its own reward.

"Rally, then, with confidence round your Commune. Facilitate its labours by devoting yourselves to necessary reforms. Brothers, be guided by brothers. March firmly and bravely upon the path of the future. Be an example to others by showing them the value of liberty, and you will assuredly attain the wished-for end—THE UNIVERSAL REPUBLIC.

"The following are the signatures of the members of the Central Committee of the National Guard:—

"AVOIN fils, ANTOINE ARNAUD, G. ARNOLD, ASSI, ANDIGNOUX, BOUIT, JULES BERGERET, BABICK, BAROUD, BILLORAY, BLANCHET, L. BOURSIER, CASTIONI, CHOUTEAU, C. DUPONT, FABRE, FERRAT, HENRI FORTUNÉ, FLEURY, FOUGERET, C. GAUDIER, GOUHIER, H. GERESME, GRÉLIER, GROLLARD, JOURDE, JOSSELIN, LAVALETTE, LISBONNE, MALJOURNAL, EDMOND MOREAU, MORTIER, PRUDHOMME, ROSSEAU, RANVIER, VARLIN."

The people followed the advice given by the Central Committee. Good and generous as ever, they placed their confidence in the newly-elected members.

They chose an immense majority of them out of their midst, from among the travailleurs-prolétaires. If they selected some from the bourgeoisie, it was only those who had for a long time given abundant proof of devotion to their cause, and whom, for this reason, they believed to be worthy of representing them.

They elevated them to the platform, and made no stipulations with them about power. They put at their service all the strength, resources, good-will, and courage they possessed.

They placed in their hands and confided to them the immense resources of the capital, namely, the administration, the ministries, the municipalities, the arsenals, the workshops, the magazines, the supplies, the finances, all the armed force of the capital, 300,000 National Guards, 1,800 cannons, all the arms, all the munitions accumulated during the siege, powerful machines, all the treasures, all public property, all domains belonging to the city and the state, the barracks, the forts, a fortified enceinte, immense means of attack and defence, destruction and production, all the resources of a city with two and a half million inhabitants, a population the best instructed, the most civilised, the best cultivated, and one of the richest in the world.

But this was not all. The people of Paris gave to the men whom they elected, for the service of the great humanising cause confided to them, not only all the social resources and collective forces of the city, but also all those of the individual; all the private property, life, and goods of each citizen and his family. In addition to this, they confided to them that which was the most inviolable, the most precious, the most sacred—that from which a nation should never alienate itself—their liberty, sovereignty, and honour!

The members of the Communal Council, then,

had in their hands all the resources, forces, and power of which the people of Paris had to dispose. It depended, then, on them to render immense service to the sublime cause whose triumph they ought to secure.

If they were devoted, capable, intelligent, honest, industrious, and courageous in the height of their mission and its circumstances, they would be able to accomplish an immense work—that of saving Paris and France from civil war, freeing them from the occupation of the foreigner, raising their country from the abyss of misery, ruin, shame, and corruption into which royalty and the Empire, the bourgoisie and Catholicism, had plunged them; they could put them upon the right track, rescue them from the deleterious influence of the oligarchical despotism of a retrograde Assembly, and from a majority worthy only of the middle ages and feudal times, which dreams of the restoration of the throne and the altar, the Popedom and legitimacy, in all their monstrous deformity and hideous reality. They would be able for ever to prevent the restoration of despotism in France; to emancipate the people for good from the threefold yoke of the Church, royalty, and capital; that is to say, to destroy religious, political, and economical tyranny, and to secure for the future, throughout the whole world, the triumph of the philosophical, political, and social Revolution.

Such was the gigantic task which the Parisian electors of March 26th and the travailleurs-prolétaires of the whole world expected from the Commune.

The Commune was perfectly aware of its important mission, but such was not always the case with some who believed themselves authorised to speak in its name. The following article, published in the *Journal Officiel*, sufficiently proves that its author had no very just idea of the spirit of this Revolution and its consequences. "All political movements," said he, "without a new, creative, and fertile idea, or which, having such an idea, are unable to produce men capable of carrying it out and defending it, are doomed, even after a brilliant victory by force, to miserably miscarry."

This is very true, but let us quote the continuation of this article, and see if the ideas which it contains are as just as the one mentioned:—

"These men of deep reflection and rapid action were found ready in the first days of 1789. They gave soul, intelligence, life, in fact, to the instinctive tumultuous movements of the crowd; they transmuted them into human, and, as it were, philosophical movements, and in a few months the instinctive crowd became a great people, conscious of itself, the people of the Revolution.

"Socratic originators of ideas were not wanting either at the Revolution of the 18th of March. After having made it, they cheered, defended, and demonstrated it. Yesterday it spoke; to-day it acts, and in this manner it still demonstrates itself.

"The champions of August 10th were not content with proclaiming liberty, equality, and fraternity: they defined the meaning of these great words, which, united in this immortal triad, had in them something strange, vague, and indeterminate for their contemporaries; they indicated the range and the consequences of them; and they showed the application of them to civil and political life.

"If the rioters of March 18th had been merely capable, on the day after their victory, of stammering out the word Commune without determining from the first its elementary principles, the primordials of the Communal organisation, perhaps nothing of its valour and strength would have remained to-day but the memory of its defeat.

"In the course of twenty years, perhaps, they would have succumbed to the outrages and calumnies of a lying history, like the insurgents of 1848, who, in order to triumph, only lacked the power of comprehending, if but imperfectly, the imperious and redoubtable question which they had felt and stated.

"We confess the task was less difficult to the men of the 18th of March. The deplorable misunderstanding which in the days of June armed two classes one against the other, both, it is true, not equally interested in the great economical reforms—this fatal mistake, which made the repression of June so sanguinary, could not be renewed.

"This time the class-antagonism did not exist; there was no other object in this war than the old one, so often renewed, and doubtlessly soon to be finished, of liberty against authority, municipal and civic right against an absorbing and arbitrary Government.

"In a word, Paris was ready to rise for the recovery of its independence, its autonomy; it wanted, until the nation should become of the same disposition, *self-government;* that is to say, the Republic.

"Oh no! the Executive was not calumniated by those who accused it of conspiring for the monarchy. The indignant Executive protested its sincerity and its good intentions.

"Well, what could the intentions of the Executive do against the people of Paris? There is something which rules the intentions of men—the force of things and the logic of principles.

"Centralisers to the extreme, on the point of depriving Paris for months, and without fixing a term for its forfeiture, of this subordinate municipality—a restriction which the governmental guardianship conceded to the smallest village—and of maintaining the humiliating stigma which the Empire had implanted, that shameful character of a caravansary town, which effaced its originality and its genius every day; centralisers by taste and system, the Executive again precipitated us into the most perfect form, the most material administrative and political centralisation, royalty.

"Let the partisans of the centralised Republic, the bourgeoisie, which is founded on the antagonism of citizen and State, of labour and capital, of the middle class and the common people—let the formalist reflect on this: their Utopia has ever served as a bridge to monarchy. It is that which for a long time has killed even the idea of a Republic in France.

"To-day this dejected idea again stands erect, more proud and triumphant, audaciously hoisting its first flag, and affixing its new name to its old patronymic title. True to its traditions, conscious of itself, the Republic is also the Commune.

"This is the return for science and labour, liberty and order, the advent of which has been retarded for nearly a century by governmental routine. Rising above the mists which enveloped it, divested of the obstacles which barred its passage, sure of its power, the Revolution comes again, by its example and its propaganda, to diffuse over the world liberty, equality, and justice."

This remarkable article contains erroneous estimations, and proves, as we have stated, that its author did not thoroughly understand the Revolution of the 18th of March, and its economical consequences.

He was right in saying that all revolutions "without a new, creative, and fertile idea, or which, having such an idea, are unable to produce men capable of carrying it out and defending it, are, even after a brilliant victory by force, doomed to miserably miscarry." These admirable words will be eternally true. But their author did not foresee that the tragical catastrophe of which he spoke would so soon be realised, and unfortunately he conjured up for himself strange illusions on the situation, men, and things, when he added, "Socratic originators of ideas were not wanting at the Revolution of the 18th of March." We could wish above everything in the world, we would give our life and shed our blood to the very last drop, that the author of this assertion had not deceived himself; but alas! events have but too truly proved that the men capable of redeeming and defending the new, creative, and fertile idea of the Revolution of the 18th of March were wanting, and were not to be found among the elected of March 26th, "since, after a brilliant triumph by force," this Revolution has "miscarried," and to-day its authors " succumb to the outrages and calumnies of a lying press, like the insurgents of June, 1848," who, according to our author, "lacked nothing but the power of comprehending, if but imperfectly, the imperious and redoubtable question which they had felt and stated."

We do not share in his ideas and estimate of the insurgents of 1848. Whatever may be said to the contrary, and notwithstanding historical calumny, they possessed, not imperfect, but very clear and complete ideas of the social emancipation for which they rose with the battle cry, "To live working, or to die fighting!" The insurgents of June, 1848, like their brothers of 1871, fought for their enfranchisement, for the abolition of the exploitation of man by man; and they knew it. If, like the members of the Commune, they succumbed, it was not the idea that caused their defeat any more than with the revolutionary socialists of 1871. No; it was because, in their sanguinary struggle, in the deadly duel in which they were engaged with the old society, their well-organised, long-standing enemies, the last-named had a well-appointed mechanism for war, were better armed, better disciplined, and possessed material elements of success far superior to them. In 1848, as in 1871, right was defeated by might; but it has not been, and never can be, definitively conquered.

The writer in the *Journal Officiel* advances

another even more venturesome and less earnest idea when he says:—

"We confess the task was less difficult to the men of the 18th of March. The deplorable misunderstanding which in the days of June armed two classes one against the other, both, it is true, not equally interested in the great economical reforms—this fatal mistake, which made the repression of June so sanguinary, could not be renewed."

This is a great error, which has been most unfortunately and cruelly belied by recent events.

This anonymous writer in the *Officiel* evinces, besides, a much-to-be-regretted ignorance of the situation of 1871, and which proves that he had formed erroneous ideas as to the cause of the Revolution of the 18th of March, when he adds:—

"This time (1871) class-antagonism did not exist; there was no other object in this war than the old one, so often renewed and doubtlessly soon to be finished, of liberty against authority, *municipal* and *civic* right against an absorbing and arbitrary Government."

The terrible events which have unfortunately been perpetrated since the 22nd of May—the massacre of the defenders of the Commune, their arrest *en masse*, and the project of transporting more than fifty thousand of them—give the flattest contradiction to this paragraph, and prove that in the year 1871 the antagonism of classes was much greater than in 1848, and that it has increased and become more envenomed during the last twenty-three years of political oppression and economical exploitation.

Blind indeed must those have been who did not perceive this, and who, like the journalist we have just quoted, saw in the Revolution of March 18th nothing "but the old war of liberty against authority, *municipal* and *civic* right against an absorbing and arbitrary Government."

To endeavour to reduce the great social demands of the Paris workmen of March, 1871, to a municipal movement is to do them the grossest injury. It is to suppose that the prolétaires of Paris rose for the sake of a municipal franchise, so as to have the pleasure and right of nominating their aldermen, replacing MM. Haussmann and Ferry by a Prefect of the Seine, or by mayors of their own choice, discussing and voting the budget of the city, watching over the sewers, the public lighting, &c.

Nothing is more certain than that the principal question of March 18th and 26th was the everlasting social demand of the disinherited, who have succeeded each other through centuries since the Gracchi, Spartacus, the Wagres, the Hussites, the peasant companions of Hutten, the Maillotins, the Jacques, the English trade-unions, the Hebertists, the Babouvistes, to the insurgents of 1848, the internationals of 1865, the Revolutionists and the Commune of 1871. This is the veritable filiation and import of the Revolution which gave rise to the Commune.

The reactionary bourgeois did not deceive themselves as to its tendency and import; they understood and judged it accordingly, which is the very reason why they carried on a war to the knife, extermination to the death, and drowned its authors in blood.

In another article the semi-official interpreters of the Communal idea confessed that the triumphant Revolution could not be confined to municipal powers only, but that it had also another mission to fulfil. They freely acknowledged it, but postponed it until its definitive triumph, the realisation of its political and economical object. The following is a comminatory article on this subject published in the *Officiel*:—

"Certain journals believe they see in the first acts of the Commune of Paris an intention of setting aside the municipal powers. It cannot be doubted that in giving to Paris decrees for the reduction of rents, the abolition of the conscription, &c., &c., the Commune has deviated from the narrow circle within which the old legislation had enclosed municipal liberty. But it would be a strange and puerile illusion to imagine that the only object of the Revolution of March 18th was to secure to Paris an elected communal representation under the despotic influence of a strong centralised national power. In France this law has never satisfied, either in Paris, the towns, or the villages, the want of independent and free administration, which is a condition absolutely necessary to the regular life, stability, and progress of a Republican state.

"It is, as has been stated from the first day, to gain and secure for the future the independence of all the communes of France, and also of all the superior groups, cantons, departments, or provinces, bound together for their common interest by a truly national compact; it is to guarantee and perpetuate at the same time the Republic, and put it on a proper basis, that the men of March 18th have fought and conquered.

"What enlightened and true spirit would venture to maintain that Paris, after the sufferings and dangers of the siege, faced the sorrowful though momentary consequences of a violent rupture in order to submit with a good grace to a law which it had not even discussed—a law which would have left it neither the administration of its police, the supreme disposition of its finances, nor the direction of its National Guard—a law which would not only involve the forfeiture of its liberty, but also be the seal of its servitude?

"In constituting itself into a Commune, if Paris renounced its apparent omnipotence, identical, in fact, with its forfeiture, it did not renounce its *rôle* as initiator; it did not abdicate its moral power, that intellectual influence which has so often given victory to its propaganda in France and Europe. Paris free, Paris autonomous, should be none the less the centre of the economical and industrial movement, the seat of the Bank, the railways, and the great national institutions, from which life is more largely distributed through the veins of the social body, which, on their side, carry it back more actively and intensely.

"While anticipating that the final triumph of its cause would give to free Paris the influential but not dominating *rôle* which the nature, economical evolution, and progress of ideas assure to it, the Commune would be content with defending its integrity, interests, and rights. In matters of municipal organisation, rent, or exchange, its legislation might be supreme, because these are its own affairs, its own interests, which can only be satisfied by those whom they concern, and not by those who ruin or deny them.

"The Commune would be right in acting in this manner in the face of a central power which, reduced to its proper functions, would be no more than the guardian and defender of the general interests. With greater reason should it do so in presence of a usurping power which only obeys reasons of State, appeals to nothing but social hatred and craven terror, and which, to those who demand a contract and guarantees, talks of nothing but repression and vengeance."

After recognising that the Commune could not confine its action within the narrow limits of a municipality, the article adds that "the men of March 18th struggled and fought to obtain and assure for the future the independence of all the communes of France, as well as of all the superior groups, cantons, departments, or provinces united to each other, for their general interests, by a truly national compact."

From what has already preceded we see that, according to this writer, the revolutionary movement of March 18th preserved the old topographical organisation—commune, canton, arrondissement, department, and province—of France. It would not, therefore, be necessary to organise the Commune on a fresh basis, to form new communes in harmony with their *rôle*, their wants, and their aim, but simply to emancipate, enfranchise, and render independent the thirty-six thousand communes, cantons, arrondissements, and departments or provinces of France.

We content ourselves here with merely noticing this declaration, reserving our criticism till later on; but before we do so, we request permission of our readers to quote another article published in the *Officiel* on the programme of the Commune. The following is this third document:—

"At the hour in which we write the Central Committee ought, if it has not done so already, to have given place to the Commune. Having fulfilled the extraordinary mandate with which necessity had invested it, it will reduce itself to the special function which gave rise to its existence, and which, violently contested by the power, compelled it to fight, conquer, or die with the city of which it was the armed representation.

"As the expression of municipal liberty legitimately, judicially insurgent against an arbitrary Government, the Committee had no other mission than that of preventing at any price the wresting from Paris of the primordial right which it had triumphantly gained. On the eve of the vote, we must say that the Committee has done its duty.

"As to the elected Commune, its *rôle* and its means will be very different. First and foremost, it will be necessary to define its mandate and fix the limits of its powers. This constituent power, so largely, indefinitely, and confusedly accorded by France to a National Assembly, it should exercise for itself; that is to say, for the city of which it is only the expression.

"The first work of those elected should be the discussion and drawing up of their charter—that act which our forefathers of the middle ages called their Commune. This done, they will have to think upon the means for getting the municipal autonomy acknowledged and guaranteed by the central power. This part of their task will not be very hard if the movement, legalised in Paris and a few other large towns, allows the present National Assembly to perpetuate a mandate which common sense and the force of circumstances limited till the conclusion of peace, which has already been accomplished some time.

"To a usurpation of power the Commune should not reply with usurpation. Federated with the free communes of France, it should in its own name, and in those of Lyons, Marseilles, and soon perhaps of ten other great towns, study the clauses of the contract which should bind it to the nation, and state the ultimatum of the treaty which it is willing to sign.

"What will this ultimatum be? Firstly, it is well understood that it should be a guarantee for the autonomy and the reconquered municipal sovereignty. Secondly, it should secure the free play of communication with the representatives of the national unity. Lastly, it should impose upon the Assembly, if it consents to negotiate, the promulgation of an electoral law, so that for the future the representation of towns may not be absorbed and swamped by the rural representation. So long as an electoral law conceived in this spirit remains unapplied, the national unity and social equilibrium, now destroyed, cannot be restored.

"On these conditions, and on these only, can the insurgent city again become the capital. Its spirit, circulating more freely over France, would soon become the spirit of the nation, the spirit of order, progress, and justice; that is to say, of Revolution."

This article then demanded:—

"1. The constituent power for Paris and for all the other communes of France.

"2. A Communal Charter containing the rights of Paris.

"3. A federative contract between all the free communes of France.

"4. An electoral law guaranteeing the free representation of towns, so that their mandataries should no longer be absorbed by the rural districts.

"5. The function of the capital to be preserved to Paris.

"6. The acceptation of the proposition, as laid down in these five paragraphs, by the central power."

This is an epitome, according to the last article we have quoted from the *Journal Officiel*, of what the programme of the Commune ought to be.

In our opinion, setting economical and social questions aside, one thing, and that the principal, is wanting in this declaration—the topographical organisation of the Commune, of which not the slightest mention is made in any one of the articles in the *Officiel*.

What ought a well-organised Commune to be, what its area, what its population, resources, &c.? These are the questions to be solved.

In our view, the Commune should be an association of citizens with a strong mutual affinity and common interests, living together in not too large a district, so that their communications may be frequent, and their interests in harmony; while, on the other hand, the territory should be large enough to afford necessary resources for the free development of all their faculties, the satisfaction of all their wants, and the guarantee of all their rights. Without these conditions a Commune cannot possess the elements necessary for the realisation of the object anticipated.

The present communal division could not be more defective. Out of the thirty-six thousand communes of which France is composed, some are exceedingly large, whilst, on the contrary, a great number are very small. Among the latter it would be vain to seek the necessary elements for a good organisation of a communal association. The majority of them count merely a few hundred inhabitants, and contain no resources in agriculture, industry, commerce, arts, science, &c. They have neither political nor social life, and scarcely participate in the civilising and progressive movements of our time. They lead a vegetative life rather than that of the modern world. They have kept beyond the pale of the progress of the nineteenth century.

The present communal division and organisation are the principal causes of the decadence of France, and must be abandoned. To seek to preserve, enfranchise, and leave to themselves the communes as they now exist would, under the circumstances, be the greatest absurdity. It would be to abandon them to the preponderating influence of the priests, the nobles, and the great proprietors; it would be to deliver up their future, the Revolution, and the liberation of the prolétaires to their most deadly enemies; and certainly this was not the wish of the Paris Commune. It desired to establish in France a certain number of large communes like its own, strong, powerful, active, progressive, full of life and movement, having, as we said before, in its territory, population, wealth, products, agriculture, mines, industry, science, arts, commerce, &c., all the necessary resources for a free development. That is the Commune which the men of the 18th and the 26th of March and the 16th of April wanted to create.

All the communes constituted in this manner should be bound to each other, as we have seen in the article in the *Officiel*, by some federative contract freely discussed and accepted. The central or federal administration, sitting, so long as it should be considered beneficial, in Paris, should have the mission of watching over the strict fulfilment of the synallagmatic contract agreed upon by all the federated communes; of causing the general principles of a superior justice, which are the foundation of the rights of men and of the citizen, to be respected; and of watching over the punctual administration of the great public services, which are of general interest to the whole Communal Confederation, such as the vast network of the central railways, the post, the telegraph, and the administration of foreign affairs. This is the sort of organisation on which, in our humble opinion, the semi-official interpreters of the Commune should have first informed themselves and then expounded to us.

Now let us see the Commune at work; let us study its acts, its means, and its aim, and, as serious historians, render to it the justice which it merits.

On the 28th of March, the day of its inauguration, the Commune held its first sitting at nine o'clock in the evening, in the deliberation-room of the Municipal Council at the Hôtel-de-Ville, under the presidency of citizen Beslay, as the oldest member.

Fifty-five members took part at this sitting, and occupied themselves in a general way with various propositions relating to the *rôle*, prerogatives, and powers of the Commune, but without coming to a decision on these diverse questions. The discussion was, nevertheless, very interesting and animated. A Commission was appointed to report on the elections. The constitution of the bureau and the limits of its powers were agitated.

The sitting lasted till half-past twelve P.M., and it was decided that the next meeting should be held at one o'clock on the following afternoon.

On that day, March 19th, the sitting of the Commune was opened with cries of "Vive la République!" Citizen Beslay, as the oldest member, again took the chair.

He begged the Assembly to elect its President, and citizen Lefrançais was nominated.

Citizens Rigault and Ferré were provisionally elected secretaries; Bergeret and Duval, assessors.

The President called upon the Assembly to regulate the composition of the bureau.

It was decided that two assessors, as well as two secretaries, should be nominated.

The nominations to be weekly.

The sittings to be secret.

On the proposition of citizens Assi, Billoray, Rigault, and Henri Fortuné, the Foreign Secretaries were to be admitted. Citizen Assi, on behalf of the Central Committee, returned the powers with which its members had been invested by the force of circumstances and the will of the National Guard. He thanked the chiefs of the National Guard for their devoted help to the Committee; and he also returned thanks to the National Guards, mayors, and adjuncts, who by their attitude had prevented bloodshed.

Citizen Eudes rose to beg of his colleagues that the new Municipal Council should be called the Commune of Paris.

Citizen Ranc seconded this proposition by saying that it was indispensable to break off from the past. The name of Commune of Paris would alone indicate that this great city desired to have its full and entire municipal franchise; in a word, *self-government*.

The name of Commune was accepted with acclamation.

The President read a proposition that the Council of the Commune should declare that the members of the Central Committee had acted like good citizens, and had deserved well of the Commune.

Citizen Delescluze seconded the proposition, and said, "The members of the Committee have well deserved the thanks not only of Paris and France, but also of the universal Republic." Citizen Cournet also supported this proposition, declaring that had it not been for the calm and energetic attitude of the Committee, France would have been a prey to terror and reaction.

The thanks were unanimously voted, except by a few members of the Committee, who were unwilling to vote for themselves.

The President charged those of the Committee who were present to transmit to the absent or non-elected members the thanks of the Commune of Paris.

On the proposition of citizens Cournet, Assi, Delescluze, Eudes, and Bergeret, the Assembly, in order to facilitate the despatch of business and the examination of motions, decided on forming themselves into ten Commissions. Each Commission was to possess the same powers as the old ministries, except that of Religion, the budget of which was to be suppressed, and placed under the jurisdiction of the Commission of General Safety. In addition to these, certain particular Commissions were instituted in order to meet the pressing necessities of the moment.

The ten Commissions were :—

" 1. *The Executive.*—This Commission is charged with the execution of the decrees of the Commune as well as of those of the other Commissions. Nothing shall be done without the consent of the Commune. This Commission will sit at the Hôtel-de-Ville, which shall also be the seat of the Commune.

" 2. *The Military Commission*, which replaces the Committee of the National Guard. This Commission is charged with the discipline, armament, clothing, and equipment of the National Guard. It is also instructed to elaborate motions relating to the National Guard.

" The staff-office of the Place Vendôme shall be

independent. In concert with the Commission of General Safety, it will watch over the security of the Commune and the proceedings at Versailles. This Commission replaces the Ministry of War. The armed boats on the Seine are placed under its orders.

"3. *The Commission of Supply*, which shall superintend the victualling of Paris, and keep detailed and full accounts of all the victuals now in the magazines.

"It is instructed to secure, by all possible means, provisions indispensably necessary for three months at least.

"It has the direction and administration of all the provisions in reserve. It is also empowered, should occasion demand it, to distribute flour to the most necessitous. Until a new law shall be made on the town dues, this Commission is charged with receiving the taxes. It will likewise keep an account of the resources of the wine stores.

"4. *The Finance Commission.*—This Commission is charged with establishing the budget of Paris on a new basis. Questions of finance, taxes, rents, exchange, &c., come under its jurisdiction, as also the Bank of France. It has likewise to collect taxes, and to inquire strictly into the position of the finances of Paris.

"Should the necessity arise, it is empowered to inquire into the best means of contracting a loan on the most economical terms.

"This Commission shall also occupy itself with the reduction of the debts of Paris by the least oppressive measures. All demands for the necessary funds of the other Commissions are to be made to the Commission of Finance, and approved of and signed by the Commune.

"This Commission shall secure, by all possible means, a quick and economical collection of the taxes. It will do away with all unnecessary employment; and the public loan offices, being in the department of the Ministry of Finance, are to be under its control.

"5. *The Commission of Justice.*—For a time this Commission is charged with raising the existing state of justice to the elevation of democratic and social institutions.

"It is empowered to take possession of the courts of justice until a decree has definitively settled the question.

"6. *The Commission of General Safety*, with the powers of the Prefecture of Police. This Commission is entrusted with the public safety and order. It will at the same time watch over the public morals, and see that individual liberty is respected as much as possible. In a word, it is charged with the general police. It is bound to preserve the safety of the Republic and to keep an eye on suspected citizens.

"7. *The Commission of Labour, Industry, and Exchange*, having in its province a part of the public works and commerce. It is also entrusted with the dissemination of socialist doctrines. It has to seek means for the equalisation of labour and wages. It will occupy itself with the advancement of national and Parisian industry. It is also the duty of this Commission to find means for the development of international exchange, so as to attract foreign industry and make Paris the great centre of production.

"8. *The Commission of Public Service.*—This Commission is charged with the supervision of the great services, the post-office, telegraphs, and public ways. It will likewise see that all these services act regularly and economically, watch over the railway companies, and organise relations with the services of the provinces.

"It is bound to study the means for putting all the railways into the hands of the communes of France, without damaging the interests of the companies.

"9. *The Commission of Foreign Affairs.*—This Commission is empowered to entertain amicable relations with all the communes of France, so as to lead to a general federation. It is enjoined to contribute to the enfranchisement of the country by its propaganda.

"It is likewise empowered, as occasion presents itself, to send representatives to the different States of Europe, and especially to Prussia, as soon as the attitude of this power towards the Commune shall become known.

"10. *The Commission of Instruction*, having for its province the public education. It will occupy itself with educational reforms. It shall also prepare a motion for gratuitous, compulsory, and exclusively secular instruction. The number of scholarships at the colleges is to be augmented."

The next proceeding was to elect the different members of these Commissions.

The following citizens were elected:—

"1. *The Executive Commission.*—Citizens Eudes,

Tridon, Vaillant, Lefrançais, Duval, F. Pyat, and Bergeret.

" 2. *The Finance Commission.*—Citizens Clément (Victor), Varlin, Jourde, Beslay, and Régère.

" 3. *The Military Commission.*—Citizens Pindy, Eudes, Bergeret, Duval, Chardon, Flourens, and Ranvier.

" 4. *The Commission of Justice.*—Citizens Ranc, Protot, Léo Meillet, Vermorel, Ledroit, and Babick.

" 5. *The Commission of General Safety.*—Citizens Raoul Rigault, Ferré, Assi, Oudet, Chalain, Gérardin, and Cournet.

" 6. *The Commission of Supply.* — Citizens Dereure, Champy, Ostyn, Jean-Baptiste Clément, Parisel, Emile Clément, and H. Fortuné.

" 7. *The Commission of Labour, Industry, and Exchange.*—Citizens Malon, Frankel, Theisz, Dupont, Avrial, Loiseau-Pinson, Eug. Gérardin, and Puget.

" 8. *The Commission of Foreign Affairs.* — Citizens Paschal Grousset, Ch. Gérardin, Antoine Arnaud, Ranc, Arthur Arnould, Delescluze, and Parent.

" 9. *Commission of Instruction.*—Citizens Goupil, Ernest Lefèvre, Jules Vallès, Demay, Miot, Blanchet, Robinet, Verdure, and Albert Leroy.

" 10. *The Commission of Public Service.*—Citizens Ostyn, Billoray, J.-B. Clément, Martelet, Mortier, and Rastoul.

Citizen Varlin, Delegate of the Finance Commission, demanded urgency for a "decree to suspend the sale of things at the public loan office until a special law for the administration of this institution on more advantageous terms to the prolétaires shall be passed."

This decree was unanimously voted.

The proposition of citizens Assi and Varlin concerning rents was also voted with urgency. On the proposition of citizen Billoray, an article was added respecting tenants in furnished lodgings. The following is the decree, including the amendment of citizen Billoray:—

"The Commune of Paris, considering that labour, industry, and commerce have had to bear all the costs of the war, and that it is nothing but just that private property should bear its share of the sacrifices, decrees:

"Art. I. Remission of rent to lodgers from October, 1870, to January and April, 1871.

"Art. II. All moneys paid for rent by lodgers during these nine months shall be adjusted on future terms.

"Art. III. Remission shall also be made of rent due for furnished lodgings.

"Art. IV. All leases may be cancelled at the option of lodgers during a period of six months, dating from the day of this decree.

"Art. V. On the demand of lodgers, all notices given shall be prolonged for three months.

"THE COMMUNE OF PARIS.

"Hôtel-de-Ville, March 29th, 1871."

The Commune organised the municipal administration of twenty arrondissements of Paris by the following decree:—

"The Commune of Paris decrees:

"Art. I. That the members of the Commune shall

have the administrative direction of their arrondissement.

"Art. II. They are invited to associate with themselves, at their own option and responsibility, a Commission for the expedition of business.

"Art. III. Only members of the Commune shall have the right to proceed with civil acts.

"The Commune of Paris."

On the proposition of citizen Beslay, the question of interest on mortgages was put as the order of the day. After hearing citizen Beslay, and on the proposition of citizen Varlin, urgency was rejected, and the question of the day was maintained.

On the proposition of the Military and Finance Commission, the conscription was abolished, and the National Guard declared to be the only regular armed force, by the following decree:—

"The Commune of Paris decrees:

"1. That the conscription is abolished;

"2. That no other military force than the National Guard shall be created or introduced into Paris;

"3. That all able-bodied citizens shall be members of the National Guard.

"The Commune of Paris.

"Hôtel-de-Ville, March 29th, 1871."

On the proposition of twenty-three of its members, the Assembly declared the Commune of Paris to be the only regular power. By another decree an act of accusation was instituted against the members of the Versailles Government, and their property in Paris confiscated.

It next decreed that the functions of all officers who recognised the Versailles Government should be revoked, and that they should be accused and prosecuted.

By another decree it ordered the suppression of the budget of Religion, and the resumption of property in mortmain.

The citizen President was empowered to sign all decrees.

On the proposition of the President, three members were nominated to draw up an address to the people of Paris. Citizens Assi, Eudes, and Bergeret were chosen.

The following is the address:—

"*Commune of Paris.*

"Citizens,

"Your Commune is constituted.

"The vote of March 26th has sanctioned the victorious Revolution.

"A cowardly aggressive power has taken you by the throat; you have, in legitimate self-defence, repelled from your walls the Government which sought to dishonour you by giving you a king.

"To-day, the criminals whom you have not even desired to pursue abuse your magnanimity by organising at the very gates of your city a focus of monarchical conspiracy. They invoke civil war; they set in motion every sort of corruption; they accept any accomplice; they have dared to tell falsehoods in order to obtain help from the foreigner.

"We appeal to the judgment of France and of the world against these execrable conspiracies.

"Citizens,

"The institutions you have just created defy all attempts.

"You are the masters of your destiny. Strengthened by your support, the representation which you have established will repair the disasters caused by a fallen power. Compromised industry, suspended labour, and paralysed commercial transactions will receive a vigorous impulse.

"To-day, the expected decision about rent;

"To-morrow, that of exchange;

"All public services re-established and simplified;

"The National Guard, henceforth the only armed force of our city, reorganised without delay:

"Such will be our first acts.

"The elected of the people only ask your confidence in order to assure the triumph of the Republic.

"As for them, they will do their duty.

"THE COMMUNE OF PARIS.

"Hôtel-de-Ville, March 29th, 1871."

The reading of this proclamation was loudly applauded.

The order of the day was then regulated for next day (March 30th) as follows:—Motion on exchange; mortgage question; the provisioning of Paris; motions on the National Guard and the priests.

On the following day the Assembly sat in Commissions.

The sitting commenced at three o'clock.

The sitting, of which we gave an account, was of all others the most remarkable.

The Commune of Paris, in constituting itself into ten sections, as the protocol of its sitting on March 29th shows, gave proof of great practical spirit. The choice and powers of its ten Commissions were the best that could be made. By means of these Commissions it concentrated in its departments all the governmental and administrative machinery of the city of Paris.

The adversaries of the Commune wanted to confine its *rôle* and circumscribe its action within the narrow circle and derisive powers of a Municipal Council in tutelage. Thus they regarded the acts of its first sitting as monstrous usurpations of power, and protested with all their might against the firm disposition manifested by the Commune to govern and administer Paris, so as to make it a free, independent, and autonomous city, preserving all its influence and powers as the capital.

To the defenders of order, the law on rents was an attack on property. No term could be found strong enough, no expression too energetic, to manifest their indignation.

The Assembly of Versailles, in its holy rage against the Communists who dared to lay their guilty hands on the sacred rights of proprietors, devoted its attention to the framing of a law on rent, which not only ordered the integral payment of the latter, but also gave security to the proprietors against every risk and danger of losses which the contingencies of the siege, the bombardment, and the suspension of business had caused to their pretended rights.

The bill of which we speak made the Commune responsible for the entire payment of the rent of insolvent tenants. This little love-law would have burdened Paris with hundreds of millions of debt. It would have been one more ruinous blow to its finances, already in so deplorable a state through the maladministration of MM. Hausmann and Ferry, and the disasters of the siege. But it mattered little to the Burgraves of Versailles whether Paris was ruined or made bankrupt, provided the principles, rights, and all the inviolable and sacred privileges of property were saved.

Between this Draconian property legislation and the decrees of the Commune there lay an abyss.

The postponement of the payment of the interest on mortgages proved another heavy blow to property, which made the gentlemen of the Versailles Government tremble with indignation.

The abolition of the conscription, of which the speedy suppression of the standing army was the most direct consequence, *and the only means of regenerating France and Europe*, raised a cry of indignation in the ranks of moderate men of all shades.

The approaching suppression of the permanent army, that fine product of the conscription, was another cause of deep pain to all privileged and designing men. How subjugate the people, how keep them under the yoke, how perpetuate despotism, the prolétariat, misery, and pauperism, without an army?

The standing army was the keystone of the building constructed by the modern bourgeoisie in France. The conscription abolished, the permanent army dissolved, there remained no power capable of keeping working men under the yoke; and the whole privileged classes were in danger.

The accusation of the members of the Versailles Government, and the sequestration of their property in Paris, were well calculated to inspire the Versailles Assembly not only with rage and reprobation, but also with horror.

In their eyes the Commune was the antichrist, the enemy of all their rights and privileges; it was the *infâme* to be crushed at all hazards. To sequestrate the property of the Thiers, Jules Favres, Jules Simons, the Picards, and the Ferrys, so swiftly and so nobly acquired since the 4th of September, by *honest* and *moderate* means known to everybody, was a dreadful crime.

But the greatest abomination of all, and which especially raised against the Commune the old men and rural Catholics of the majority of Versailles, was the decree suppressing the budget of Religion, and the return of mortmain property into the Communal domain. In the eyes of the pious sons of the Crusaders this law was more than a crime against property; it was a dreadful, an abominable sacrilege.

It will be seen that since the *début* of the Commune the abyss which separated Paris from the Versailles Government grew wider and wider, and the idea of ever filling it up had to be at once abandoned. Versailles and Paris were in every sense two opposite powers, each repelling the other. Versailles, or the majority of the Assembly, represented feudalism, the middle ages, the old royalist and Catholic society, with all its prejudices and antiquated privileges, anti-revolutionists for whom the years 1789, 1792, 1830, 1848, 1870, 1871, and the whole nineteenth century, had no existence; Paris, or the Commune, personified the aspirations and hopes of the travailleurs-prolétaires for a new and better world by the complete transformation of society; it was the negation, the destruction, the absolute overthrow of present institutions, and the radical abolition of all exploitation. This was how the question stood from the first sitting of the Commune.

In saying this we do not mean to assert that all the members of the Commune were revolutionary Communists. No; many, the greater part, even the immense majority, were not Communists. The greater number, indeed almost all, were individualist socialists; but the circumstances, the wants, and absolute necessities of the moment were such as to force all members of the Commune to the most radical reforms, each of which, in the opinion of the reaction, was a violent attack against the so-called principles of order.

The natural conclusion to be drawn from the facts and phenomena we have just stated is, that any transaction, conciliation, or synthesis between the resistance of the past and the wants of the present was impossible, and that the existing social order in France had attained such a degree of incompatibility with the necessities of the actual situation of the times that it could only be maintained by force; that from the day of its abandonment, as on the 18th of March, all religious, political, and economical institutions would be powerfully menaced and attacked; and that even if those who were charged with the overthrow of the old social order should act unconsciously, it would nevertheless be destroyed by the force of circumstances.

It is possible, however (and facts have since proved it), that by a series of circumstances beyond the control of those to whom the accident of events had confided the mission of the present Revolution, the latter has been a failure; but it will not be so for long; its triumph is only postponed; every stand-still renders it more necessary and more indispensable.

But let us set aside previsions of an inevitable future, and return to the realities of a past of a few weeks only, and to the present.

The Commune, on its first sitting, instructed a Commission to report on the elections. The following was the result:—

"*Report of the Commission on the Elections.*

"The Commission charged with the verification of the elections had to inquire into the following questions:—

"'Is there any incompatibility between the mandate of a deputy of the Versailles Assembly and that of a member of the Commune?'

"Considering that the Versailles Assembly, in refusing to acknowledge the Commune elected by the people of Paris, does not deserve to be recognised by that Commune;

"That plurality ought to be interdicted;

"That it is, besides, absolutely impossible to attend to the labours of two Assemblies;

"The Commission considers that the functions are incompatible.

"'Can foreigners be admitted to the Commune?'

"Considering the flag of the Commune to be that of the universal Republic;

"Considering that every city has the right of bestowing the title of citizen upon foreigners who serve it;

"That this custom has existed for a long time among neighbouring nations;

"Considering that the title of member of the Commune is a greater mark of confidence than that of citizen, which latter quality has been tacitly permitted;

"The Commission is of opinion that foreigners may be admitted, and proposes the admission of citizen Frankel.

"'Can the elections be considered valid according to the law of 1849, which requires that an eighth part of the registered electors shall vote for those returned?'

"Considering it has been stipulated that the elections should be made according to the law of 1849, the Commission is of opinion that an eighth part of the registered votes is legally indispensable.

"But considering that an examination of the electoral lists of 1871 has brought to light such important irregularities that no reliable estimate of the number of electors can be obtained; that the causes of this inaccuracy are of different kinds, namely, the imperial Plébiscite, which produced an unusual augmentation; the Plébiscite of November 3rd; the deaths during the siege, the number of inhabitants who left Paris after the capitulation, and, on the other hand, the vast number who sought refuge in Paris during the siege, &c., &c.;

"Considering that it was almost impossible to rectify all these errors in time, and that no reliance could be placed on such an evidently erroneous legal basis;

"The Commission proposes, in consequence, to declare valid all elections which obtained an eighth part of the votes, as well as the other six in suspense, in consideration of the relative majority of those who discharged their duty as citizens by going to the ballot.

"On behalf of the Commission,
"The Reporter,
"PARISEL."

The decision of the Commission was very justly approved of by the Communal Assembly.

The incompatibility of the mandate of the members of the Commune with that of the representatives of the Versailles Assembly is incontestable. Besides, as the Commune was labouring for the triumph of the universal Republic, it was bound, after its election, to admit citizens of all nationalities who were willing to fight in its ranks for the same object.

The reasons which the report assigned for the non-observance of the clause enacting an eighth of the votes of all registered electors in order for an election to be valid, were most serious and just. The Commune, then, acted wisely in declaring valid the elections of which we have just spoken.

Citizens Delescluze, Cournet, Gambon, &c., elected as members of both the Commune and the Versailles Assembly, did not wait for the promulgation of the law made by the Commune to give in their resignation as deputies of the people to the Versailles Assembly. The following is a letter from citizen Delescluze justly estimating the political spirit of that Assembly:—

To the Citizen President of the Assembly at Versailles.

"Citizen,

"Having for eight days taken no part in the deliberations of the Assembly over which you preside, and in which I only remained during the time of the accusation against the dictators of the 4th of September, and being, besides, unwilling to associate myself either *with its insanity or its passions*, I have the honour to inform you that I give in my resignation as a representative of the people for the department of the Seine.

"I may add that, having had the honour of being elected by two arrondissements for the Commune of Paris, I accept that delegation.

"Salutation and fraternity.

"Signed: DELESCLUZE."

The letters of Cournet and Gambon are quite as severe against the Assembly as that of their colleague Delescluze.

Citizens Floquet and Lockroy, members of the Versailles Assembly, also tendered their resignation in the following letter:—

"Monsieur le Président,

"We have done all in our power to prevent civil war in the face of the armed Prussians still on our soil.

"We swear before the nation that we are in no way responsible for the blood which is being shed at this moment; but since, notwithstanding our past efforts, and those which we are still making to bring about a reconciliation, the battle has commenced by an attack on Paris, we, the representatives of Paris, feel that our place is no longer at Versailles.

"Our place is with our fellow-citizens, with whom, as during the Prussian siege, we shall share the dangers and sufferings in store for them. We have no other duty than that of defending as citizens, and according to the inspirations of our conscience, the menaced Republic. We return into the hands of our electors the mandate confided to us, and we are ready to give them an account of our acts.

"The representatives of the people of Paris,
"CH. FLOQUET.
"EDOUARD LOCKROY."

This letter, so remarkable for its dignity and appropriateness, was an honour to its authors.

Citizen Millière, another deputy of the Versailles Assembly, was also unwilling to take part any longer in its sittings. The disgust and indignation with which it inspired him are plainly shown by the following letter to his electors:—

"Citizens,

"Notwithstanding the profound disgust with which the heinous and violent passions expressed by the majority inspired me, I considered it to be my duty to remain as long as possible in the National Assembly, in order to fulfil the mandate entrusted to me by the people of Paris; that is to say, as long as I was able to contend for the cause of justice, and to combat the party of disorder, coalesced against the Republic.

"Without taking the liberty of judging, and still less of blaming those citizens who, from a conscientious and disinterested sentiment, viewed their duty in a different light from myself, I considered that a resignation, pure and simple, was not the best method of accomplishing the task imposed on a representative of the people.

"I was confirmed in this opinion by the advice of a great number of members of electoral committees who had proposed my candidature; and I was enabled to appreciate the justness of it when I saw with what satisfaction our enemies received the resignation of several deputies who had been elected by the Republican party.

"But the abominable outrage of the Executive, the crime perpetrated by the Versailles Government against right and humanity, affords an opportunity to the deputies of Paris of making a last use of their mandate by solemnly reproving a policy whose evident aim is to deluge the Republic in the blood of the people, which knows no other means of pacification but civil war, the end of which, if realised, would be the absolute ruin of our country.

"It was in this spirit that I wished to present myself at to-day's sitting.

"I intended to question the Government about the attack on Paris, and to demonstrate to the country, deceived by the falsehood of M. Thiers, what was the true situation of the capital.

"It is well that the whole of France should know that Paris is not in a state of insurrection, but rather in a state of legitimate self-defence; that it has only peaceably exercised its right—the right which belongs to it as to every other commune of France; that after having, in a most infamous and treacherous manner, unparalleled in history, delivered it up to its enemies, these miserable men, who have sacrificed our country to their ambition, seek to stifle the spirit of municipal liberty and independence, which would not allow them to enjoy with impunity the fruit of their treason; and that, notwithstanding outrages, defiance, and provocations, the calm, peaceable, and unanimous population of Paris had attempted no aggression, committed no violence, and caused no disorder when the Government attacked them with the old imperial police organised into pretorian troops, and commanded by ex-senators of the Empire.

"This is what I consider to be the duty of a representative of the people. It is thus that I should have fulfilled my duty could I have been at Versailles. I should have declared to the world from the tribune that the reactionary majority and its Executive were responsible for the new calamities which they let loose on our unfortunate country; and, on quitting the Assembly, I should have shaken the dust from my shoes.

"MILLIÈRE."

Never to our knowledge, from the Rump Parliament of Cromwell's time to the Undiscoverable Chamber of 1816, has an Assembly been treated with such disdain, and never has one inspired such an aversion in any of its members.

If some of the Versailles deputies retired from it in

disgust, several of the reactionary members of the Commune, actuated by far less honourable motives, likewise tendered their resignation. They had only allowed themselves to become candidates in order to prevent the nomination of devoted Republicans; but finding, on its first sitting, that it was too revolutionary, they retired.

The following are the names of the principal gentlemen who resigned :—MM. Desmarest, E. Ferry, Nast, Chéron, Rochart, Tirard, Leroy, Brelay, Adam, Méline, Barré, Robinet, Frimeau, Loiseau, Marmottan, De Bouteiller, Ranc, &c.

Most of these gentlemen considered the Commune had usurped power in occupying itself with other matters besides the municipal administration. They voluntarily forgot that the Commune of Paris was not a Municipal Council, and ingeniously confounded these two very distinct institutions.

Their retreat gave more homogeneity to the Commune, and increased its strength. It was, therefore, no misfortune.

CHAPTER II.

THE BATTLE.

SINCE March 19th two armies encamped within sight of each other, the one at Versailles, the other at Paris.

The former, that of the reactionary Government at Versailles, consisted of all those soldiers of France who were hostile to the Republic and enemies of the people. It was composed of the ban and arrière-ban of the most reactionary military elements; namely, the old Municipal Guard of the monarchy, transformed by the Empire into the guardians of Paris, and by the Government of the National Defence into Republican Guards; different regiments of provincial gendarmes, accomplices of the authors of the ambuscade of the 2nd of December, 1851; all the ex-sergents de ville of the Empire, Corsican bravoes, slaughterers and garrotters of the people for twenty years, transformed into guardians of the peace by the Government of the 4th of September; Chouans, Vendéans, and Pontifical zouaves of Charette; royalist and Catholic volunteers, with mobiles of the departments; sailors and marines; rough and fanatical Bretons; half-savage turcos; a few regiments of the line, forced to march in the midst of these reactionary hordes; and a corps of cavalry under the command of the Marquis de Galifet, an old friend at the Tuileries, and a ferocious and bloodthirsty officer; full of valour when women, children, and disarmed and chained-up prisoners were to be butchered, but a coward in the face of a foreign enemy invading our country. This saloon-hero, antechamber soldier, and alcove-runner, had only recently returned from Germany, whither the Prussians had sent him prisoner after the shameful defeats at Sedan and Metz. All this heap of corrupted and besotted old soldiers of the Empire, rude gendarmes, police assassins, wild bravoes, degraded mercenaries, royalist Bretons, Catholic Vendéans, and fanatical Chouans, were commanded by traitor generals, felons of the 2nd of December; among whom the Vinoys, Ducrots, Galifets, L'Admiraults; the royalist officers Cissey, Daurelle, Besson, &c.; and leaders of bands like that of Charette, distinguished themselves. The whole of them were placed under the commandership-in-chief of a marshal of the Empire, Mac-Mahon, who proved himself as incapable as cowardly at Sedan, and, next to the sinister man of December, the principal author of all our evils, defeats, invasion, ruin, misery, humiliation, and shame. Such, as a whole, was the army of Versailles.

The despatches from this town of April 1st said:—

"All precautions have been taken to protect Versailles against a surprise. Fresh troops arrive every day. We are on the point of erecting new camps near Porchefontaine and Villeneuve-l'Etang. Three battalions of the foreign legion have arrived here from Besançon. The troops at this moment at Versailles are composed of eight divisions of infantry and three of cavalry.

"The Government has taken care to send all the troops not to be depended upon into the provinces. Yesterday morning several emissaries from Paris, who attempted to collect adherents among the soldiers to the Central Committee, were arrested.

"A great many soldiers, late prisoners in Germany, are continually returning to swell the ranks of the Versailles army."

The army of Paris formed a complete and striking contrast to that we have just described. It was composed of the same heroic National Guard of Paris which had defended the capital for six months, and fought with such perseverance, courage, and fearlessness against the formidable Prussian army. It numbered among its ranks the whole Parisian population, comprising the most intelligent, energetic, courageous, devoted, and heroic men of France.

At the head of the battalions, nominated and chosen by them, were the most devoted and popular Republican chiefs; and they were led by young citizen generals who had won their rank in a few months by marching at their head against the enemy, and the greater number of whom had been the principal actors on the memorable day of March 18th. The best known among them were Generals Flourens, Duval, Bergeret, and Eudes.

The first of these two armies had been in the service of the most backward monarchical and clerical reaction that ever sullied France, dreaming of nothing else but the restoration of the throne, the altar, and the monarchical institutions of the period before

1789; seeking not only to re-establish the divine right of royalty and the supremacy of Catholicism as the State religion, but also to destroy all that remained of the economical state of affairs brought about by the conquests of the great French Revolution. The little liberty, franchise, and rights enjoyed by the working class were menaced. The humbler citizens and prolétaires of Paris knew perfectly well that if the Government of Versailles, which had fled from Paris on the 18th of March, should return victorious to the capital, it would place them more rigorously under the triple yoke of royalty, clergy, and the exploitation and monopoly of capitalists.

The second of these armies—that is to say, the National Guard of Paris—had firmly resolved to resist to the very knife this restoration of the past, which it would not have at any price, and to fight to the last extremity, to death, to massacre, and, if necessary, even to annihilation, in the defence and preservation of the Republic, menaced by the reactionary majority of the Versailles Assembly. It desired the independence, liberty, and autonomy of Paris and of all the other communes of France— *a free Paris in a free France*. It wanted to secure all the rights of the man and of the citizen. Above all, it demanded the first, most just, most useful, most indispensable, primordial, and, at the same time, the most contested of all its rights—that which it had never possessed to this day—the entire, absolute, and complete benefit of the produce of its labour, without the loss of the slightest part, the smallest particle.

The armed people of Paris were fighting then, above all, for the abolition of the *exploitation of man by man;* for the destruction of all privileges, monopolies, despotism, and economical, political, and religious tyrannies; for the suppression of the prolétariat, of misery and pauperism; in a word, for the complete, radical, and absolute emancipation of all the working classes.

These were the two diametrically opposite ends for which the armies of Versailles and Paris were going to war, which were now facing each other in battle array, and between which the slightest contention, the most trifling accident, would cause the fight to commence.

Versailles was the pole of iniquity, Paris that of justice.

We shall soon see how the frightful storm we are describing broke out between these two opposite elements.

But let us first explain the situation of these two armies at the end of March.

The Communal troops, and those of Versailles, were face to face, and the outposts could bid defiance to each other. Whilst in Paris every barricade gave way to peaceful occupations, outside the walls the footstep of war was plainly visible. The forts on the left bank of the Seine, as well as the redoubt of the Hautes-Bruyères, were each occupied by three battalions of National Guards, who were on duty, on an average of six times, twenty-four hours. The forts were armed with pieces of artillery, and furnished with everything requisite for service in the way of *personnel* and ammunition. From the Barrière Fontainebleau to Bas-Meudon the different gates were each protected by four cannons levelled against the exterior of Paris.

Sorties and reconnaissances went on day and night, and several battalions, organised as marching companies, were continually directed against divers points.

The outposts of the Commune extended from Vincennes to Mont Valérien. There was a corresponding cordon of the enemy on the other side of the Seine. Through the again budding woods, on the slopes at the entrance of the park, the eye encountered nothing but municipal guards and sergents de ville.

The marines and foot-soldiers remained at Versailles; the cavalry at both Versailles and Saint-Germain. The chasseurs d'Afrique and the zouaves were likewise close to the Assembly, as also the mobiles and volunteers, all but too well prepared to show no mercy to Paris.

On April 2nd, at eight o'clock in the morning, troops from Versailles marched against the outposts of the National Guards. About a hundred mètres from the Courbevoie circus, the advanced guard, composed of troops of the line, made a halt. The commanding officer advanced towards the commander of the 118th battalion of the National Guard; but the latter, not wishing to fire on their brethren of the army, turned their butt-ends up. The commander of the line requested the defenders of Paris to lay down their arms. On their refusal, the Versailles soldiers fell back, likewise unwilling to be the first to fire upon their countrymen. Several companies of gendarmes, men capable of anything, then marched upon the National Guards up to the point previously occupied by the line. The officer of gendarmerie then spurred his horse, and advanced towards the Parisian battalions. A sentinel of the latter, crossing his bayonet, called out, "Who goes there? Halt!" The gendarme seized his revolver and aimed at the sentinel; but before this madman had time to discharge his weapon the sentry fired, and the officer of gendarmes fell from his horse mortally wounded. The horse was taken and brought into Paris, and immediately a fight commenced between the gendarmes and National Guards.

At the same moment the Versailles troops unmasked their mitrailleuses, which gave fire and spread confusion in the ranks of the Federals, who, having been joined by five hundred National Guards from Courbevoie, retired fighting to the bridge, pursued by the gendarmes.

While this was going on, the Versaillists placed some pieces of artillery at the circus of Courbevoie, and no sooner had the National Guards reached the Avenue de Neuilly than the aggressors sent their bombs into them, which put the finishing-stroke on the disorder of their ranks.

Mont Valérien also hurled some projectiles: about thirty cannon-shots were fired. Two bombs fell in the Avenue de la Grande Armée between eleven and twelve o'clock in the day. The house No. 79, and the fifth on the side of the fortification, were struck.

Towards one o'clock the white flag of the Versaillists was hoisted on the lamp attached to the pedestal from which the statue of Napoleon I. had been thrown down.

The dead and wounded were picked up, those of the National Guard being laid on litters and carried into Paris by the inhabitants of Courbevoie.

At two o'clock the drawbridge of the Porte Maillot was lowered for the passage of the ambulances and surgeons.

Battalions came successively to the Porte de Neuilly, and were sent off to the different bastions.

The gates on the right and left banks had been closed from Montrouge to Ternes, where, through mismanagement, a line of waggons waited in vain for the lowering of the bridges.

The drums beat to arms in several quarters. The 208th battalion, occupying the Saint-Lazare Terminus, received orders to depart.

Embrasures were made, and the ramparts armed with cannons, and along the whole of the west line work was actively carried on.

Commander Flourens arrived at the head of his battalion, and marched through the Porte des Ternes. Battalions continually succeeded each other, until the Avenue de la Grande Armée was completely covered with National Guards and spectators.

Some deserters, Versailles soldiers of the line, entered Paris.

The zouaves of Charette fought under the white flag. Each of them wore a Jesus-heart of white cloth on his breast, with the inscription, "Stand still; the heart of Jesus is truth." It was also stated that they cried "Vive le roi!"

"The gendarmes," says the *Vengeur*, "having made prisoners some of the 93rd battalion of the National Guards, fastened them to the tails of their horses, and dragged them to Mont Valérien to be shot. The mangled bodies of these unfortunate men were subsequently found and brought to the mairie of Neuilly, where crowds of people flocked to see them. One of the bodies had been mutilated in a most outrageous and barbarous manner."

These were the first acts of ferocious cruelty committed by the troops of Versailles, soon to be followed by many others which excited the defenders of Paris to desperation, and resulted in their making terrible reprisals.

By four o'clock several batteries descended the avenue, and the National Guards assisted in drawing the cannons up the ramparts and fitting them into the embrasures. Ammunition was collected and stored in the magazines.

At half-past four General Bergeret, with some of his staff, arrived in a closed carriage, escorted by several officers.

At that moment the firing of cannons was heard in the distance, which, without doubt, proceeded from the army of Versailles. But be that as it may, there was not the least doubt that during the night or the next day a serious engagement would take place; and the National Guards marched out in great numbers with artillery and mitrailleuses.

At six o'clock battalion after battalion defiled along the boulevards, through the Rue de Rivoli, towards Neuilly. Eight seven-pounders passed through the Rue Richelieu in the same direction.

At eight the drums beat to arms in the quarters of the Palais-National.

It will clearly be seen that on April 2nd, as on January 2nd and March 18th, the troops of the

Versailles Government commenced the attack, and were the first to inaugurate those long series of atrocious crimes which were fraught with such terrible consequences.

Let the responsibility of this war, and of the bloodshed, misfortunes, disasters, executions, massacres, and barbarous execution of prisoners, that followed as a necessary consequence of the attack of April 2nd, fall on the heads of the guilty and cruel aggressors, the authors of our first disasters, of our defeat in the foreign invasion, and of the surrender of Paris; who, for the sake of personal interests and a royalist, clerical, and bourgeois reaction, after having provoked a foreign war, did not hesitate to kindle civil war, to shed rivers of French blood, to bombard Paris after the Prussians, to set it on fire again, to cover it with ruin and disaster, and to plunge it into an abyss of evils, misery, and desolation, unnamed and unparalleled in history; and all this in the face of a foreign enemy, brought there by them, and still occupying our territory.

The following are the eloquent terms in which Paul Meurice stigmatises in the *Rappel* the crime of high treason against humanity committed by the Versailles Government:—

"Well! we did not believe it; no, we did not, could not believe that the Versailles Government would have dared to attack the people of Paris. We had registered its provocations and its threats, but if we had been asked whether we believed it would put them in execution, we should have replied, 'We think not.'

"We said to ourselves, 'M. Thiers speaks in a

high tone; he tries to intimidate Paris by the clatter of his swords and the enumeration of his forces; he holds reviews and councils; he writes circulars: these are his diplomatic tricks and parliamentary artifices to secure for himself better conditions in a possible treaty. But he is too clever a politician, and perhaps too good a Frenchman at bottom, to risk his reputation, and also to precipitate his country into that horrible adventure of civil war.'

"Well! we deceived ourselves. See how bravado turns into outrage, and a profligate act becomes a crime! That braggart phrase in his circular of April 1st which made us laugh, '*One of the finest armies France ever possessed* has been organised at Versailles,' became one of the most abominable by-words ever uttered when that 'fine army' really threw itself upon this great Paris!

"They have attacked!

"They dare not deny it! The fact is averred and incontestably proved; the most moderate journals give in to it; the signal was given by two cannon-shots fired from Versailles. Besides, the National Guards only occupied Courbevoie since yesterday, where they were surprised; they had not fortified themselves, and were in small numbers, with only a few cartridges against cannons and mitrailleuses. . . . . There cannot be any doubt or equivocation: those of Versailles commenced the attack!

"We will not for the moment look upon anything else; we set aside every political question, all estimation of principles; we will not try to find out which side is right, or which ought to be victorious;

we content ourselves with stating this fact: the Government of M. Thiers, which may or may not be legal or even right, which may or may not be victorious, is and must for ever stand arraigned and condemned of having commenced the civil war in the presence of the enemy, the still threatening Prussians, the National Guard and the French army still wounded and bleeding: the Government was the first to set one against the other. Whatever may happen, and even if it should gain the day, this Government is doomed: ruined by its own partisans, now and for ever. Never, never can it rise again before history and before our country.

" In fact, the country, like a mother between two contending sons, neither knows nor wishes to know which of the two is in the right or wrong, which is the stronger or the weaker; but, in order that it may decide which shall be arraigned and condemned, it simply asks—

"' Who commenced?'"

On the news of the attack on the troops of the Commune by those of Versailles, and the atrocities committed by the latter, the Executive Commission made the following proclamation:—

"*To the National Guard of Paris.*

"The royalist conspirators have *attacked*.

"Notwithstanding the moderation of our attitude, they have *attacked*.

"Not being able to trust the French army, they have attacked with Pontifical zouaves and the imperial police.

"Not content with cutting off all communication with the provinces, and making useless efforts to defeat us by hunger, these infuriated men have imitated the Prussians, and bombarded the capital.

"This morning the Chouans of Charette, the Vendéans of Cathelineau, and the Bretons of Trochu, supported by the gendarmes of Valentin, bombarded the inoffensive village of Neuilly, and commenced the civil war against our National Guard.

"There have been some killed and wounded.

"Elected by the population of Paris, it is our duty to defend the great city against the guilty aggressors. With your help we will defend it.

"The Executive Commission,
"Bergeret, Eudes, Duval, Lefrancais, Félix Pyat, Tridon, and Vaillant.

"Paris, April 2nd, 1871."

The Government of Versailles also gave an account of these facts, dissembling all the odiousness of the criminal attack of which it had been guilty against Paris.

The following is the address which it sent to the provinces:—

"Versailles, April 2nd, 1871, six o'clock in the evening.

"For two days movements have commenced near Reuil, Nanterre, Courbevoie, and Puteaux; and the Pont de Neuilly having been barricaded by the insurgents, the Government could not allow these attempts to go unpunished, and has given orders for them to be immediately suppressed.

"General Vinoy, after having assured himself that a demonstration of the insurgents near Châtillon was not of a serious character, departed at six o'clock with the Audel Brigade of the Faron

Division, and the Bernard Brigade of the Bruat Division, protected on its left by General Galifet's division of chasseurs, and on its right by two squadrons of the Republican guard.

"The troops advanced in two columns, one by Reuil and Nanterre, the other by Vaucresson and Montretout.

"They effected a junction at the circus of Bergeries. Four battalions of the insurgents held the position of Courbevoie, as well as the barracks and the circus round the statue.

"The troops carried these barricaded positions with remarkable spirit; the barracks were taken by the marines; the great barricade at Courbevoie by the 113th of the line. The troops then rushed at the descent which adjoins the Pont de Neuilly, took the barricade, and closed the bridge.

"The insurgents beat a precipitate retreat, leaving a number of dead, wounded, and prisoners in our hands. The spirit of the troops accelerated this result. Our losses were almost *nil*.

"The exasperation of our soldiers was extreme, especially against those deserters who were recognised. At four o'clock the troops re-entered their cantonments, having rendered good service to the cause of order, which will not be forgotten by France. General Vinoy never quitted his command for an instant.

"The miserable men whom France is forced to fight have committed another crime. M. Pasquier, the chief surgeon, who advanced too near the enemy, has been killed."

It will be seen from this report that the authorities of Versailles, while dissembling their crimes and exaggerating their successes, themselves declare that their troops attacked those of the Commune; and they own, besides, that "the exasperation of their soldiers was extreme." We need not, therefore, be astonished that the gendarmes, municipal guards, and sergents de ville of M. Thiers's army were guilty of atrocious crimes, and that they should be reproached with having murdered the prisoners of the Commune in a most cruel and barbarous manner.

But neither this sudden attack, the cruelties committed by their enemies, the furious ardour of the Versailles gendarmes, the fanatical ferocity of the Pontifical zouaves of Charette, the rough dash of the Breton marines, the superiority of the armament, nor the precision of the fire of the Versailles soldiers, could discourage the defenders of the Commune.

The whole night was spent in assembling and rallying together the battalions of the National Guard.

Next day, April 3rd, at daybreak, a great number were ready, and moved off in the direction of Versailles.

The troops of the Commune destined to act on that day were divided into three army corps.

The first column, forming the right wing, was commanded by General Bergeret. It had orders to advance along the Avenue de la Grande Armée, clear the fortifications through the Porte Maillot, march along the Avenue de Neuilly, cross the Seine, pass to the circus of Courbevoie, wheel round Mont Valérien, and march on Versailles by

Reuil and Bougival. General Flourens, with the battalions of Belleville and his own volunteers, formed part of this column.

The centre, under the command of General Duval, supported by the cannons of Fort Issy, was to advance by the heights of Meudon and Sèvres, take them, and then march on Versailles.

The left, commanded by General Eudes, was to march on Versailles by Vitry, Villejuif, Bourg-la-reine, Sceaux, Plessy, Viroflay, &c., under the protection of Forts Ivry, Bicêtre, and Montrouge.

These three columns formed an effective force of nearly one hundred and twenty thousand men, with about two hundred cannons and mitrailleuses.

General Bergeret's column began moving at five o'clock in the morning between Neuilly and Courbevoie. For a long time he encountered no resistance, and a part of his corps marched on Versailles by the road which defiles close to Mont Valérien.

The latter was silent, and did not appear to be guarded: not a single soldier was to be seen. The officers, and a commander of mobiles who was at the head of the column advancing directly within the fire of Mont Valérien, assured their men that friendly troops occupied that citadel, and that the commander of the fort had promised not to fire on the National Guards. The troops of the Commune, full of confidence in these promises, continued their march, the 118th battalion of the National Guard being at the head. But no sooner had the latter entered the road which encircles the glacis than the hitherto silent and inanimate fortress was lit up by a circle of fire; a frightful rolling of the thunder of cannon was heard; and the guns of the citadel vomited balls, bombs, and grape-shot on the imprudent and too-confiding National Guards, whom their chiefs had inconsiderately led within the very mouths of the cannons.

Many of the National Guards fell dead, and a still greater number were wounded. Fortunately for them, the commander of the fort had allowed them to approach too near, and being in a hollow of the road, the greater part of the projectiles passed over their heads.

But this formidable welcome, totally unexpected as it was by the National Guards, inflicted great disorder and absolute panic among their ranks. Many fled, crying out "Treachery!" which spread disorder among the other troops, and even into the midst of those encamped at the ramparts. Some of the fugitives found their way into the fortified enceinte, and re-entered the city, spreading the most alarming news about the début of the expedition.

Before proceeding with our narrative let us observe that the chiefs of the Federals, in so imprudently leading their men within range of Mont Valérien, had acted honestly in saying that this fortress would not fire. This rumour had been spread some days before, and they imprudently re-echoed it; but we must confess that they were guilty of an unpardonable fault in acting as they did. Some of them considerably aggravated their guilt by asserting that the fort was occupied by friendly National Guards, who would not only not fire, but give up the fortress to the Federals.

These lying promises were productive of very serious consequences. They threw the ranks of the

National Guards into the greatest disorder, and exercised a most melancholy influence on the commencement of the campaign.

During this accident the bulk of the column, consisting of about fifteen thousand men, with General Bergeret at its head, had succeeded in passing Mont Valérien, and marched on to Nanterre.

Some of the chiefs of the Federals maintained that the direct march of the 118th battalion on Mont Valérien was undertaken with the view of diverting the attention of the defenders of the fortress, and of occupying their artillery while the principal columns rounded the fort and effected their passage to the other side.

A hot engagement took place at Nanterre, Reuil, Bougival, and Courbevoie. Attacked by superior forces, without ammunition and provisions, the National Guards defended their position foot by foot. A member of the Commune was at their head. The rural troops of Versailles were continually reinforced; and the battalions of the Commune found themselves compelled to fall back to the Seine, leaving behind them a number of killed, wounded, and prisoners.

Soldiers of the line taken prisoners from the ranks of the National Guard were immediately shot without pity by the murderous armed bands of Versailles, which mostly consisted of gendarmes and sergents de ville.

Some honest soldiers of the 58th of the line, comprehending the odious work for which the Thiers Government had destined them, refused to fire on their fellow-countrymen who were fighting in defence of their rights, which were likewise those of the prolétaires of the entire army.

The brigands who furnished them with weapons for the sanguinary and liberty-destroying work which the pitiless reaction expected them to do, ordered the sergents de ville to seize, disarm, and immediately shoot in front of their regiment the unfortunate men who had refused to commit the most detestable of all crimes—the murder of the defenders of right and justice.

The following is the proclamation of one of the chiefs of the Versailles hordes to his soldiers :—

" War has been declared by the bands of Paris.

" Yesterday, the day before, and to-day they assassinated my soldiers.

" I declare war without truce or pity against these assassins. This morning I made an example. May it be beneficial! I do not wish to be driven to such an extremity again.

" Do not forget that the country, the law, and right are on the side of Versailles and the National Assembly, and not on that of the grotesque Assembly of Paris, calling itself the Commune.

" The General commanding the Brigade,
" GALIFET.

" April 3rd, 1871."

Citizen Flourens commanded a column of the right wing, composed of the battalions of Belleville, Montmartre, Batignolles, and La Villette. At daybreak these troops crossed the Seine by a bridge constructed on the island opposite Puteaux, and sheltered from the projectiles of Mont Valérien.

But at the circus of Bergeries, on the heights of Puteaux, bombs from the fortress struck the battalions of Flourens. This threw the ranks into the greatest disorder, some were killed and wounded, and three or four battalions fell back and recrossed the Seine.

Commander Flourens, with a part of his troops, nevertheless continued his advance on Reuil, which was occupied by from about twelve to fifteen hundred men, who quartered themselves partly in the barracks and partly on the inhabitants.

Flourens immediately constructed barricades in the broad avenue leading to Saint-Germain, and posted a cordon of tirailleurs along the Seine, in order to guard against a surprise from the Versailles troops. In company with some of his staff-officers, he stationed himself near the terminus.

Notwithstanding the surveillance of the tirailleurs, which had been very badly executed, a squad of gendarmes on a reconnoitring tour crossed the Seine in boats, and unexpectedly presented themselves in front of the terminus. On seeing the enemy, Flourens fired his revolver and wounded one of the gendarmes badly; his aides-de-camp immediately surrounded him, and a hand-to-hand fight commenced, in which the unfortunate general of the Commune fell mortally wounded by two sword-cuts on the nape of the neck. It was the officer in command of the squad who killed him.

His two aides-de-camp were disarmed and made prisoners, one of them being seriously wounded. The body of Flourens was conveyed to the house of a cultivator in the avenue, and, being placed in a dung-cart filled with straw, was sent to Versailles, where it was publicly exposed in order to gratify the brutal curiosity of the abject mob of the royal town of the Parc-aux-Cerfs, the Great and the Little Trianon. This populace made itself remarkable for its rage against the unfortunate prisoners of the army of the Commune.

To reform the human race, the poor modern people, after the model of the great Hellenes, by a free life, free thinking, and free speech, was the fixed idea of the unfortunate Flourens. *La Science de l'Homme* was the title of his great work, which by his premature death has been left unfinished. Science teaching the art of life, the philosopher becoming the instructor of the people, as in the time of the Greek legislators—it was this conviction which brought him to the sword of the gendarmes, and which cost him his life. The Revolution was his means of action. He precipitated himself into it with ardour, without any reserve, staking his life, and losing it. From plot to conspiracy, from insurrection to revolution, he had just reached the day on which the Commune risked its first great battle, when he became one of its first martyrs. He consecrated with his blood the great cause of the prolétariat, which may succumb to-day, and perhaps even to-morrow, but which nevertheless will and must be victorious in the end.

The day is not far distant when social doctrines will lead to the application of such reforms as must infallibly result in the emancipation of the working classes. Neither right nor science can be stifled. The demands of those in misery, the cry of the ignorant for instruction, and the desire of the abject to rise from their humiliation, cannot for ever be rejected. No; they are not to be stifled by executions, cannonadings, and massacres *en masse.*

Never is a cause so near its triumph as when its apostles fall beneath the blows of the enemy. Nothing more advances the budding and fructification of just ideas than the blood of its martyrs.

The defenders of Paris honoured the brother of General Henry, who was also killed, with a grand funeral, worthy of the heroic young man and of themselves. Fifty thousand National Guards followed him to his grave. .

While the right wing was undertaking its heroic but imprudent attack, General Duval, who commanded the centre of the army of the Commune, made a movement with twenty battalions in the direction of Arcueil, Bagneux, Châtillon, Clamart, and Meudon.

The first shots were fired from Bas-Meudon at seven o'clock. The fight soon extended in the direction of the woods, across the territory of Moulineaux and Val-Fleury, where it assumed the proportions of a battle.

The guardians of the peace and the gendarmes occupied the heights of Meudon, and two batteries were hastily erected on the terrace of the château.

Everywhere the musketry fire was very lively. The fire of the mitrailleuses intermingled its sinister crackling with the roll of the cannons of Fort Issy, which fired on the batteries at the Château de Meudon. The field-pieces of the Federals vomited grape-shot. The thunder was even greater than the heaviest cannonading of the Prussians.

The outposts of the Versaillists were vigorously attacked and everywhere dislodged, while the gendarmes ran as fast as possible from the glass-works of Sèvres.

The artillery, with their batteries, retired from Meudon to Montalets, in order to oppose the passage of the Federals, and likewise to get beyond the reach of the fire from Fort Issy. Two seven-pounders attempted to force the battery from Val-Fleury, and some of the horse artillery were placed on the heights of Meudon, above the château.

The following was the hourly progress made by the Federals against the Versaillists :—

At nine o'clock the attack extended along the whole line. Attacked in the rear by the Federals, the fire of whose muskets and cannons was heard in the woods of Meudon, Viroflay, Jouy, the hamlet of Vélizy, and Grâce-de-Dieu, the Versaillist artillery was forced to remove its scarcely-erected batteries to the heights of Meudon.

The glass-works of Meudon, used as a station by the gendarmes, were attacked, and all resistance proving fruitless, they descended and fled as fast as their legs would carry them before the musketry fire of the Federals.

At ten o'clock the National Guards climbed, by cross-roads and fields, the heights of Clamart and Châtillon; others marched through the village of Clamart towards the redoubt of Châtillon. Fifteen well-horsed pieces of artillery defiled in the streets. A detachment from Fort Issy encamped at the entrance of the village.

At eleven o'clock a desperate fight began on the

line of the Bois de Meudon and in the streets of Val-Fleury.

The fire of small arms was sharp. The shots fell thick and fast.

At Moulineaux the National Guards, in ambush at the back of the houses, fired at the gendarmes posted on the right, and in less than five minutes thirty of them were *hors de combat*, and eight lay dead at the Bellevue Station. The artillery of the forts, the batteries, and the field-pieces mingled with the crackling of the mitrailleuses. The projectiles whistled and crossed each other in the air. It rained bombs. Some burst at the top of the village, others in the centre; and the whole population was in a dreadful fright. All the shops were closed.

At noon the cannons roared with greater violence, and the small-arm fire very nearly equalled it.

The heights of Châtillon and the Clamart woods were in possession of the Federals, as also part of those of Bas-Meudon, where the Versaillists still maintained a battery.

At two o'clock Fort Issy fired on the two batteries of the Château de Meudon, which replied vigorously.

A well-sustained fire from the tirailleurs was unceasingly heard in the woods of Clamart, and from time to time the rolling of the mitrailleuses drowned the noise of the small arms.

Several wounded officers arrived from Fleury in ambulances, and many of the dead were placed in waggons requisitioned from the villagers of Clamart.

During the whole of this day the National

Guards displayed the greatest courage, and fought like old soldiers. They vigorously attacked and handled the enemy, whom they several times dislodged and forced to retreat. In a word, the citizen soldiers were admirably heroic and cool, and there is not the least doubt that if they had possessed a little more experience and better commanders they would have been victorious.

Their attack on Meudon was not only made with great courage, but with a good deal of skill. At first they advanced in skirmishing order in two lines; but, on account of the resistance they encountered, they were unable to dislodge their adversaries. Finding these tactics would not do, they reformed into columns, and, by a clever movement, turned the viaduct of Val-Fleury, and attacked the enemy in flank, supported by the artillery of Fort Issy. But the precision of the fire from the Versailles artillery posted on the terrace of Meudon caused heavy losses. It rained bombs, and heavy carnage among their ranks was the result. Nevertheless they maintained their position well, and continued to advance against the enemy, who was forced to remove his cannons to the heights.

Had it not been for a sad accident the success of the Federals at this point would have been complete. Their battery at the redoubt of Moulinet was so badly served by inexperienced artillery-men that most of their bombs, instead of reaching the troops of Versailles, found their way into the ranks of the National Guard, causing considerable disorder and confusion, and killing and wounding great numbers. These losses were the more to be regretted as they were inflicted by friends, and were the principal cause of the failure of the attack on the château and heights of Meudon.

At four o'clock the retreat was sounded, but the fire did not cease until six. After the signal for retreat, a great number of National Guards wanted to continue the fight, and retired behind the entrenchments of Issy in a state of fury.

During these events a desperate fight took place in the Clamart woods, occupied by the Federals, who disputed their ground foot by foot for four hours. From this dangerous position they fell back, in order to avoid being cut off by the troops of Versailles; but they retired in good order, notwithstanding the fire from the concealed batteries of Meudon, which showered bombs into the column of General Duval, causing it to suffer greatly, as it was taken in a hollow, slanting road.

Towards four o'clock the ammunition began to fail, and the soldiers of the Commune, harassed and tired out by thirty hours' work, effected a retreat in good order, and established themselves in ambush in and behind the houses of the villages of Issy and Vanves. The 61st and the 79th suffered heavy losses, a great number of the officers being killed by grape-shot.

Another column then took possession of the plateau of Châtillon; a detachment occupied the redoubt; whilst the 41st, 81st, and 125th battalions advanced to the farm-house of Chavillé. Night having come on, and ammunition and victuals being very short, they were also compelled to retire. This retreat was the signal for a furious attack by the gendarmes, sergents de ville, and

Breton mobiles. The field-pieces and mitrailleuses committed fearful execution in the ranks of the National Guards, compelling them to hasten their flight and take refuge in the redoubt, closely followed by the enemy. A great number of killed and wounded was the result of this day's battles.

At night the retreat of the Federals commenced along the whole line. The fire slackened, and a few cannon-shots were heard at intervals, but the action was over.

The wounded were brought in by ambulances. The Necker Hospital received a great number of the 67th, 127th, 129th, and 194th battalions of the National Guard. The wounds being generally of a serious nature, many amputations were necessary. Most of these wounds had been received at close quarters. All these men were wounded in the morning at the fight of Meudon. Fortunately some doctors from Issy, Moulineaux, and Meudon most laudably lent their assistance in the first dressing of the wounds. During the day several ambulances were re-established on the left bank of the river.

The 67th battalion suffered badly during the fight at Moulineaux in the morning. This battalion had engaged in a narrow lane of Meudon, and was assailed by a murderous fire from the windows.

The 101st battalion of the Twelfth Arrondissement (Gobelins) took a mitrailleuse by storm near Châtillon. During the night the National Guard occupied the trenches between the redoubt of Moulin-de-Pierre and Châtillon. Some houses in Moulin-de-Pierre were set on fire by the cannons of Fort Issy.

At Belleville, Montmartre, and La Villette no

able-bodied men remained at home: all were at battle.

To-day, at two o'clock in the afternoon, a great number of National Guards reached Villemombes, about five English miles from Versailles, but were beaten by the Government troops, with a loss of two hundred and fifty men.

The left wing, under the command of General Eudes, had but a small share in that day's fighting, and consequently did not suffer much. It marched by the south of Paris on the road to Choisy-le-roi, Sceaux, and Bagneux, turning its back to the heights. But behind the Meudon woods and Villacoublay the head of the column was received by a heavy musketry fire, to which the Federals promptly replied. The small band of assailants was driven back.

As we have seen, the whole was a great battle offered by the Commune to the disciplined troops of Versailles, who were commanded by a marshal of the Empire, old and experienced generals, and skilled officers. To oppose these the Commune had only young generals, inexperienced in warfare, whose audacity, courage, and genius had to stand in place of study, art, and practice.

The army of the Commune was to a great extent composed of married men with families, and we need not, therefore, wonder that they were deficient in the practice, stability under fire, and especially in the discipline of the regular army. Its officers had neither the military knowledge which study alone can give, nor the habit of command or experience only to be acquired by long practice.

There was no cavalry, and the artillery was very

inferior in comparison with that of the enemy. The artillery-men, being National Guards, were but insufficiently instructed. The conductors of the teams did not understand how to manœuvre, and the horses, sadly deficient in number, had never been under fire.

Such were the principal causes of the inferiority of the army of the Commune. But, in spite of all this, they did not hesitate to give battle outside the fortifications of the city, to face the fire of Mont Valérien, and to march on Versailles. Yes, perhaps it was audacious. And yet up to three o'clock in the afternoon the chances of battle were not so very unfavourable to this bold undertaking. If the rear-guard of the columns of Bergeret and Flourens had retreated fighting under the fire of Mont Valérien, the bulk of these two corps had succeeded in doubling that fortress and marching on the road to Versailles. And, further, if the centre, under the command of Duval, had had sufficient provisions and ammunition, and had been properly supported by the right and left wings, so as to allow the reserve to be brought forward, it was quite possible they would have won the battle. Up to three o'clock in the afternoon the Federals gained positive successes over the Versaillists, who were forced back, while some of their batteries were silenced.

The ammunition and victualling departments were badly arranged, and greatly contributed to the defeat. For three days the greater part of the National Guard had nothing to eat but bad biscuits; other victuals were not to be had; and at the plateau of Châtillon even water was unobtainable.

In consequence, the National Guards suffered considerably from hunger and thirst. Badly as the administration was managed during the siege, it was even worse after the 18th of March.

The National Guards were frequently forced to abandon their positions and beat a retreat from want of ammunition. The direction and management of the staff-office and administration were very inferior. Nevertheless the National Guards gave abundant proofs of courage, spirit, and gallantry. They stood fire, bombs, and bullets like old soldiers. This their enemies have acknowledged, declaring their astonishment that the Government of the National Defence should have made no better use of these elements of resistance and attack against the Prussians.

The days of the 2nd and 3rd of April proved that the army of the Commune wanted nothing but a skilful chief, a Hoche or a Marceau, in order to win the battle and take Versailles. Perhaps the Commune might have found such a commander-in-chief in the person of General Duval, had time been granted him to develop his talent.

The young generals commanding-in-chief the columns marching against Versailles, being at the same time members of the Executive Commission, the Commune, in order to give them greater freedom of action, replaced them in the latter by three of their colleagues—citizens Delescluze, Vermorel, and Cournet, and nominated General Cluseret Delegate to the Ministry of War.

The following decree confirmed these different nominations:—

To Citizens Bergeret, Duval, and Eudes.

"Citizens,

"We have the honour of acknowledging to you that the Commune has entrusted the direction of the War Administration to General Cluseret, in order that you may have full scope for the performance of your military operations.

"The Assembly has thought fit, under the grave circumstances in which we are placed, to establish unity in the administrative services of war.

"The Commune also considers it indispensably necessary to replace you provisionally in the Executive Commission, as your military work will not permit of your attending to its duties.

"In arriving at this twofold decision there is no necessity to add that the Commune is far from being displeased with you, or desirous of weakening your important position as commanders-in-chief of corps. You will see nothing in this act but the necessities of the moment.

"Salutation and fraternity.

"The members of the Executive Commission,

"CH. DELESCLUZE.
"FÉLIX PYAT.

"Paris, April 3rd, 1871."

On its side, the Government of Versailles addressed the following despatch to the prefects:—

"Versailles, April 3rd, evening.

"The insurgents returned in great force from Courbevoie to Nanterre, Reuil, and Bougival. At the same time columns from Paris marched on

Besons and Château-Croissy. At daybreak Mont Valérien opened fire against the insurgents, and compelled them to seek shelter at Nanterre, Reuil, and Bougival. They subsequently attacked our positions.

"The Garnier, Dandel, and Dumont Brigades opened a cannonade and repulsed the enemy. General Vinoy, with the cavalry brigade of Dubreuil, threatening to take them in flank, the insurgents fled in the greatest disorder, leaving many killed and wounded behind. A total rout ensued.

"While this was going on, Sèvres, Meudon, and Petit-Bicêtre were attacked by strong forces of the enemy. The Lamariouse Brigade and the gendarmes pushed forward to Meudon, and were received by shots from the windows of the houses. But the brigade dislodged the insurgents, who left a great number of dead and wounded behind.

"The Bruat and Derocrat Brigades, under the command of Admiral Pothuau, bombarded Petit-Bicêtre on the right. The day ended in the flight of the insurgents in the direction of the Châtillon redoubt.

"This day caused heavy losses to those who allowed themselves to be blindly led by such malefactors, and gave a decisive blow to the insurrection, which, finding itself powerless, will be forced to abandon Paris.

"THIERS."

We have seen that the troops of the Commune, after their first success on April 3rd, were compelled to take flight in the evening and to abandon some positions, and that a great part of the troops sought refuge under the protection of the cannons of Forts Issy and Vanves. But the National Guards did not abandon all the positions they had occupied on the plateau of Châtillon: they still retained some of them, including the redoubt. They also took possession of the trenches between the redoubt of Moulin-de-Pierre and Châtillon, lately occupied by the Prussians.

During the night the Federals, to the number of about fifteen thousand, had massed at Bel-Air, between Forts Vanves and Issy. Batteries were erected in front of the forts, but they were badly protected by weak trenches. The line of battle extended from the Versailles Railway, on the left, to a place called Croix-d'Arcueil, on the left of Fort Montrouge.

At midnight the conflict recommenced with renewed vigour; but notwithstanding their obstinate resistance the National Guards were compelled to give way before the foot-chasseurs and soldiers of the line, who were in superior force.

The Versailles troops marched on Châtillon, and gained some ground. At daybreak they strongly entrenched themselves on the plateau, in the positions constructed by the Prussians. The line of battle extended from Bagneux to Meudon.

Both parties commenced reconnoitring early in the morning, and at half-past five the batteries of Châtillon gave the signal for a fresh attack. The trenches of the Federals were simultaneously attacked with a well-sustained fire of artillery, which threw their ranks into disorder. It was not without great difficulty that the commanders succeeded in rallying their battalions. The trumpets sounded, the drums beat, and Forts Montrouge, Vanves, and Issy replied vigorously. Commander Ranvier directed a part of the military operations, and sent a great number of orderlies in all directions.

In order to reform their lines the Federals sought the shelter of the undulating bends in the hilly country between Châtillon and Vanves; but the troops of Versailles left them no time to accomplish this, charging them with great vigour, and again forcing them to fall back under the protection of their two forts, the fire from which, as well as that of the batteries established on some neighbouring ridges, converged on the opposite plateau, occupied by the regular army of Versailles. The Versaillist batteries erected in the trenches constructed by the Prussians fired furiously. It was a perfect artillery duel. Some of the battalions of the National Guard suffered heavy losses, especially the 219th, half of which was *hors de combat*.

The Châtillon redoubt, constructed at the commencement of the siege to protect Paris against the Prussians, and a few other neighbouring positions, were still in possession of the soldiers of the Commune. The Versaillists, who already occupied a part of the plateau of Châtillon, sent the Pelle Division and the Derojo Brigade, with two twelve-pounder batteries, to attack and to take this small fortress. The battalion in charge of this position was only five hundred strong; but they defended themselves vigorously against a far superior force. Several assaults with cannon and small arms were repulsed. The besiegers, finding it impossible to take the fort from its heroic defenders by force, resolved to try stratagem.

The *Daily Telegraph*, a journal unfriendly to the Commune and sympathising with the Versaillists, describes this deed of April 4th in the following terms :—

"The soldiers of the Government advanced with butt-ends in the air, crying, 'Vive la Garde Nationale!' The latter replied, 'Vive la ligne!' and in their turn raised their butt-ends in the air. The Communists, fancying this a defection of the line, looked upon it as a confirmation of their hopes. Without fear they allowed the troops of Versailles to approach, and even marched out to meet them; but they were soon cruelly undeceived.

"Seeing that they might approach with impunity, the Government troops were no sooner close to the insurgents than they levelled their muskets at them, and sent a volley of bullets into their ranks. The National Guards retired in stupefaction, closely followed by the enemy, who, after a lively engagement, succeeded in capturing the redoubt."

Such, in truth, was this odious piece of treachery, for which the *Daily Telegraph* has not a single word of blame.

But the *honest journalist* forgot to mention that the traitors in red trousers who were guilty of such infamy were not soldiers of the line, but despicable disguised sergents de ville.

Nearly two hundred of these far too confiding National Guards were killed or wounded. Three hundred of the 219th battalion, with Commander Henry and the commanders of the 105th and 127th battalions, were compelled to lay down their arms, and taken prisoners. A drummer, who refused to give up his drum-sticks, was disembowelled by a sergent de ville. A lieutenant of the 219th battalion shot this miserable man dead, and by unexpected good fortune was enabled to break through and escape.

This frightful act of felony committed by the troops of the defenders of order not only led to the loss of the Châtillon redoubt, but also caused the greatest disorder, and had the worst effect among the ranks of the National Guards, several battalions of which, encamped near the plateau, fell back skirmishing to the side of Forts Issy and Vanves.

Such was the shameful treachery to which the soldiers of the honest Versaillists resorted to surprise and beat the defenders of the Commune. Such infamous ambuscades, frequently repeated, were a dishonour to the Government and its party, and deserve to be made known to, and stigmatised by, all men of heart and honour.

La Commune branded them in the following manner :—

"Citizens, the monarchists sitting at Versailles do not go to war like civilised men; their warfare is that of savages. The Vendéans of Charette and the agents of a Piétri shoot their prisoners, assassinate the wounded, and fire on ambulances. Twenty times have these wretches, who dishonour the uniform of the line, raised their butt-ends in the air, and then traitorously shot the gallant men who too confidingly approached them.

"Citizens, such treachery, such atrocity, cannot bring victory to the eternal enemies of your rights.

In the energy, courage, and devotedness of the National Guards we have a pledge for the Republic. Their heroism and constancy have been admirable. The artillery-men have directed their fire with remarkable precision; so much so, indeed, that it has several times silenced that of the enemy, who have left a mitrailleuse in our hands.

"National Guards, the Commune congratulates you, and declares that you deserve well of our country."

After this defeat a great number of wounded were brought in through the Porte d'Issy.

On the news of all these atrocities, treachery, and massacres, M. Thiers exclaimed in the Versailles Assembly, amidst the applause of the Right, "France has recovered its army!"

On the day before he had already said:—

"The insurrection showed itself in force at Meudon. The foot-gendarmes were heroic. Fresh divisions arrived in the evening. The insurgents fell back, but a certain number of them remained in the Châtillon redoubt. It was then too late to attack them.

"The bulk of the insurgent army was driven back under the walls of Paris.

"To-morrow a few cannon-shots will suffice to dislodge the last insurgents; and we have not the least doubt that these unfortunate men, misled by malefactors, will soon be but too happy to implore clemency from the Government, which will readily accord it. (Applause on the Left.)

"*A voice on the Right.*—Yes, the clemency of the gendarmes.

"*M. Thiers.*—Mind, I should not think of according indulgence to crime; it will only be bestowed on those who have been misled. (On the Left, 'Very good, very good!')"

The following is an account of the combats as they occurred on that day :—

The Federals could not leave their trenches until half-past ten o'clock. At that time the forts slackened their fire—Meudon, Châtillon, and Clamart were almost silent—and the Federals, profiting by this, erected batteries parallel with the railway, with the intention of cutting off the columns coming from Châtillon.

At eleven o'clock a company of National Guards left the fort, and directed its course in quick march to the Issy redoubt, where the troops of the Commune had erected a battery.

At one o'clock Vanves and Issy, having received a supply of ammunition, opened a tremendous fire on Meudon, in order to protect an advance movement of the Federals. Suddenly some waggons covered with blinds arrived by railway from Meudon, and vomited grape-shot along the whole line of the advancing column, so that the Federals were once more obliged to seek the shelter of Forts Issy and Vanves.

An artillery battle recommenced in the finest style.

Some reinforcements arrived for the Federals: on the right wing from Billancourt, and on the left from Montrouge, which until now had been very little engaged.

At half-past two some batteries descended from Meudon, and, protected by a shower of grape-shot, effected a turning movement. The Federals defiled to the right of Issy, and opened a terrible artillery fire and a lively fusillade on the advanced columns of the enemy; but being again forced to abandon their position in consequence of the fire from Meudon, Clamart, and Châtillon, they for the third time retired under the protection of their forts.

Meudon now slackened its fire, and Fort Issy, profiting by it, launched its projectiles at a column of the Versailles army, which, nevertheless, continued its flank march, and succeeded in joining the troops occupying the Châtillon plateau.

At three o'clock, following up this manœuvre, the army of Versailles succeeded in advancing its line of battle, and the cannons of Meudon, Clamart, and Châtillon protected the erection of fresh batteries in the valley.

The Federals sustained heavy losses; there were not enough ambulance waggons to carry off the wounded, and many remained lying on the ground with their wounds undressed. There was a great deficiency of surgeons. The troops of Versailles likewise suffered very heavy losses. Among their officers wounded on April 3rd and 4th were M. de Dumast, struck by two pieces of shell; Captain Lesur, by two bullets in the chest, who succumbed to his wounds; and ten other superior officers, more or less seriously wounded.

The military hospital at Versailles received one hundred and twenty wounded men, of whom forty were National Guards. The prisoners at Versailles were treated very badly.

While these deadly combats were going on, citizen Duval, commander of the centre of the Communal army, at the head of fifteen hundred or two thousand men, had a battle to the knife with the Versaillists, and advanced for the purpose of re-taking the plateau and redoubt of Châtillon, but, on account of the general retreat of his army corps, he was soon isolated and surrounded by a superior force, and he and his detachment were made prisoners.

General Vinoy, one of the accomplices of the ambuscade of the 2nd of December, 1851, who had won his general's epaulets by massacring the defenders of the Constitution and the Republic, was commander-in-chief of the troops who took Duval and his soldiers prisoners.

The old hired imperial assassin, now in the service of a Republic—and a fine one too!—which he helped to destroy in the year 1851, galloped to the front of the prisoners.

"Is there among you," said he, "a gentleman who calls himself General Duval? Where is he?"

"Here I am," said Duval, stepping from the ranks with two other chiefs of battalion, who were also called out.

"If you had taken me prisoner," said the imperialist general, "would you have had me shot?"

"Without hesitation," coolly replied the courageous Duval.

"March these prisoners to this field, and shoot them immediately," said the ferocious Vinoy, pointing to a place near at hand.

The intrepid Duval and his two heroic companions walked resolutely and without moving a muscle to the place appointed for their execution. Their calmness and composure never deserted them for a single instant. They took off their coats themselves, and proudly regarded their assassins, who were deeply moved by so much firmness and courage. These three stoical heroes, after laying bare their breasts, gave the signal for execution themselves, exclaiming in a firm voice, "Vive la Commune!" "Vive la République!"

Eighty other unfortunate prisoners were slaughtered by the troops in the service of the royalist and clerical reaction of Versailles.

The simple and laconic reply of Duval to Vinoy, when he asked him whether he would have had him shot, was admirable. Those two words, "Without hesitation," so simple, so laconic, and so energetic, were the sublimity of expression, idea, courage, audacity, and heroism.

This Lacedæmonian reply was worthy of a Leonidas, and the "Let him die!" of old Horace.

Vinoy, the stupid soldier, besotted since 1851 by the massacres of which he had been guilty, was quite unconscious of the fresh infamy he had committed by ordering the execution of his prisoners. This guilty man, blinded by crime, did not even dream that in assassinating Duval he had murdered a true hero.

CHAPTER III.

THE POLICY OF THE COMMUNE.

THE terrible war which the Commune maintained against the Versailles army did not prevent it continuing its philosophical, political, and social reforms. Like the National Convention, it was at once the soldier and the legislator of the Revolution. It defended the latter by cannon and decrees.

Several of its members having sent in their resignation, the Commune issued the following decree :—

"The electors of the First, Second, Sixth, Eighth, Ninth, Twelfth, Sixteenth, Seventeenth, Eighteenth, and Nineteenth Arrondissements are convoked for Wednesday, April 3rd, to elect new members."

The Commune, being of opinion that the possession of the entire military power by one man was fraught with great danger to public liberty, promulgated the following decree :—

"1. The title and functions of the commander-in-chief are suppressed;

"2. Citizen Brunet is unattached;

"3. Citizen Eudes is nominated Delegate of War, Bergeret delegate to the staff of the National

Guard, and Duval to the military command of the ex-prefecture of police.

"The Executive Commission.
(*Signatures.*)

"Paris, April 1st, 1871."

In order to do away with the abuse of over-pay, the Commune issued another wise decree. It was as follows:—

"The Commune of Paris,

"Considering that the highest posts of the public service have up to this day been looked upon as places granted by favour;

"Considering that sinecures and over-pay should have no existence in a genuine democratic Republic;

"Decrees:

"*Sole article.*—The highest salary for the different services of the Commune is fixed at £240 per annum.

"THE COMMUNE OF PARIS.

"Hôtel-de-Ville, April 2nd, 1871."

In order to ameliorate the condition of labour and industry as much as possible, the Commission of Labour and Exchange decreed as follows:—

"*Sole article.*—A Sub-commission is nominated, composed of citizens Bertin, Lévy Lazare, Minet, and Rouveyrolles, to present, with the shortest delay, a detailed estimate of unfinished public works, and to furnish a plan for the execution of such works by the Commune of Paris.

(*The Signatures.*)

"Hôtel-de-Ville, April 1st, 1871."

To secure the payment of the provisional contributions towards the maintenance and pay of the National Guard, the Delegates of Finance issued the following decree:—

"Citizens Simon, Langlois, Delamarche, Champeval, and Lefranc are nominated as a Commission for the reorganisation and regulation of town dues. They will act in concert with citizen Volpénile, whom we have nominated Director-General, and will take such measures as they may think necessary for the financial interests of the Commune of Paris.

"The Members of the Commune of Paris,
Delegates of Finance,
"VARLIN, D.-TH. RÉGÈRE."

The Commune and its delegates devoted themselves from the first to the different branches of the public administration. The finances, labour, industry, exchange, taxes, public security, commerce, rents, the means of defence, the organisation and armament of the National Guard, &c., took up the time of their first sittings.

Unfortunately, the violence, cruelties, ferocities, and atrocities of the troops of Versailles compelled the Commune to depart from this wise and moderate course, and, much against its will, to engage in reprisals for the sake of its own security.

The police hordes, and the rude, corrupt, and fanatical bands in the service of Versailles, were daily guilty of the greatest crimes and cruelties against the unfortunate National Guards who were made prisoners. Contrary to every law of war, they massacred them without pity, or outraged them in the most inhuman and barbarous manner. On arriving at Versailles they were most abominably ill-treated. The correspondent of the *Indépendance Belge,* who surely cannot be suspected of too much good-will towards the Communal prisoners, and who was an eye-witness of these repulsive and inhuman scenes, was so indignant at them that he could not dissemble his reprobation.

"I returned to Versailles," said he, "just in time to see the entry of the prisoners. I cannot speak without regret of the over-excited attitude of the crowd. Not only did it demand the instant death of all the prisoners, but even assailed them with stones. The calmer spectators carefully suppressed every manifestation of pity; no sort of appeal to the laws of humanity could be breathed without running the risk of becoming a victim of the popular fury. Some spectators were maltreated and arrested for imprudently manifesting a feeling of pity.

"The women especially behaved in the vilest and most odious manner. They filled one's heart with disgust."

Another correspondent, speaking on the same subject, expressed a similar horror of the conduct of the Versaillists:—

"*To the Members of the Commune of Paris.*

"Paris, April 5th, 1871.

"I have arrived from Versailles much affected and profoundly indignant at the horrible deeds I have witnessed.

"The prisoners were received at Versailles in a most atrocious way. They were struck down without pity. I saw some bleeding, with their ears wrenched off, and their face and throat torn to pieces as if by the claws of wild beasts. I saw Colonel Henry in this state, and to his honour and glory must I confess that, scorning this band of barbarians, he walked proudly and calmly to his death.

"Under the eyes of the Government there exists a provost-court; that is to say, death cuts down our fellow-citizens taken prisoners.

"The cellars into which they were thrown were wretched holes, confided to the tender mercies of gendarmes.

"I thought it the duty of a citizen to inform you of these cruelties, the memory of which, for a long time to come, will fill me with indignation.

"BARRÈRE."

Citizen Barrère is a relative of the well-known Girondin of that name. Citizen Leroux, commander of the 84th battalion of the National Guard, testified to the truth of the above letter.

Well, who would have believed that these frightful atrocities, which were enough to move the most unfeeling to pity, could have inspired M. Picard with the following odious and cruel language?

"Never," said he, speaking of the unfortunate prisoners who were so cruelly insulted by an infuriated crowd, "did low demagogues present to the afflicted view of *honest men* figures more vile."

Well, these "vile figures" were the electors *whose vote was belied by M. Picard.*

Another witness of similar facts says in the *Indépendance Belge:*—

"The soldiers loaded the prisoners with injuries and curses. One of the latter, in the uniform of a soldier of the line, was beaten with the butt-ends of muskets. Three were summarily shot by soldiers. Even the most seriously wounded received no indulgence, but were pitilessly mocked. Greater animosity could not have existed.

"The gendarmes were the most insensible to pity. I heard one of them say there was no necessity to look for cords to bind the prisoners, for if they made the slightest attempt to escape they would be shot. Another assured me that all the superior officers would undoubtedly be shot."

The *Mot d'Ordre* relates the following abominable execution:—

"At about nine o'clock in the morning two boats containing eighteen National Guards crossed the Seine from Reuil to Chatou, to breakfast with a wine merchant. At ten o'clock fifteen of them returned in the boats to Reuil. The captain, a sergeant, and a guard of the 4th company, remained to finish their meal.

"The Marquis de Galifet, apprised by a miserable informer of the presence of the three National Guards at the wine merchant's house, marched thither at the head of five or six hundred cavalry, among whom were many gendarmes. He took the three guards prisoners, and had them immediately shot in the Route de Saint-Germain."

They all had families, and left their unfortunate wives and little ones without support, without bread, and in the greatest misery.

Executioner Galifet enjoyed this sanguinary orgie, thinking only of the noble debauchery in which he would soon be enabled to revel on his entrance into Paris.

Neither the ambulances nor the medical corps were respected by the soldiers of the Versailles Government. The war against the Commune was a war of savages.

This is irrefragably proved by the following letter to the journal *La Commune:*—

"Citizen Editor,

"We bring to your notice an unheard-of fact accomplished by the artillery of Mont Valérien on the 3rd of April. About twenty surgeons, accompanied by seven waggons belonging to the International Ambulance Society, bearing the red cross of the Geneva Convention on white flags, were made targets of, and had it not been for a bend in the ground, in which they took shelter, the shells would have struck the surgeons and the wounded, &c. . . . . .

"The Physician-in-Chief of the Hôtel-de-Ville,
"Dr. HERZFELD."
"Deputy Physician,
"Dr. CLAUDE."

French soldiers in the pay of the royalist and clerical reaction were guilty of deeds never enacted by the Prussians during the siege—they bombarded the ambulances. Never had such a thing been seen. But we need not be astonished that this or any other infamy should have been perpetrated by men who violated and murdered honest ambulance women, who, at the risk of their lives, devoted themselves to the care of the wounded.

While these horrible scenes, worthy only of savage hordes, were being enacted, the Government of Versailles, finding that the courts-martial were too slow, and that French blood was not flowing fast enough, laid a bill before the Assembly for the more speedy acceleration of proceedings before the military tribunals engaged in trying prisoners. Urgency was voted. Could anything be of greater urgency to the Versaillists than the shooting of their fellow-citizens?

But massacre and shooting were not enough for the wild beasts of Versailles. In their eyes virtue was a crime. The exercise of hospitality, which is respected even by barbarians, was punished as the greatest of offences by these insensate fools, who seemed possessed by a sanguinary monomania for carnage.

M. Baratte, a peaceable citizen of Courbevoie, living in the Route de Saint-Germain, gave shelter to two wounded National Guards. Five sergents de ville not only shot the two unfortunate wounded men, but murdered M. Baratte, his wife, and two daughters, after having most shamefully outraged the latter under the very eyes of their despairing parents, whom they had bound together.

Such are the crimes with which the defenders of order, the throne, and the altar—the support of the family, religion, property, and the entire civilised society—have sullied themselves.

We could cite thousands of infamous cruelties: speak of the violation and murder of many ambulance women and cantinières; the massacre of hundreds of prisoners in the most atrocious manner; of horrors so dreadful that none but the hired assassins of Versailles, the reiters of the Empire escaped from German prisons, and the fanatical Chouans of Charette, could have been capable of them; but we have no wish to afflict our readers too much by the recital of this repugnant carnage. The examples we have cited will more than suffice to give a true idea of the ferocity and lewdness of the saviours of order. The summary executions, not only in contempt of the laws of war, but in gross outrage to every feeling of humanity—all these atrocities not only inspired the most violent indignation and the greatest horror, but also the desire for just reprisals, and forced the Commune to seek means for protecting its defenders—the National Guards of Paris—from the massacre, shooting, and murder to which they were exposed on being taken prisoners.

The Commune hesitated a long time before taking any measures for reprisals, which were, unfortunately, but too well justified; but with its elevated sentiment of respect for human life, it felt instinctively repugnant to use the only means in its power for putting an end, if possible, to the shedding of the blood of their fellow-citizens like water by the hired assassins of Versailles.

A week had nearly passed since the Versaillists had dragged at the tails of their horses and murdered some unfortunate prisoners; it was already some days after the horrible and cowardly murder of Flourens, Duval, and their courageous companions, when the Commune voted the law concerning hostages with which it has so often been reproached, but which was nevertheless very mild in comparison with the courts-martial which

M. Dufaure, the sanguinary Minister of Justice of Versailles, found to be too weak and slow. Yes, the hostage law was indeed too mild and too just for the barbarous practices of the lynchers of Versailles, who day after day killed their prisoners without even according them a summary judgment, which the terrible American Judge Lynch never refused to the greatest criminal.

Vinoy and Galifet, those sinister executioners, burdened with more crimes than they could count hairs on their guilty heads, did not even interrogate their victims. Without anything being known of them, they were killed simply because they had the misfortune to attract their attention or to displease them. At a sign their hired bravoes precipitated themselves on the unfortunate innocents, and instantly murdered them without the least sign of pity. Even women found no favour with these ferocious janizaries, who first violated and then massacred them.

The following is the hostage law of the Commune. If read with care it will be found, as we have already remarked, very humane in comparison with the crimes for the prevention of which it was made.

"The Commune of Paris,

"Considering that the Government of Versailles has openly trampled every law of humanity and war under foot; that it has been guilty of horrors with which even the invaders of French soil did not sully themselves;

"Considering that it is the imperative duty of the representatives of the Commune of Paris to defend the honour and lives of the two millions of inhabitants who have placed the care of their destiny in its hands; that it is important at once to take all necessary measures which the situation requires;

"Considering that the politicians and magistrates of the city are bound to insure the common welfare, with due respect for individual and public liberty;

"Decrees:

"Art. I. All persons accused of complicity with the Versailles Government shall be at once arraigned and imprisoned.

"Art. II. A jury of accusation shall be instituted within twenty-four hours to take cognizance of crimes brought before it.

"Art. III. The jury shall make a report within forty-eight hours.

"Art. IV. All accused persons found guilty by the verdict of the jury of accusation shall be hostages of the people of Paris.

"Art. V. All executions of prisoners of war, or of partisans of the regular Government of the Commune of Paris, shall immediately be followed up by the execution of a triple number of hostages retained by virtue of Art. IV., and who will be drawn by lot.

"Art. VI. All prisoners of war shall be taken before the jury of accusation, which shall immediately decide whether they are to be set at liberty or retained as hostages."

If we coolly examine the spirit of this law, we shall see at once that it only applies to accomplices of the Versailles Government; that is to say, to spies and traitors, and not to prisoners of war, properly so called. It never entered into the mind of the members of the Commune to put this law in force towards soldiers made prisoners. According to Article I. all those accused of complicity with the Versaillists were to be brought before the jury of accusation, which was to decide as to the liberation or retention of them as hostages. By this it will be clearly seen that soldiers, properly so called, who had not been traitors, were set at liberty. It is well known with what kindness and regard soldiers of the regular army who were made prisoners were treated by the Commune. If gendarmes and sergents de ville were declared hostages, it was not in their military capacity, but for their acts in the police service of the enemy. The Government of Versailles, by enlisting into its army the whole *personnel* of the police, exposed them to reprisals, justified over and over again by the infamous conduct of the whole police corps, not merely since the 18th of March, but even from the 2nd of December, 1851.

Article II. of the hostage law instituted a jury of accusation, before which all persons accused of complicity with Versailles were to be taken; and by another law it enacted that this jury should be chosen by lot from the delegates of the National Guard. Ordinarily, in time of war, accomplices of the enemy are not judged by a jury, but by a court-martial, or they are condemned as spies. To be brought before a jury, composed of honourable citizens elected by universal suffrage, was a great safeguard to them. The National Guards, prisoners of war at Versailles, would have thought themselves very fortunate if they had had such juridical securities. But the reactionary Government of Versailles arraigned them in batches before courts-martial which were passively submissive to its authority, and which pitilessly condemned them either to death or hard labour, according to orders.

By the hostage law, if any one was accused of complicity with the enemy, and found guilty by the jury of accusation, he was neither condemned to death nor to hard labour, nor even to imprisonment, but merely retained as a prisoner of war until peace should be concluded; and only when his allies or partisans, the defenders of the Government of Versailles, committed fresh cruelties towards the prisoners of the Commune, contrary to the laws and usages of war, was he in real danger.

The Government of Versailles and its military chiefs had it, therefore, in their power to prevent the application of it. It would have sufficed for them not to assassinate the prisoners, and to treat them in conformity with the laws of war. Was this asking too much?

The hostage law was a just one, since it only applied to accomplices of the Versailles Government found guilty by a jury which offered abundant security in point of honesty, impartiality, and independence. The utmost liberty and facility of defence were freely accorded.

It was a very humane law, for it guaranteed the lives of accomplices of the enemy, and even those of traitors and spies. They had only to put up with temporary imprisonment, which could not have been prolonged beyond the war.

This exceptional measure, necessitated by circumstances, and rendered indispensable by the cruelties perpetrated by the Versailles soldiery, was inspired by the ardent wishes of the members of the Commune to put a stop to these pitiless massacres.

It only depended, then, upon the so-called defenders of order to prevent the shedding of a single drop of blood of prisoners of war, or even of a spy. It would have sufficed to respect the laws and usages of war, and to treat the prisoners of the Commune with the same humanity as the latter displayed towards theirs.

What earnest, conscientious, and really honest man, taking into consideration the terrible situation of the Commune, created as it was by the shortcomings and crimes of the Versailles Government, would be so foolhardy as to condemn this measure of the defenders of Paris?

We well know that, regarded from the standpoint of absolute right, as represented by the Commune, human life should have been sacred. But we may observe, in extenuation of the Government at the Hôtel-de-Ville, that the war of Versailles forced it to defend itself—to fight with equal arms. It was its absolute duty to employ all means consistent with the rights of man for protecting the lives of the National Guards, honest citizens and fathers of families; and under no pretext whatever could it allow their massacre to pass unpunished. If on philosophical principles inviolability of human life be admitted by one party and contested by another, nobody can deny that there should always exist an absolute equality and reciprocity of procedure between combatants until the advent of true civilisation has abolished war. This principle of justice does not allow one adversary to shoot prisoners, and at the same time enact that the other shall respect their lives.

The only reason of any real weight against the hostage law is this—a man can only be held responsible *for his own acts*. Offences and crimes are personal. It is unjust, therefore, to make hostages expiate the crimes to which they were strangers, and to which they had not in any way contributed, since they were prisoners at the very time they were committed. This is a serious reason, and we are bound in justice to mention and acknowledge it. Had we been a member of the Commune at the time, we should not have voted for the hostage law without proposing, as an amendment, that this law should have no retroactive effect on the hostages who were in prison at the time of the perpetration of punishable crimes. Those who were arrested after the committal of such crimes should have the facility of proving their complete innocence before the jury, and, if they did so prove it, they should be liberated, and simply kept in Paris till the conclusion of peace. We consider that under no pretext whatever should the great principles of justice and immutable right, which ought to be the basis of all the acts of honest men as well as of social order, be departed from. And we are fortunate, whatever our enemies may think or say to the contrary, in never having violated these principles, for they have invariably regulated our conduct.

The following proclamation of the Commune preceded the promulgation of the hostage law:—

"Every day the banditti of Versailles massacre or shoot their prisoners, and we are constantly hearing of the perpetration of assassinations. You are well aware who are guilty of these crimes—the gendarmes of the Empire, the royalists of Charette and Cathelineau, marching on Paris with the cry, 'Vive le roi!' and with the white flag at their head. The Government of Versailles acts contrary to the laws of war and humanity, and if it continues to disregard the common usages of civilised nations, we shall be forced to make reprisals. If our enemies assassinate a single one of our soldiers, we shall retaliate by executing the same or double the number of prisoners. The people of Paris, even in their anger, detest the shedding of blood as they detest civil war; but they must protect themselves against the savage outrages of their enemies, cost what it may—eye for eye, tooth for tooth.

(Signed) "THE COMMUNE OF PARIS."

The assassinations of Flourens, Duval, several commanders of the National Guard, and a great number of privates, as well as of the cantinières and ambulance women, the latter of whom were first shamefully outraged by the bravoes of Versailles, with all the other horrors, might logically provoke the Commune to reprisals and the adoption of rigorous measures.

On the 5th of April the Archbishop of Paris and M. Daguerry, vicar of the Madeleine, were arrested on the charge of conspiring against the Republic and of complicity with Versailles. For the same reasons, M. Isard, superior of the Seminary of Saint-Sulpice; M. Bertans, vicar of Saint-Sulpice; the vicar of Saint-Séverin; the chaplain-general of prisons; the rector of Notre-Dame de Lorette; M. Blondeau, vicar of Notre-Dame de Plaisance; M. Croses, ordinary of the Roquette Prison; M. Ducoudray, rector of the Sainte-Geneviève School; M. Bertaux, vicar of Saint-Pierre de Montmartre; Father Bosquet, superior, and eleven other fathers and one brother of the Congregation of Picpus; M. Bagle, vicar-general; Miguel, first vicar of Saint-Philippe du Roule; Brother Calixte, of the Christian Doctrine; Lurtèque, vicar of Saint-Leu; Millaud, vicar of Saint-Roch; Geslain, vicar of Saint-Médard; Sire, professor at Saint-Sulpice; the vicar of Saint-Bernard la Chapelle, &c., &c., were also imprisoned.

In effecting the arrests of these ecclesiastics the Commune had principally in view the stopping of the massacre of Parisian prisoners by the Versailles army. It hoped that M. Thiers would not expose the Archbishop of Paris and the principal ecclesiastics of the capital to such terrible reprisals, and that these arrests would suffice to put a stop to the cruelties and barbarities of the Versailles Government. The best proofs of the sincerity of these intentions are the two letters addressed to M. Thiers by the Archbishop of Paris and the vicar of the Madeleine, imploring the Chief of the Executive power to discontinue the massacre and ill-treatment of prisoners. M. Bertaux, vicar of Saint-Pierre de Montmartre, took the two letters to Versailles, promising to return in three days with the answer.

This he did, bringing back the written reply of M. Thiers, in which the executioner of Duval, Flourens, and so many others, impudently denied all the crimes committed by his police assassins. The bombarder of Paris remained deaf to the entreaties of the archbishop and the vicar of Sainte-Madeleine, and, as we shall see further on, notwithstanding their prayers, continued to have the prisoners massacred, without taking into consideration the dangers to which the hostages of the Commune were consequently exposed. M. Bertaux was liberated on his return.

The Commune was also forced to take severe measures against the Press. On March 19th the Central Committee suppressed the *Figaro* and the *Gaulois*. All the reactionary journals of the capital had not only openly attacked the Central Committee and the Commune, their members and their acts, in a most unworthy manner, with lies, gross calumnies, injuries, and defamation, but they had publicly preached revolt and civil war against them. It was, therefore, the duty of the Commune and the Central Committee to take the most energetic measures for defending themselves against this venal and criminal press, which was in the pay of the enemy, and a real danger to Paris in its critical situation.

All Europe knows well enough the unworthy *rôle* which a portion of the French press has played for twenty-two years. It has been a scandal and a disgrace to France. The Commune had not only the right and the power, but it was also its duty to suppress it; and it did well to put an end to the culpable excesses of that *venal, degraded,* and *vil-*

lainous press, which for twenty years had only existed by the toleration of the police, as a regular branch-office of the Rue de Jérusalem.

By the suppression of all these immoral organs, defenders of the Versailles Government, the Commune, at war with the latter, did no more than defend itself by using the right of legitimate reprisals. It could not reasonably be expected that it would permit the enemy to have his organs, defenders, and devoted partisans, who were nothing more nor less than spies, in the very heart of Paris, which was being besieged by the Versaillists. By this act it only made a just use of reciprocity.

The Versailles Government not only did not allow the publication of any journal favourable to the Commune, but seized all the socialist Republican journals issuing from Paris. The following is the verbatim decree on this subject by M. Picard: —" I order the seizure of all the Paris journals, and their circulation is interdicted." Every one was seized; even friendly papers were not excepted.

But the Government of the National Defence had already, previously to the war, suppressed six popular journals; and all these honest and very moderate organs, which had for eighteen years applauded the suppression of the liberty of the press, now loudly complained of their own suppression, which was all the more unwelcome on this account.

While Versailles continued the war to the very knife, the representatives of the free associations of Paris endeavoured to put an end to hostilities by well-meant intervention. The delegates of the

Republican League of the Rights of Paris and of the General Syndicate of the National Union also tried to interpose between the belligerents. The Republican League adopted the following programme:—

"Rocognition of the Republic;

"Recognition of the right of Paris to self-government, to regulate its police, finances, public charities, and instruction by a freely-elected and supreme council, as well as to the exercise of liberty of conscience;

"The guarding of Paris exclusively by the National Guard, which is composed of all valid electors;

"A full and complete amnesty to all citizens who have taken part in the Revolution of the 18th of March and in the acts of the Commune;

"And the conclusion of an armistice for the laying down of the conditions of a definite peace."

The propositions of the General Syndicate of the National Union were similar to those of the Union for the Rights of Paris.

The delegates of these two associations were only able to obtain the favour of an interview with M. Thiers on condition that they did not present themselves in the name of the Commune, with which the Chief of the Executive, the man elected by the departments under the Prussian yoke, would not treat, not acknowledging its right as a belligerent.

The delegates, after declaring that they had received no mandate from the Commune, and were only the representatives of a free and independent meeting which had nothing in common with the Government of the Hôtel-de-Ville, had an audience of M. Thiers, who, having listened to the object of their mission, replied:—

"That negotiations of an official character could only be broached provided it was first admitted in principle that Paris would lay down its arms.

"That as long as he (M. Thiers) was in power the Republic should not be overthrown.

"That Paris should enjoy the same municipal franchise as the other towns of France, in accordance with a law to be voted by the Versailles Assembly.

"That to Paris should be given the common right—nothing more, nothing less.

"That the National Guard should be reorganised, but that the guarding of Paris could not belong exclusively to the National Guard, nor could the exclusion of the regular army be admitted in principle.

"That the right of belligerents to men engaged in strife against the National Assembly being inadmissible, he could not and would not treat with them for an armistice; but that if no musket nor cannon were fired by the National Guards, the troops of Versailles likewise should not fire until a certain time to be fixed, when the Executive power should resolve on action and commence the war.

"That all those who discontinued their armed strife—that is to say, who abandoned their hostile attitude and returned to their homes—should be exempt from prosecution, except those whom M. Thiers called the assassins of Generals Lecomte and Clément Thomas, who, if discovered, should be condemned."

Such was the answer given to the delegates of the Union of the Rights of Paris, according to a circular of M. Thiers to the prefects, dated April 13th :—

"Delegates have arrived at Versailles. Had they been sent by the Commune, they would not have been admitted; but, being true Republicans from Paris, they were received. I have invariably said to them, 'None but assassins menace the Republic. The lives of the insurgents shall be saved. The unfortunate workmen shall be provisionally assisted. Paris must return to the common right. All secessions shall be suppressed in France, as they were in America.' Such was my reply."

It is easy to see that the reply of M. Thiers afforded no chance of success, because the National Guards would never consent to lay down their arms, nor could they accept the reactionary municipal law elaborated by the Versailles Assembly, or the insufficient and humiliating alms accorded by M. Thiers, in his munificence, to the needy workmen. The Commune also refused to put itself in relation with the Versailles Government, and interdicted the meetings of the conciliators.

The Commune, comprehending the grave inconveniences arising from its secret sittings, decided, not on holding them publicly, but on publishing reports of every one of them.

In its sitting of April 12th the Commune decided upon the formation of a council of war for every legion of the National Guard, and reduced the price of passports to fivepence. But the decree of this sitting which caused the greatest sensation and resentment was the following :—

"The Commune of Paris,

"Considering that the imperial column in the Place Vendôme is a monument of barbarity, a symbol of brutal force and false glory, an affirmation of Chauvinism, a negation of international rights, a permanent insult of the victor towards the vanquished, a perpetual outrage against one of the three great principles of the French Republic, fraternity;

"Decrees:

"*Sole article.*—The column of the Place Vendôme shall be demolished.

"Paris, April 12th, 1871."

It would be difficult to say whether the adoption of this decree inspired hatred or anger against the Commune. We attach little importance to monuments dedicated to the memory of false glory and the flattery of national vainglory. We believe they merit nothing but disdain and contempt. But it is always a good and moral thing to obliterate them, so that they may no longer recall to the mind of the present and future generations the ephemeral triumph of tyranny and the butchery of nations for the sole benefit of crowned banditti, who are pleased to call pillage, arson, and the destruction of human life *glorious war*. And of all the monuments symbolising , the epochs of carnage and heroic brigandage none better deserved to be razed to the ground than the column of the Place Vendôme. Were it only to obliterate and trample under foot the statue of the imperial scoundrel in the costume of a Roman emperor standing on the top, the Commune, in demolishing this remembrance of the first Empire, the cursed forerunner of the second, would have rendered important service to France and to humanity.

Next day the Commune ordered the formation of ambulance companies.

A Commission of five members, composed of citizens Theisz, Vermorel, V. Clément, Parisel, and Lefrançais, was nominated to examine different projects respecting the postponement of the bills of exchange due and becoming due, and to report thereon.

The following proposition of citizen Tridon was adopted :—

"The Commune decides to send two of its members to attend the funeral of Pierre Leroux; declaring that this homage was not to be considered as due to the partisan of a mythical philosophy, but to the politician who courageously defended the vanquished of June."

The proposition of citizen Vermorel to notify every arrest immediately to the Delegate of Justice was adopted by the Commune.

This exceedingly useful decree permitted citizen Protot to control all arrests in a serious manner, and to immediately set at liberty all who were arrested by mistake.

The conflict now daily became greater, and the Commune thought it necessary to address another manifesto to the provinces, in order to enlighten them as to its intentions, to put a stop to the misunderstandings which existed amongst them, and to call upon the departments to prevent the further progress of the sanguinary conflict which was devastating the capital. But alas! this appeal never reached the departments. The Versailles Government prevented all communication between the provinces and Paris. It drew closer and closer the circle of iron and fire with which it had surrounded the latter, so that the provinces might be kept in ignorance and apathy. Paris stood alone in its struggle to the knife against the Versailles Government.

The great towns which had followed its example —Lyons, Marseilles, Toulouse, Bordeaux, Avignon, Limoges, Grenoble, and Creuzot—and tried to gain their autonomy by proclaiming the Commune, had been vanquished and placed under the yoke of the centralising Government of Versailles. The manifesto of the Commune, then, had no chance of producing any effect in the provinces.

On April 20th the Commune decreed:

"1. The executive power remains provisionally confided to the delegates of the nine Commissions into which the administrative powers are distributed;

"2. The Commune will nominate the delegates by a majority of votes;

"3. The delegates shall meet every day, and decide the propositions in each department by a simple majority of votes;

"4. A report of all measures proposed or executed shall be presented daily to the Secret Committee of the Commune."

The following were the citizens nominated to the Executive Commission:—

War	CLUSERET.
Finances	JOURDE.
Subsistence	VIARD.

Foreign Minister	PASCHAL GROUSSET.
Justice	PROTOT.
Instruction	VAILLANT.
Public Safety	R. RIGAULT.
Labour and Exchange	FRANKEL.
Public Service	ANDRIEUX.

This new organisation of the Executive Commission laboured under a great inconvenience, which its author, a politician of some experience, ought to have anticipated.

The delegates of the different public services or ministries were all burdened with so much administrative work that most of their time and power were absorbed by it. To confide to them the executive power likewise was to overwhelm them with a new and important mission which they were unfit to fulfil. It was materially impossible for them to meet every day for deliberation as members of the Executive Commission, in order to imprint an intelligent and energetic direction on the progress of public affairs, the war, and the armament and defence of Paris. To watch over the progress of events was quite as impossible, for time and strength were necessary to do this efficiently, and these were daily absorbed by administrative work.

At a time of such great difficulties and laborious work this bad organisation soon made itself felt and bore its fruits. The Committee of Public Safety speedily followed as a modification.

In the sitting of April 21st it was decided that a large number of copies of the *Journal Officiel* should be posted up, and that its price should be reduced to a halfpenny; but, notwithstanding this vote, it continued to be sold for three halfpence.

On April 22nd, a decree proposed by citizen

Protot, the Delegate of Justice, for the institution of a jury of accusation was adopted. The following were its principal provisions:—

"Art. I. The jury shall be chosen from the delegates of the National Guard;

"Art. II. The jury of accusation shall consist of four sections, each comprising twelve jurymen, chosen by lot at a public sitting convened for the purpose by the Commune. . . . . The accused and the prosecutor shall alone have the right of exemption. . . . .

"Art. V. The accused shall have the right of summoning his witnesses at the cost of the State. The sittings shall be public. The accused shall be freely allowed to choose his own advocate, even though the latter should not belong to the corporation of advocates. He may propose any exception which he thinks will prove beneficial to his defence. . . . .

"Art. IX. The accused shall not be pronounced guilty unless there is a majority of eight out of twelve votes. . . . ."

This was a very liberal decree, and it afforded substantial guarantees to the accused.

The unfortunate National Guards of Paris, who had lingered for four months in the casemates and on the pontoons, would have been but too happy to be tried before so equitable a jurisdiction.

The following was another decree, proposed on the next day by the Delegate of Justice, and adopted by the Commune:—

"Art. I. The ushers, notaries, appraisers, and registrars of all courts nominated from this day shall receive a fixed salary. Security may be dispensed with.

"Art. II. All moneys collected by virtue of their office must be paid every month into the hands of the Delegate of Finance.

"Art. III. The Delegate of Justice is charged with the execution of this decree."

Citizen Vallès proposed, and the Commune adopted, an additional security to arrested persons, the object of which was to prevent them being secretly kept prisoners behind the prison gates by arbitrary acts. It was as follows:—

"Every member of the Commune shall have the right to visit the prisons, and all the public, civil, and military establishments."

A most touching incident happened during the sitting of April 26th. Delegates from the Freemasons announced that a considerable number of their brethren wished, in the interests of humanity, to be received by the Commune. The latter assented, and they were at once received in the court of honour.

Several thousands of the venerable brethren, dressed in all their insignia, were introduced. They declared themselves willing to make a last effort of conciliation with the Government at Versailles, namely, to plant their banners of peace on the ramparts, to march before the army of Versailles, and to adjure their brethren in the ranks to put an end to this fratricidal war. If their supplications were not heard, and if a single ball struck their flags of peace, all the Freemasons, young and old, would enlist in the ranks of the National Guards, and march against the common foe.

The Freemasons, with a Commission of the Commune at their head, then quitted the Hôtel-de-Ville, and took the direction of the Place de la Bastille, following the line of the great boulevards to the Avenue de la Grande Armée.

More than fifteen thousand Freemasons in full dress, decorated with their insignia, and carrying all their banners, took part in the procession, which was joined by nearly all the members of the Commune, and forty or fifty thousand citizens. They were everywhere received with the greatest sympathy and enthusiasm.

On its arrival at the Arc de Triomphe de l'Etoile, the peace procession was assailed with a shower of bombs and shells from the savage banditti in the pay of the traitorous Government which had delivered France over to the foreigner, and which now wanted to reign over the ruins of Paris.

This fresh act of savage ferocity committed by the barbarians under the command of Mac-Mahon was received with a tremendous cry of "Vive la Commune!" "Vive la République universelle!" The procession halted. Some citizens were wounded. The venerable members of the Masonic lodges advanced alone, under the fire of the enemy, to the ramparts, where they planted their banners as symbols of peace. A few of them were wounded. Some of the flags were pierced by bullets, and the staff of one of them was broken in two.

The white banner of Vincennes, on which were inscribed the words "*Love one another*," floated in the air. Doubtless some of the assassins could read this admirable and fraternal legend from that distance, for the fire was suspended, and the bullets ceased to fall.

About forty delegates advanced by the Route de

Neuilly to the Courbevoie barricade, then in the possession of gendarmes. General Leclerc received them in front of the bridge, and conducted them to General Montandon, the superior commander of the division occupying Courbevoie.

This officer, himself a Freemason, received them courteously, and proposed that three Masons should be sent as a deputation to M. Thiers. This was done.

The bombarder of Paris gave the most unfeeling and frigid reception to the devoted and humane men who had braved his bombs, shells, and bullets in order to stop bloodshed, and to put an end to this fratricidal war.

"We do not negotiate with rebels," he repeated. "Let the Parisians lay down their arms. To those who do so we guarantee the safety of their lives: only the assassins of Generals Lecomte and Clément Thomas will find no clemency." With this haughty declaration the delegates were drily dismissed.

When Paris heard next day of the haughty and unbecoming reception of the Freemasons, it was highly indignant.

On the proposition of citizen Léo Meillet, the following decree was adopted by the Commune in its sitting of April 27th:—

"The Commune of Paris,

"In consideration that Bréa Church, erected in memory of the general of that name, one of the assassins of the combatants of June, 1848, is a standing insult to the vanquished of June who fell while defending the cause of the people,

"Decrees:

"Art. I. That Bréa Church shall be demolished;

"Art. II. That the place where it stood shall be called the Place de Juin;

"Art. III. That the municipality of the Thirteenth Arrondissement shall be charged with the execution of this decree."

Citizen Vésinier, considering it only just to take cognizance of the victim as well as the executioner, proposed the following additional articles, which were adopted:—

"Art. IV. The Commune declares and grants amnesty to citizen Nourry, who for twenty-two years has been a prisoner at Cayenne for the execution of the traitor Bréa. He shall be set at liberty as quickly as possible.

"Art. V. It grants to his mother, the widow Nourry, who for twenty-two long years has bewailed her innocent son, the same pension as to widows of National Guards killed in battle."

In a previous sitting, citizens Gambon, Langevin, and Vésinier were instructed to hold an inquest on the bodies of four National Guards cowardly assassinated by the murderers of Versailles, of which the following was the report read to the Commune by citizen Vésinier:—

"Citizens Langevin, Gambon, and Vésinier were sent to Bicêtre to hold an inquest on four National Guards of the 185th battalion. Accompanied by citizen R. Rigault, procurator of the Commune, and citizens Ferré and Léo Meillet, they visited citizen Scheffer, a guard of the said battalion belonging to the Thirteenth Arrondissement, in the hospital at Bicêtre.

"Citizen Scheffer was bedridden in consequence of a bad wound in the chest. The doctor having declared that the invalid was able to answer any questions, citizens Gambon and Vésinier examined him. Citizen Scheffer declared that on April 25th, at Belle-Epine, near Villejuif, he and three of his comrades were surprised by horse chasseurs, who demanded their surrender. Surrounded by a large force, resistance was impossible, so they laid down their arms and surrendered. The soldiers made them prisoners without violence or threat.

"They had only been prisoners a few minutes when a superior officer of chasseurs came up on horseback, and fell on them with his revolver. Without saying a single word, he fired at one and killed him on the spot, after which he shot at Scheffer, who received the bullet in his breast, and fell by the side of his comrade.

"The other two guards drew back in terror at these infamous acts; but the ferocious captain killed both of them with his revolver.

"The chasseurs retired with their chief after these brutal, atrocious, and cowardly acts, leaving their victims on the ground.

"After their departure citizen Scheffer rose, and, by a desperate effort, reached his battalion, which was encamped at some distance.

"Two of the slain National Guards could not be found.

"The body of the fourth was discovered not far from the place of the murder.

"The condition of Scheffer is all that can be wished. His wound is very serious, but there is no danger, and the doctor says that he can answer for

his recovery. He has a young wife, who has only been confined ten days.
"The Members of the Commune:
"FERDINAND GAMBON.
"VÉSINIER.
"C. LANGEVIN.

"April 27th, 1871."

A subsequent inquest proved that the miserable author of this quadruple assassination was the ferocious beast in human form named Galifet.

By a decree of April 28th the Executive Commission interdicted night-work in bakehouses.

On April 30th the capture of Fort Issy by the Versaillists was rumoured in Paris. The facts were that the fort was in a most critical position, as it was completely dismantled, and covered with bombs and shells. Its defenders spiked the guns and left it, all except one man, a young citizen, who quietly remained within its half-demolished ramparts.

This news caused the greatest excitement in Paris. The Commune deliberated in a secret committee, energetic measures were adopted, and Fort Issy reoccupied.

The Executive Commission declared that "the thoughtlessness and carelessness of the Delegate of War had compromised the possession of Fort Issy, and the Executive Commission considered itself bound, in consequence, to propose the arrest of citizen Cluseret, which was accordingly decreed."

At the same time the following decree appeared in the *Officiel*:—

"Citizen Cluseret is dismissed from his functions as Delegate of War. His arrest is ordered by the

Executive Commission, and approved of by the Commune.

"The provisional replacement of citizen Cluseret is provided for. The Commune is taking all necessary measures for security.

"The Executive Commission decrees:

"Citizen Rossel is provisionally charged with the functions of Delegate of War.

"The Executive Commission:
"JULES ANDRIEUX, PASCHAL GROUSSET, ED. VAILLANT, F. COURNET, JOURDE.
"Paris, April 30th, 1871."

Scarcely was citizen Rossel installed in office when he issued the following decree :—

"Citizen Gaillard, sen., is charged with the construction of barricades behind the fortifications as a second line of defence. In conjunction with the municipalities, he will appoint engineers or delegates to each of the exterior arrondissements, who shall work at these constructions under his orders.

"He will receive orders from the Delegate of War as to the sites and armament of the barricades.

"In addition to the second line of defence of which we have just spoken, barricades, forming three citadels, are to be erected at the Trocadéro, the Buttes Montmartre, and the Panthéon.

"The laying out of these citadels will be determined on the ground by the Delegate of War as soon as the engineers shall have been appointed for their construction.

"General Wroblewski will have the entire command of the left bank of the Seine, and of the troops and forts of Issy and Ivry.

"The commanders of forts, commanders of troops, and all other officers of the Commune, will acknowledge his quality and obey his orders.

"The Delegate of War,
"ROSSEL.

"Paris, April 30th, 1871."

The check experienced by Fort Issy was productive of another result: it proved the defectiveness of the Executive Commission of which we have already spoken, and led to its replacement by the Committee of Public Safety.

On the proposition of citizen Miot, and after two days' noisy discussion, the following decree was adopted by forty-five against twenty-three votes :—

"Art. I. A Committee of Public Safety shall be at once organised.

"Art. II. It shall be composed of five members, voted separately by the Commune.

"Art. III. The most extended powers over all the Commissions are given to this Committee, which shall only be responsible to the Commune."

The Committee of Public Safety, with the object of increasing the order, energy, and regularity of the War Department, decrees:

"The War Delegation is composed of two divisions: the military direction and the administration.

"Colonel Rossel is charged with the chief direction of military operations.

"The Central Committee of the National Guard

is charged with the different services of the War Administration, under the control of the Military Commission."

Citizens Ferré, Dacosta, Marainville, and Huguenot were nominated as deputies of the procurator of the Commune.

After several days of laborious deliberation, the Commune issued the following important decree concerning goods in pawn establishments :—

"Art. I. All pledges in pawn prior to April 25th, 1871, such as clothes, furniture, linen, books, tools, and bedding, under the sum of twenty francs, shall be returned gratuitously from the 12th of May.

"Art. II. The above-mentioned articles are only to be delivered up to the original ticket-holders, who will have to prove their identity.

"Art. III. The Delegate of Finance is instructed to come to an arrangement with the administration of the pawn establishments concerning the settlement of the indemnity to be allowed according to the present decree."

During the night of May 4th a fresh misfortune overtook the Commune. The Versaillists, dressed as National Guards, treacherously entered the redoubt of Moulin Saquet, after having given the watchword to the sentinel. The 55th and 120th battalions, which occupied it, were driven out, the artillery-men killed, and six cannons and three hundred prisoners captured.

The news of this great disaster created the utmost excitement, which, three days later, was destined to be still further augmented by the evacuation of Fort Issy for the second time.

Citizen Rossel, the Delegate of War, was called before a secret sitting of the Commune to give explanations respecting these fresh calamities.

Citizen Rossel answered the questions of the President and other members with great accuracy, clearness, and laconism.

He complained bitterly against the Committee of Public Safety for having given orders for the displacement of Generals Dombrowski, Wroblewski, and Lacécilia, without either communicating with or consulting him, by which act the defence had been disorganised and compromised.

Citizen Pyat, member of the Committee of Public Safety, declared, in the presence of the Delegate of War, that he had sent no direct despatches to the generals under the command of Rossel, neither had he displaced any of them.

Citizen Rossel insisted upon his statement, and further declared that he had himself seen the despatches to Dombrowski, Wroblewski, and Lacécilia, but that he had not got them in his possession. He also declared that he could not answer for the safety of Paris till the evil caused by the said despatches had been repaired.

On the following day citizen Arnold communicated to the Commune and the members of the Committee of Public Safety the different orders in question addressed by the latter to the generals. The most important of them was signed by Ch. Gérardin; Ant. Arnaud, and Léo Meillet, with a postscript signed by Félix Pyat. Having looked at it, the latter declared that he had no recollection of it, but candidly admitted that his memory had become weakened by excessive work; and he gave in his resignation as a member of the Committee of Public Safety.

In consequence of this Rossel published a bitter letter, in which he accused the Artillery Committee, the Central Committee of the National Guard, the commander and garrison of Fort Issy, the chiefs of legions, and the Commune of indecision, inaction, weakness, and incapacity. He ended his violent letter by giving in his resignation and demanding " a cell at Mazas."

At the same time, he had placarded bills on the walls of Paris, announcing, in the strangest terms, the occupation of Fort Issy by the Versaillists.

" The tricoloured flag," said he, "floats over Fort Issy, abandoned by its garrison."

After the publication of these two documents the Committee could only do one thing—accede to the wishes of citizen Rossel by granting him " a cell at Mazas," which was done. But the Delegate of War, after reflection, very reasonably preferred the pure air of liberty.

After having been consigned to the Hôtel-de-Ville, under the charge of Ch. Gérardin, member of the Committee of Public Safety, citizen Rossel and his obliging guard profited by the occasion, and vanished. Unfortunately, however, after escaping out of the hands of the too good-natured Commune, Rossel fell into those of the executioners of Versailles, who arraigned him before a court-martial on the charge of desertion to the enemy. He is now condemned to death, and we sincerely hope that he may escape execution. When before the Commune, citizen Rossel committed only one fault, that of giving way to his irritable and violent temper. He might have afforded great assistance in the war if he had only contented himself with exerting his talent in the service of the popular cause.

After the explanations concerning the despatches of the Committee of Public Safety which had given rise to incidents so greatly to be regretted, and compromised the defence of Paris, this Committee was recomposed of citizens Gambon, Eudes, Billoray, Ranvier, and Ant. Arnaud.

In the sitting of the Commune of May 8th citizen Vésinier was nominated secretary to the above Committee, and, on the 15th of the same month, chief editor of the *Journal Officiel*. The price of this journal was reduced to five centimes, in consequence of which its daily circulation rose from 2,500 to 25,000 copies.

Citizen Ferré was nominated Delegate of General Safety in place of citizen Cournet.

M. Thiers not only continued to bombard Paris and massacre the prisoners, but also made public appeals to treachery by means of a bill placarded slily on the walls of Paris. The Committee of Public Safety resolved, therefore, to punish these atrocities in the most exemplary manner, and issued the following decree:—

"In view of the placards of M. Thiers, in which he styles himself Chief of the French Republic;

"Considering that this placard, printed at Versailles, has been posted on the walls of Paris by the orders of M. Thiers;

"That in this document he asserts that his army did not bombard Paris, whilst every day women and children are victims of the fratricidal projectiles from Versailles;

"That, feeling the absolute impossibility of vanquishing the heroic population of Paris, and taking the city by other means, he has appealed to treachery;

"The Committee of Public Safety decrees:

"Art. I. The furniture belonging to M. Thiers shall be seized by the administration of the domain.

"Art. II. The house of M. Thiers in the Place Georges shall be pulled down.

"Art. III. Citizen Fontaine, delegate of the domain, and citizen J. Andrieux, Delegate of Public Service, are charged, as far as it concerns each of them, with the immediate execution of the present decree.

"The Members of the Committee of Public Safety:

"ANT. ARNAUD, EUDES, F. GAMBON, G. RANVIER.

"Paris, Floréal 21, year 79."

This decree was immediately executed.

On May 12th, on the report and by the proposition of citizen Delescluze, the Commune decreed that the 128th battalion of the National Guard had "deserved well of the Commune and the Republic," for having, under the command of General Dombrowski, destroyed the Parc de Sablonville, occupied by the Versaillists.

"The Committee of Public Safety decrees:

"Art. I. The Military Commission shall in future be composed of seven instead of five members.

"Art. II. Citizens Bergeret, Cournet, Geresme, Ledroit, Sicard, and Urbain are nominated members of the Military Commission, in place of citizens Arnold, Avrial, Johannard, Tridon, and Varlin.

(*The Signatures.*)

"Hôtel-de-Ville, Floréal 25, year 79."

"The resignation of citizen Gaillard, sen., charged with the construction and command of barricades, is accepted under the twofold title.

"The battalion of barricaders under his orders is dissolved, and the men who composed it are placed at the disposal of the director of the engineer corps, who shall proceed as far as he thinks fit with the works already commenced.

"The Civil Delegate of War,
"DELESCLUZE.

"Paris, May 15th, 1871."

"The Committee of Public Safety calls upon the workmen, excavators, carpenters, masons, and mechanics over forty years old.

"An office will immediately be opened in every municipality for the enlistment and forming of brigades from these workmen, who shall serve during the war under the orders of the Committee of Public Safety.

"Their pay will be 3 fr. 75 c. per day.

(*Signatures.*)

"Paris, May 16th, 1871."

The decree ordering the demolition of the Vendôme column was executed on May 16th in presence of a vast crowd. This cursed bronze, the statue of tyrants whose glory was made up of blood and tears, fell to the ground amidst vociferous exclamations of "Vive la République!" "Vive la Commune!" and the red flag replaced the monument of glory of the Empire.

In the sitting of May 17th a report was laid on the table respecting a fresh act of brutal and ferocious cruelty perpetrated by the janizaries of Versailles, and which was far more infamous than any of which they had been guilty up to that time. Citizen Butin, lieutenant of the 3rd company of the 105th battalion, testified, in a written report, that a young ambulance woman had been assaulted, violated, and massacred by the criminal, savage, and degraded soldiers of Versailles, who were animated by the basest, most infamous, and most shameful passions.

On the reading of this report a thrill of horror ran through the Assembly, and several members demanded that energetic measures should be taken to put a stop to the unparalleled atrocities of which these degraded beings in the pay of Versailles, lost to all sense of honour, and covered with the foulest crimes, were daily guilty. Propositions to this effect were put, but, on the demand of citizen Protot, the following order of the day was adopted:—

"The Commune, referring to its decree of April 7th concerning hostages, demands its immediate execution."

This incident and this vote are the best reply to the accusation of ferocity brought against the Commune. It was a month and six days since the decree respecting hostages had been voted, which ordered that all executions of partisans of the

Commune by the bands of Versailles should at once be followed up by a threefold execution of Versaillist prisoners. But notwithstanding the daily execution of prisoners by the Versaillists, and the quadruple assassination proved by citizens Gambon, Vésinier, and Langevin, the Commune allowed the hostage law to slumber, and had executed no one. It needed the proof of a new and atrocious crime of violation and murder perpetrated on an innocent ambulance woman to recall the existence of the hostage law. And, as we shall show further on, notwithstanding the order of the day which it had just voted, the Commune would not have made reprisals had not the Versaillist hordes again sullied themselves with greater crimes.

The following is the report of the staff of the Seventh Legion, read in the sitting of the Commune, and inserted in the *Officiel*, confirming the infamous facts previously narrated by Lieutenant Butin, and others, if possible, still more odious and disastrous :—

"The staff of the Seventh Legion lays the following facts before the Military Commission :—

"To-day we sent Lieutenant Butin with his company, accompanied by Dr. Leblond and M. Labrune of the infirmary, as parlementarians to Fort Vanves and its environs, to seek and pick up the dead and wounded which our legion left behind in evacuating the fort.

"At our outposts they met a commander at the head of his men, who shook hands with them and bade them adieu, affirming that he had no occasion to say, 'Till we meet again.' And in order to confirm his words the commander added, 'This morning I saw with my telescope a wounded man abandoned on the plain. I immediately sent to his assistance an ambulance woman, furnished with armlet and papers *en règle*. Scarcely had she arrived at the place where the guard lay, when the Versaillists seized, outraged, and shot her on the spot, without our being able to afford her any help.'

"Notwithstanding this, Lieutenant Butin and his companions advanced, preceded by a trumpeter and a white flag, as well as the flag of the Geneva Society.

"At a distance of about twenty mètres they were received by a lively musketry fire. The lieutenant, thinking this a mistake, marched on. A second platoon fire proved to them the sorrowful reality of this violation of parlementarian usages and the rights of civilised nations. A third fusillade induced them to fall back.

"This lieutenant was compelled to return with his men, leaving seventeen killed and seventy wounded in the hands of the enemy.

"On his arrival he made his report to us, and I have hastened to communicate it to the Military Commission in order that Lieutenant Butin may be cited before it to give his explanations.

"The Chief of the Staff of the Seventh Legion."

Let those who accuse the Commune on account of the hostage law remember all these abominable and criminal executions, all the horrors committed by the troops of Versailles; and let them not forget that the law on hostages was only voted for the prevention of these crimes.

In the sitting of May 17th citizen Vésinier laid on the table of the Assembly of the Commune the projects of the following decree, to be put on the order of the day, and to be sent before competent Commissions :—

" 1. Titles, coats of arms, liveries, aristocratic privileges, and all honorary distinctions are abolished. The pensions, revenues, and appanages accruing therefrom are suppressed.

" 2. Entailed estates of all kinds, with their revenues, pensions, and privileges, are abolished.

" 3. The Legion of Honour and all other orders are abolished.

" Another decree shall determine the pensions of the legionaries which are to be preserved."

Other propositions :—

"The law of May 8th, 1816, is re-established; and the decree of March 21st, 1803, promulgated on the 31st of the same month, is put in force.

" All acknowledged children are legitimate, and shall enjoy the same rights as legitimate children.

" All natural children are acknowledged by the Commune as legitimate.

" All male citizens of eighteen, and female citizens of sixteen years of age, who shall declare before a magistrate their wish to be united in marriage, shall be considered as united, on condition that they make a further declaration that they are not already married, and are not within the degree of consanguinity which the law regards as a hindrance to marriage.

" All other formalities are dispensed with.

" Their children, should they have any, will be considered legitimate on their simple declaration."

All the so-called *honest journals* put themselves in a rage on account of these propositions, which they declare to be very immoral. To bring marriage and the family within reach of all appears, to Conservatives and pretended Liberals, very immoral; to abolish concubinage and bastardy by declaring natural children legitimate, and to let the legitimacy of a union depend only on mutual consent, is called immoral. We frankly confess that we do not understand this modest and honest *morale*, and are astonished that such a decree should be reproached with immorality.

In one of its last sittings, that of May 19th, the Commune, which has been so unjustly accused by its enemies of theft and crime, promulgated the following decrees, which are sufficient proofs of its disinterestedness, probity, and morality.

The first of these decrees was proposed by citizen Cournet:—

"Considering that in times of Revolution the people, by their instinctive respect for justice and morality, have always proclaimed this maxim, 'Death to thieves!'

"The Commune decrees:

"Art. I. All functionaries guilty of extortion, depredation, or theft, shall, as long as the war lasts, be brought before a court-martial. All those found guilty shall be punished with death.

"Art. II. As soon as the bands of Versailles are defeated, an inquiry shall be instituted against all those who have had the management of the public funds."

The second was proposed by citizen Vaillant:—

"Considering that a Communal Government should provide a sufficient indemnity for the subsistence and dignity of those whom it employs,

"The Commune decrees:

"Plurality of salaries is interdicted.

"All functionaries called upon to perform services not appertaining to their normal occupation shall have no right to additional indemnities for such services."

Citizens Miot, Régère, and Pothier proposed the third, which was as follows:—

"The Commune decrees:

"Art. I. The authorisation of a superior Commission for accounts.

"Art. II. It shall be composed of four accountants nominated by the Commune.

"Art. III. It shall take charge of the general verification of accounts of the different Communal administrations.

"Art. IV. It shall furnish a monthly report of its labours to the Commune.

"Paris, May 19th, 1871."

The last sitting of the Commune, on May 21st, was devoted to the examination of citizen Cluseret, and resulted in his liberation.

CHAPTER IV.

THE INVASION OF PARIS.

WE had wished to relate the heroic struggle sustained for two months by the National Guard outside Paris against the Versailles army; but we are obliged to suppress a very important part of this epoch, that between the death of Flourens and Duval on April 3rd and 4th, and the entry of the Versaillists into Paris on May 21st.

This important and very dramatic period, comprising forty-eight days of heroic combat, will find its place in another volume, which we intend to publish under the title of "The Siege of Paris under the Commune." In the same volume will also be found the history of the Commune in the Provinces, for which, likewise, we have no space here.

Should circumstances permit, we also intend to publish a biography of our colleagues of the Commune, the martyrology of the National Guards, women, and children, defenders of the Commune, who had the misfortune to fall into the hands of their enemies—executioners we should have said—the slaughterers of Paris and its heroic population. In our opinion this will be the most interesting of the three volumes, which will form a complete history of the Commune.

From the 2nd of April the troops of the Commune sustained a war to the knife against the army of Versailles. Terrible battles took place every day. Between Forts Issy, Vanves, Montrouge, Bicêtre, Ivry, the batteries of the Hautes Bruyères, Moulin Saquet, Moulineaux, the ramparts of Paris, and the bastions on one side, and Mont Valérien, the batteries of Châtillon, Clamart, Meudon, Montretout, &c., on the other, a gigantic struggle was constantly going on. All the positions of the Versaillists had been occupied by the Prussians a few months ago.

These tremendous battles, in which the artillery played the principal part, and in comparison with which those against the Prussians sank into insignificance, met with alternate success and defeat. The National Guards fought with spirit and courage against the veteran troops of Versailles. But serious and competent observers did not fail to perceive that the progress of the Versaillists, though slow—often very slow—was none the less sure. Little by little did they advance their positions against the forts and fortifications of Paris.

On the other hand, the *matériel* and *personnel* of the Versaillists were daily reinforced. Batteries, siege and marine pieces, mortars, howitzers, and field-artillery were sent every day from the strongholds and seaports to Versailles. Recruits, also, arrived daily from the provinces or from Prussia to swell the ranks of its army; the prisoners of the French army in Germany were allowed to depart in great numbers to augment the forces of Versailles; whilst those of the Commune could not be

T

recruited from the outside, and were constantly diminishing by losses.

Every day the Versaillists advanced their works of attack nearer to the forts, and contracted their line of investment. By the help of their reinforcements of artillery, new batteries were erected daily, and their fire grew stronger and stronger.

Under such circumstances, the Commune had not only to renounce the hope of conquering the army of the Versailles Government outside the ramparts, but likewise to look forward to an attack under the walls and in the streets of Paris. Since the defeat of the provincial towns which had sided with the Commune, only one chance remained for Paris—that of annihilating the Versaillists in its streets. This was where the final struggle, which would decide not only the triumph or defeat of the Commune, but also of the Revolution or counter-revolution, would have to be made.

With the prospect of such a street war all the efforts, plans, means, and powers of the defenders of the capital should have coincided. It was their duty to provide for and protect themselves against this terrible event. All necessary measures, precautions, and dispositions should have been taken to turn this struggle, on which the success of all their undertakings, and perhaps the destiny of their sublime cause, depended, to their advantage, so as to come victorious out of the battle.

The people of Paris knew that all their great battles had been won, and the Revolution made triumphant, behind the barricades; and they believed they would again be victorious behind their ramparts of stone and earth.

Under the Government of the National Defence, a laughable Barricade Commission, at the head of which were citizen Rochefort and some other barricade builders of the same stamp, had ordered a few old barrels and some baskets full of earth and stones to be placed at the entrances of the principal avenues. But these playthings of barricades were as far from being made in earnest as every other step taken by the so-called Government of the National Defence. After the 18th of March a great number of barricades of paving-stones had been erected by the National Guard. Some time afterwards citizen Gaillard, sen., was charged by the Administration of War with the construction of strong barricades at strategical points indicated to him.

Citizen Gaillard worked zealously at the important task confided to him. His barricades were built with much art and considerable good taste. Some were really small fortresses. That at the angle of the Rue de Rivoli and the Rue de Saint-Florentin was a veritable redoubt, supporting itself to the right on the Ministry of Marine, and to the left on the Tuileries. It was constructed of earth, and sacks filled with earth, and pierced with five embrasures. Four other barricades defended the Place de la Concorde. The Places Vendôme, Madeleine, and that of the Hôtel-de Ville were very strongly barricaded, as were also a great many streets in the heart of the city and in the most populous arrondissements, inhabited by the working classes. But most of these barricades were built for the purpose of protecting certain districts rather than for the general strategic defence of Paris.

It was necessary, before everything, to secure the inviolability of the fortified walls of the capital. Should the besiegers succeed in forcing a gate or making a breach in the walls, it would then be imperative to prevent them passing through and spreading into the interior of the city. This would necessitate a second line of defence; and, in case that should fail, a third, fourth, or even a fifth would have to be constructed.

This plan had been broached by General Cluseret before he became Minister of War, and he reprinted it in the *Mot d'Ordre* of May 16th as follows:—

"Dear Fellow-Citizens,

"The difference between the state of the defence as I left it and as I found it on the 15th of May forces me to break the silence which I had imposed upon myself.

"Before my arrest I had several times told citizen Gaillard to leave off constructing useless barricades in the interior, and to concentrate all his energies on the Barrière de l'Etoile, the Place du Roi de Rome, and the Place d'Eylau.

"This triangle forms a natural place of defence; and, by connecting with it the Place Wagram and barricading the space between the Porte de Passy and the Pont de Grenelle, we should have a second fortress considerably stronger than the first.

"I had ordered Colonel Rossel to get these works constructed, and, for greater security, I deviated from hierarchical rules, and issued this order direct to citizen Gaillard in presence of Colonel Rossel, being afraid he would not obey the latter.

"Not content with this, on the second day after my arrest I wrote to citizen Protot and to the Executive Commission, recommending them to devote all their attention to this indispensable work.

"Were my orders executed? I was told they were not. It is of importance that they should be executed at once. If the population will only commence in earnest, they may be accomplished in twenty-four hours.

"But the works at the Barrière de l'Etoile, at the Trocadéro, at Wagram, and at the circus of Grenelle must be no playthings; they should be as solid as those of the Rue de Rivoli.

"These works, which I had ordered as precautionary measures, have now become works of urgency, since in my absence Issy has been taken, and the enormous fault committed of allowing the Bois de Boulogne to be invaded—a movement which I had watched day and night, and which under my command should never have been accomplished.

"Now we have to submit to a regular siege.

"If you do not wish to awake one of these mornings and find the enemy in Paris, you must oppose to their siege works counter siege works. Battery must be opposed to battery, earth to earth. In a word, you must make the war one of positions.

"To oppose nothing but human breasts to projectiles is simply insane.

"*It is professional skill, nothing but professional skill, always professional skill, that is wanted;* and that is the reason why I was not astonished on perceiving what a difference there was between the situation of the defence on April 30th and May 15th.

"But recriminations are useless: it is action and science that are required.

"I tell the people what they ought to do: let them do it, or have it done. Let us construct a third line of defence, extending from the Pont de la Concorde to the Porte de Saint-Ouen, which will utilise the famous barricade of the Rue de Rivoli.

"E. CLUSERET."

When Cluseret wrote this letter a great part of these useful recommendations had been executed, and had he been at liberty he might have seen them.

A young colonel, commanding the engineers, had been charged with the execution of Cluseret's plan, and he performed his duty zealously and skilfully. Having been nominated to the direction of the corps of engineers by the Committee of Public Safety, and having, consequently, to watch over the construction of the barricades, we regularly assisted, during the last eight or ten days previous to the entry of the Versaillists, in all the defensive works, and since comparatively few are acquainted with these matters, we deem it advisable to give a description of them here.

It had long been known by competent military men that the Point du Jour, between the Porte de Passy and that of Saint-Cloud, was one of the weakest and most exposed places of all the fortifications of Paris. It was, therefore, easy to foresee that an attack might be made from this side, and that it was consequently necessary, before everything, to strengthen this position. Preparations for this event were made.

The commander of the corps of engineers, of whom we have just spoken, had the viaduct of the Auteuil Railway walled, barricaded, and fortified as a second line of defence between the Porte de Passy and the Seine. He barricaded the passage of the Portes du Point du Jour, Saint-Cloud, Auteuil, Passy, Muette, Dauphine, &c. A battery placed between the railway viaduct and the fortifications opposite Bastion 62 took the Portes de Saint-Cloud and Point du Jour on the slant, and defended the approach to the Porte de la Muette. Another battery, near the barricades at the intersection of the same railway viaduct and of the streets leading to the Portes de Saint-Cloud and Point du Jour, defended the two entrances of the latter, as well as the covered waggons laden with artillery at the Ceinture Railway, and made this position almost impregnable.

A strong barricade at the Quai d'Auteuil, near the Rue Guillon, commanded the quay, the Auteuil Viaduct, and the Porte de Billancourt. Facing this, on the Quai de Javel, on the other side of the river, another barricade swept the quay, and defended the Porte du Bas Meudon.

Between the Porte de la Muette and the Seine, from Bastion 58 to 67, barricades had been erected at all the intersections of the streets, avenues, and roads in the neighbourhood. Gunboats defended the passage of the Seine, and threatened the environs occupied by the enemy.

The place in front of the Porte d'Auteuil, at the intersection of the Rues Molière, La Fontaine, Boileau, and Pèrechamps, as well as the one before the Passy Station, at the angle of the Avenues de la Muette and Beauséjour, were barricaded. Finally, the Place d'Eylau, an important strategical point, was fortified in a formidable manner. Strong barricades were placed at the angle of the Avenues Malakoff, Bugeaud, Eylau, and the Rues Léonard de Vinci, Sablons, Boissière, and Copernic, which terminate here.

These four places were united by covered roads, and their barricades connected with each other by underground trenches. The cellars of the houses in the neighbourhood served as casemates. These habitations, which had not been occupied since the siege, were crenellated, and the windows protected by sacks of earth, thus forming so many small fortified places for the use of the National Guards.

The four fortified places formed a very strong first line of defence behind the enceinte, and were capable of opposing a serious resistance to the taking of one or more of the gates, or the storming of the walls.

A strong barricade at the Quai de Passy, near the Jesuits' College, commanded the quay and the Pont de Grenelle, and defended the Porte de Billancourt.

The religious institution which we have just mentioned is a large building, admirably adapted for being transformed into a stronghold; and this was done. The walls were crenellated; the windows blocked up; the terrace surrounded with sacks of earth, through which loopholes were made; and a large gallery in front, commanding the Portes du Point du Jour and Saint-Cloud, was furnished with sacks of earth and loopholes, and made fit for artillery, the fire of which would destroy any attacking force trying to enter between Bastions 62 and 68. These cannons protected, besides, the barricades and batteries under the viaduct of the Circular Railway. The walls of the college garden and of others in the neighbourhood were all crenellated; all of them communicated with each other by holes in the walls, or by covered ways. The whole of the neighbouring streets were barricaded, and the terraces so adjusted as to be capable of receiving mitrailleuses and cannons. All the gardens, houses, and streets between the Rue Beethoven and the Avenues de Passy and Ingres were similarly barricaded and fortified. This sort of irregular quadrilateral, comprised within these limits and the line of fortifications, formed a veritable labyrinth of barricades and fortified places, inextricable and impregnable if furnished with cannon and mitrailleuses, and properly manned by National Guards. The earthworks, trenches, embankments, barricades, covered ways, crenellated houses, and fortified yards would have made of these positions an impregnable fortress, if properly armed and occupied by a proportionate number of troops. Some months would have been required to dislodge their defenders and to conquer them; and the troops of Versailles could never have taken the Portes du Point du Jour and Saint-Cloud by surprise, and invaded the interior of Paris, as they did.

But in order to give greater strength to the defence, and to prevent the forcing of the Portes Dauphine, Maillot, Ternes, Neuilly, Villiers, Courtelles, and Asnières, three other important strategical points, the Trocadéro, the Place de l'Etoile, and the Place Wagram, were barricaded.

Citizen Gaillard, sen., was charged with fortifying the first and most important of these positions, the Trocadéro, and he did it in a most perfect manner.

The Avenue de la Muette was obstructed by an enormous barricade of earth to the height of the first floor, upon which a huge platform, capable of holding five or six pieces of artillery, had been constructed. This platform not only commanded the avenue and defended the Portes de la Muette and Passy, but it was also enabled to cannonade Mont Valérien. An enormous trench in front, and a covered casemated way on its right, served as impregnable supports to its defenders.

A very strong barricade defended the Rue Franklin. The Avenue du Prince Impérial, leading to the Porte Dauphine; the Avenue Malakoff, leading to the Place d'Eylau and the Porte de Neuilly; the Avenue du Roi de Rome, leading to the Arc de Triomphe de l'Etoile; the Avenue de l'Empereur and the stairs of the Trocadéro, leading to the quay, were barricaded in such a manner as to form a large entrenched camp. Siege-pieces and mitrailleuses were to be placed behind the barricades, and field-pieces in such situations as to be immediately available at menaced points. This most important position of the Trocadéro was capable of preventing troops invading the right bank of the Seine, after they had forced the fortifications from the Point du Jour to the Porte Maillot; and, in addition, its batteries commanded the left bank, and could easily destroy the enemy, should he try to settle down in the Champ de Mars, at the Ecole Militaire, or upon the Esplanade des Invalides; they swept the quays and bridges of both banks, from the Porte du Bas Meudon to Pont Neuf; and, in case the enemy should take the Prefecture of Police, the Conciergerie, the Palais de Justice, and the barracks in the neighbourhood, the bombs and shells of the Trocadéro would drive them out.

A large cemetery, situated on a terrace formed by nature between the barricades of the Rue Franklin and the Avenue de la Muette, was also fortified and crenellated, to serve as an advanced post and entrenchment against attacks from the line of fortifications on the side of Point du Jour.

The Place de l'Etoile was as strongly fortified as the Place du Roi de Rome. All the avenues which end there—namely, those of the Grande Armée, Roi de Rome, Wagram, Champs-Elysées, Joséphine, Jéna, Esseling, &c.—had been strongly barricaded. The Arc de Triomphe de l'Etoile had been transformed into a veritable citadel. On a high platform, surrounded by sacks of earth and trenches, were placed eight cannons and mitrailleuses, capable of cannonading and bombarding at a great distance, and sweeping all the surrounding avenues. This miniature fortress had been stocked with provisions and ammunition, as well as water, for a fortnight. The Place Wagram, which had a park of artillery, was solidly fortified. It defended the Portes de Courcelles, Asnières, and Clichy, and commanded the Versailles, Saint-Ouen, and Ceinture Railways. These three important points, the Trocadéro, the Place de l'Etoile, and the Place Wagram, were connected with each other by covered ways; the surrounding houses were protected by earth in sacks, and loopholed; and their cellars communicated with the barricades by underground passages, and were available as casemates. The gardens, yards, and all other enclosures in the neighbourhood communicated with each other by openings. This third line of defence was formidable, and if it had been well defended, an army of a hundred thousand men, after having succeeded in clearing the fortifications at the Point du Jour and the next line of defence, might have been kept in check for several months.

The circus of the Champ-Elysées and the Parc de Monceaux, two important points lying in the rear, were well fortified.

But another strong point of defence was that of the Place de la Concorde and the Tuileries. All Paris visited the forts and strong barricades at the entrance of the Rues de Rivoli and Saint-Florentin, the Rue Royale, the Avenue Cardinal, the Cours de la Reine, and the quay. The railings and terraces of the Tuileries gardens were likewise barricaded. The terrace at the water-side, the one in front, and that at the other side of the garden, were secured by sacks of earth, loopholes, and cannons; and the windows looking into the private garden, and those of the pavilion facing the Pont Royal, were defended by cannons, which swept the quays, bridges, and avenues, and defended the roads leading to the palace. All these were transformed into impregnable citadels by citizen Gaillard. Gunboats under the bridge were ready to sweep the approaches and defences of that position.

The Rue de Castiglione and the Rue de la Paix, as well as the Place Vendôme, which, with the Rue de la Madeleine and the Rue de l'Opéra, form a triangle protecting the right side of the Tuileries, were strongly barricaded.

The Western Railway Terminus and the Place de Clichy, in the same line of defence, were solidly barricaded and well armed.

Finally, the Buttes Montmartre, armed with two hundred cannons, surrounded by barricaded streets, and protected by the cemetery metamorphosed into an entrenched camp, defended the Portes de Clichy, Saint-Ouen, Montmartre, and Clignancourt. The Buttes Montmartre, thus armed, and commanding, by their elevation, the whole town, could bombard all the positions in the interior of the enceinte, cover them with fire and iron, and prevent the invader taking foot there. Montmartre was the Mount Aventine, the Capitol of the defenders of Paris, and the key of the capital.

We have thus shown the formidable lines of defence, on the right side of the Seine, from the Point du Jour to the Tuileries and Montmartre. If these positions had been properly defended, the enemy could never have forced the wall of the enceinte between the Porte de Billancourt and that of Clignancourt, from Bastion 57 to Bastion 37.

The fortified enceinte on the left side of the Seine, between the Porte de Meudon and the Orleans Railway Station, from Bastion 58 to Bastion 94, was defended by Forts Issy, Bicêtre, Montrouge, Vanves, Ivry, and the redoubts of Hautes Bruyères, Moulin Saquet, and Moulineaux, against the exterior approach of the enemy. Up to May 21st, the day on which the Versaillists took the Porte du Point du Jour, only one of these forts, Issy, had succumbed to the enemy. But this check would not have endangered the fortified enceinte on the left bank had it been properly defended. Works similar to those on the right bank of the river should have protected it.

Well, the principal strategical points on the left bank had been fortified. We will not go further into detail on this subject; it will be sufficient to say that interior barricades defended the Portes de Meudon, Sèvres, Issy, Versailles, Plaisances, &c.; and that other fortified places situated behind these formed a second strategical line of defence, of which the strongest were those at the Quai de Javel, Rue Lecourbe, Rue de Vaugirard, Rue de Vanves, Rue de la Santé, Petit Montrouge, Place d'Enfer, Place d'Italie, Boulevard de Montparnasse, Rue Vavin, Deux Moulins, the quay of the Orleans Railway Station, &c.

A second line behind this had as its principal points the Champs de Mars, the Ecole Militaire, the Montparnasse Railway Station, the Place de l'Observatoire, &c.

The third line commenced at the Invalides, and extended to the Luxembourg, the Panthéon, and the Jardin des Plantes.

The last was erected at the Corps Législatif, in the Rue du Bac, Rue des Saints-Pères, Rue de Verneuil, Rue des Ecoles, Place Saint-Michel, Place Mouffetard, and in all the streets between the Boulevard Saint-Michel, the top of the Boulevard Saint-Germain, and the Halle aux Vins and Jardin des Plantes.

This line of defence was as solid as that on the right bank. Defended in this manner, and protected as they were by the exterior forts, the fortifications on the left were almost impregnable. Considerable fortifications had been made during the Prussian siege, in the form of terraces in front of the Ceinture Railway, from the Rue de Vaugirard to the quay at the Orleans Railway Station. They formed a series of round points, horseshoes, forts, small barricaded redoubts, surrounded by trenches, &c., which afforded considerable shelter and solid strategical positions, and in which a hundred thousand men and a great number of artillery might easily have been placed to render the fortified enceinte insurmountable.

Such were the means of defence at the disposal of the military chiefs of the Commune on the 20th of May last. Five or six thousand workmen laboured day and night, under the surveillance of the auxiliary corps of engineers, to complete the works of defence which we have described.

Having been, as we have already observed, a delegate to this corps of engineers, to watch over and push forward the construction of barricades and other artificial works requisite for the defence of the capital, and to prevent the besieging army from taking the enceinte of the fortifications, we, after working at night at the editing of the *Journal Officiel*, with which we had been charged, made a surveying tour of the works, the oversight of which had been confided to us. As soon as they were sufficiently advanced for arming, we drew up a report to the Delegate of War and the Committee of Public Safety, urging that they should be occupied by the National Guard, and armed with mitrailleuses and cannon in such numbers as to be able to destroy the enemy, should he succeed in taking the enceinte.

The colonel charged with the superior direction of these works made a similar request to the Delegate of War.

But alas! notwithstanding these demands and many other proceedings of a similar nature, these strategical lines were never armed nor occupied; and those constructed for the defence of the Porte de Saint-Cloud and the Porte d'Auteuil at the Point du Jour, the weakest and most exposed parts of the fortifications, had neither been occupied nor armed on Sunday morning, May 21st, when we made our tour around these greatly-jeopardised points, especially since the taking of Fort Issy and the occupation of the Bois de Boulogne by the Versaillists.

At five in the morning the ramparts between the Porte de la Muette and those of Saint-Cloud and Versailles, which we visited, were very severely bombarded, and we ran a great risk. This part of the fortifications was riddled by shells, bombs, and shot from Forts Mont Valérien, Issy, and Montretout, which fired with all their pieces; by the redoubts of Châtillon, Meudon, and Gennevilliers; and by the siege batteries at Clamart, Bagneux, Sèvres, Saint-Cloud, Bellevue, Grande Jatte, Château de Bécon, Courbevoie, and Asnières, some of which had as many as seventy-six pieces of heavy calibre, and most possessed large siege and marine pieces. The situation was terrible, and became more and more critical. The fortifications were so ploughed by shell and ball that it was almost impossible to stop on the ramparts, or on the roads near them; and it was easy to see that these gates could not be occupied much longer, and would have to be abandoned, as they were already half demolished. It was then of the greatest and most urgent necessity that the solid works behind the fortifications should at once be armed and occupied.

We could not understand the reason why the armament we had persisted in demanding had not been effected. We feared lest the place should be taken; but all the superior officers to whom we communicated our fears assured us that there was no danger of the fortifications being forced.

At six o'clock in the evening, at the close of the sitting of the Commune, Dombrowski sent a despatch announcing the taking of the Porte du Point du Jour, without expressing much uneasiness, saying that he had no fear of repulsing the Versaillists. This communication created great sensation in the Commune, and seemed to considerably agitate the members of the Committee of Public Safety. Citizen Delescluze, the Delegate of War, appeared very anxious.

As to ourselves, we were in the greatest disquietude, for we knew that the defences behind the Porte du Point du Jour and the Porte de Saint-Cloud were neither armed, guarded, nor defended, and that by a *coup de main* the enemy could invade Paris as far as the Trocadéro and the Arc de Triomphe.

In the evening, after the sitting of the Commune, we, in company with citizen Gambon, went to the Ministry of War to recommend the execution of those measures which, in our opinion, were the only means of averting the imminent danger which threatened Paris. We met citizen Cluseret first, to whom we submitted the plan of defence. This general, who, as we have already shown, had himself recommended these means of defence, told us that he was going to speak of it to the Delegate of War, and that he hoped the necessary measures would be taken to prevent the further progress of the enemy. A moment afterwards General Lacécilia entered the Ministry of War, and we made the same observations and recommendations to him, begging him to have the works of defence on the left, adjoining the fortifications, immediately armed, and to oppose the passage of the Pont de Grenelle and the railway viaduct with all his strength, so that in the event of the troops of Versailles entering by the Point du Jour, they might not be able to spread over the left bank. General Lacécilia promised to take our observations into consideration, and to watch over the positions confided to him. Arriving at last, with citizen Gambon, in the presence of citizen Delescluze, the Minister of War, we repeated to him all we had said to Generals Cluseret and Lacécilia. We made him understand the utility and indispensable urgency of the measures proposed, telling him that if they were neglected a third of Paris would be taken possession of by the enemy the next morning, and that then we should be lost. General Henry, who had visited the works with us, joined in our demand for their armament. Citizen Delescluze promised to issue orders according to our wishes, and that he would not forget our recommendations.

General Henry said that he himself would watch over their execution. We also recommended that citizen Gambon should at once visit the points in jeopardy, and secure their defence. He departed immediately for Passy and Auteuil. We greatly regretted our inability to accompany him, as our occupations kept us all night at the *Journal Officiel*, the editing and management of which had been confided to us.

The shells and bombs from the Trocadéro and the Arc de Triomphe, where the Versaillists had settled down, fell the whole night on the office of the *Officiel*, situated on the Quai Voltaire. One shell burst its door open.

At four o'clock in the morning we observed a great number of National Guards traversing the Pont Royal. On inquiring the reason of this movement, we were informed that the Portes du Point du Jour and Saint-Cloud had been taken by the enemy; that they had been outflanked on the left at Muette, and on the right at Vaugirard; that the enemy had passed the Seine by the Pont de Grenelle; that the whole of the left bank was taken, and probably the right as far as the Trocadéro and the Arc de Triomphe de l'Etoile. These National Guards added that they had fought for nearly two months as outposts, and were now going to defend their own quarters. We readily understood the meaning of all this: our recommendations, so often repeated for eight days, and renewed only the day before, had not been executed; our sorrowful prophecy had been fulfilled; the enemy's troops had advanced into the city, and captured, without meeting any serious resistance, the very considerable works of defence before they had been manned or armed; and that it was now high time to organise the defence at other points.

The following is what had happened. Commander Trèves, astonished at the silence of the defenders of Paris, which had lasted for some time, advanced, at three o'clock in the afternoon of May 21st, to the Porte de Saint-Cloud. During his examination of that gate he perceived a man in civilian dress at the left bastion, who was hoisting a white flag on it. This unknown man said something, which the commander believed to be, "Come on, there is nobody." On this invitation he leaped into the trench, followed by Sergeant Constant of the 3rd battalion of the 91st regiment, ran to the bastion, sprang on to the drawbridge, only a single plank of which remained, and joined his interlocutor.

"My name is Ducatel," said he. "I am an overseer of roads and bridges, and an old officer of marines. You can trust me and my words. Paris is yours if you will only take it. Let your troops enter without loss of time. See, everything is abandoned."

And the bastions on the right and left were, in fact, completely evacuated, and neither near nor far was a National Guard to be seen.

Commander Trèves invited M. Ducatel to accompany him out of Paris, and give an account of the situation to the general-in-chief. He then addressed the following despatch to Generals Douay and Vergé at Villeneuve l'Etang and Sèvres:—

"I have just entered Paris with M. Ducatel through the Porte de Saint-Cloud. Everything is abandoned. I am going to cut the wires of the torpedoes."

Half an hour later the fire along the whole line was silenced.

Commander Trèves, accompanied by M. Ducatel, Captain Garnier, and a section of his engineers, entered Paris.

Two companies of the 37th of the line from the Vergé Division, with a few sappers and artillerymen carrying a 0·15 mortar, penetrated one by one into the place at half-past three. Some National Guards, having observed this invasion, returned and commenced a charge of musketry. A twelve-pounder was immediately levelled against them, whilst a foot-bridge was erected on the ruins of the drawbridge. The guards in the trenches and the workmen were hastily led on to sustain the fight.

General Mac-Mahon, whose head-quarters were then at Mont Valérien, on being informed of the event, immediately gave orders to all commanders of corps to make the necessary dispositions for entering the place in the track of General Douay's Corps.

General Berthaut, commander of the Seventeenth Division of the Fourth Corps, followed the two companies of the Thirty-seventh which entered the place first. The Gandil Brigade of that division penetrated it at half-past six, followed by the Carteret Brigade. General Berthaut had orders to take the square formed by Bastions 62 to 67, the Seine, and the viaduct of the Ceinture Railway, a very important position, which formed an excellent battle-field inside the walls.

This operation was executed by marching along

the fortifications by the Boulevard Murat, so as to turn the defences of the viaduct bridge facing the Portes du Point du Jour and Saint-Cloud. The invaders soon afterwards took the Porte d'Auteuil, and gave access to other troops.

The Vergé Division entered Paris at half-past seven, and took the direction of the Versailles road to the Pont de Grenelle, which it traversed in order to take the Portes de Meudon, Sèvres, Issy, and Versailles, open them to the besieging troops on the left bank, and allow them to take Grenelle, Vaugirard, and Montrouge.

If the line of defence of the Auteuil Viaduct between the Seine and the Porte d'Auteuil had been properly armed and defended; if the batteries under the viaduct facing the Portes du Point du Jour and Saint-Cloud, and the covered waggons had assailed the attacking party as soon as they issued through these two openings; if the batteries of the strategical road at Bastion 62 had swept the Boulevard Murat, and taken the assailants in flank, they could never have advanced to the Porte d'Auteuil. If the barricade armed with cannons, situated on the quay near the Pont de Grenelle, which commanded the Porte de Billancourt and the Quai d'Auteuil, had properly swept the latter, the Vergé Division could never have marched in the direction of the Pont de Grenelle; and if the cannons of the barricade at the Quai de Passy, at the angle of the Rue Beethoven, had fired at the Pont de Grenelle, the latter would have been impassable. If the Jesuits' College at Passy, which had been transformed into a fortress, had been manned and armed; if its terrace, capable of holding eight or ten cannons, had been armed; and if this terrible battery, which commanded the famous square between Bastions 62 and 67, the Seine, and the railway viaduct, had fired on the besiegers, it is certain that they could not have occupied it for a single minute. The Auteuil Viaduct might also have been armed by flying batteries and mitrailleuses, capable of defending the approach to and the taking of the Portes d'Auteuil, Point du Jour, and Saint-Cloud.

Nothing could have been more easy than to prevent the invasion of Paris from this side. It would have been sufficient to arm and defend the strategical positions forming the second line of defence—positions which were truly formidable. Through the neglect of this, the army of Versailles penetrated into Paris, massacred forty thousand National Guards, took as many prisoners, and vanquished the Revolution. May the responsibility of this misfortune fall on the heads of the guilty!

These remarks made, let us continue the recital of the invasion of Paris by a quotation from the report of the general-in-chief of the Versaillists, Mac-Mahon :—

"The Berthaut and Hérillier Divisions (Fourth Corps), after taking the Porte d'Auteuil and the railway viaduct, advanced to attack the second line of defence, situated between Muette and the Rue Guillon. They took the Saint-Périn Asylum, the church, and the Place d'Auteuil.

"On the right the Vergé Division took a formidable barricade on the quay at the top of the Rue Guillon; it then advanced to the strong position of the Trocadéro, taking 1,500 prisoners."

The *Gaulois* narrated the capture of the barricade in the Rue Guillon, the principal defence of the Quai de Passy in the following style:—

"The capture of the Guillon barricade was one of the most fortunate affairs. This extremely strong barricade belonged to the so-called second line of defence. It was armed with three twelve-pounders. Captain Jacquet, commander of the picked sharp-shooters of the 90th, entered the barricade at the very moment in which six hundred National Guards came running to secure its defence. With remarkable self-possession, this officer commenced by taking the revolver from the chief of the insurgents before entering into conference with him. During this time a deserter of the army named Monthus, formerly secretary to Colonel Monclat, arrived by mistake amidst us, provided with an order from Dombrowski to escort a flying battery to be placed at the Point du Jour Viaduct. The commander of the Federals took on himself to order the 247th, in charge of the battery, to retire, and made us masters of the barricade after the firing of only about twenty musket-shots."

If this account be correct, which we very much doubt, it would appear that the order to defend the second fortified line and to arm the Auteuil Viaduct had been given too late; that the Point du Jour had been occupied by surprise; and that the barricade of the Rue Guillon was taken by the enemy through the weakness or the treachery of its commander.

Even after the forcing of the enceinte and the first position behind it, the Trocadéro could never have been taken if the enormous and formidable barricades at the entrance of the Avenue de l'Impératrice, Avenue de la Muette, and the Rue Franklin had been armed and defended. As we said before, these barricades were really covered redoubts, crenellated and provided with loopholes and casemates. Had they been defended, a whole army might have been detained for a long time.

The report of Mac-Mahon adds: "General Clinchant entered the place at about nine o'clock in the evening with the Blot Brigade, through the Porte de Saint-Cloud, followed by the Brauer Brigade; he turned to the left, and following the Boulevards Murat and Suchet, took the Porte de Passy. The Courcy Brigade then entered through this gate.

"The important position of the Château de la Muette," continues the official report, "which rested its defences on the ramparts, and prolonged them to the Seine, became the object of General Clinchant. Defended by ditches, walls, and iron railings, it was almost unassailable from the rampart side. The general moved to the east, turned, and took it."

The taking of the Château de la Muette, which was defended by so skilful and courageous a general as Dombrowski, appears to us inexplicable. This superior officer was thoroughly acquainted with the ground on which he fought; he could not have been ignorant of the considerable defensive works executed at this part of Paris, with the defence of which he had been entrusted; he must have known that the weakest and most threatened position was the Point du Jour; and we never could comprehend why he did not formidably arm and vigorously defend these positions and works, which commanded the Portes de Saint-Cloud and Point du Jour, and which rendered them impregnable. To us this is an inexplicable mystery, since the intelligent and able Dombrowski was well aware of this; and we are convinced that he might have prevented the taking of the Portes de Saint-Cloud and Point du Jour by the Versaillists.

The Grénier and Laveaucoupet Divisions of the First Corps penetrated into the place at three o'clock in the morning. The Bruat and Faron Divisions of Vinoy's army entered Paris at two o'clock in the morning. The Faron Division remained at Passy as a reserve. The Bruat Division crossed the Seine for the purpose of taking the Porte de Sèvres and of facilitating the entry of the Second Corps. With this view the Bernard de Seigneurens Brigade of this division passed over the viaduct bridge. It met with some difficulties in attacking Grenelle, but it overcame them at the moment when the troops of General de Cissey, who had forced the Porte de Sèvres, came to rejoin them.

It was sixteen hours since the invading troops passed through the Porte de Saint-Cloud before they encountered any resistance. The reason of this is very simple : the strong barricades at the angle of the Rues de Vaugirard and Desnouettes were armed.

As soon as this position had been occupied the Porte de Versailles was opened, and the Bocher Division entered. The head-quarters of Mac-Mahon were then shifted to the Trocadéro. General Douay, on the right, was ordered, on the evening of the 22nd, to occupy the Palais de l'Industrie, the Palais de l'Elysée, and the Ministry of the Interior.

"General Clinchant," says Mac-Mahon in his report, "will endeavour to make himself master of the Western Railway Station, the Pépinière Barracks, and the Collége Chaptal.

"On the left bank General de Cissey will wheel round the Ecole Militaire, the Invalides, and the Montparnasse Station on the east.

"At the close of the day the Bruat Division will occupy the Emperor's stables and the tobacco manufactory.

"The Faron Division of General Vinoy's army will remain near the Trocadéro as a reserve."

It will be seen that notwithstanding the weakness of the defence, the Versaillist troops advanced with considerable hesitation. It was only on the evening of the 22nd that the Place de l'Arc de Triomphe de l'Etoile and that of Eylau were occupied. The Palaces of the Elysée and Industrie were taken on the same day.

All the formidable defences erected with so much art and at the cost of such enormous labour, from Point du Jour to the Champs-Elysées and the Saint-Lazare Railway Station on the left, to the Rue de Vaugirard on the right, which would have secured the inviolability of the enceinte of Paris, east and south, for months, if they had been properly armed and defended, fell with scarcely a struggle in the short space of twenty-four hours. The enemy was permitted to take all those parts of Paris between Bastions 44 and 72, which gave free passage to a torrent of the invaders, who precipitated themselves on the interior, and took a third of Paris in a day.

CHAPTER V.

THE BATTLE IN THE CENTRE OF PARIS.

ON seeing this frightful result of the 22nd, we readily comprehended that no other resource remained to the devoted defenders of the Commune than that of resisting to the death in those parts of Paris still in the power of the people, and that it was of the utmost importance to secure an efficacious resistance in the popular quarters of the capital, the hearth of the Revolution. We knew the bloodthirsty ferocity, the blind rage with which the royalist, clerical, and police hordes in the service of the Versailles Assembly were animated; we knew the thirst for vengeance and blood, the savage cruelty of the ferocious generals who commanded the pretorians of the second Empire, now the hired assassins of the reaction. We resolved to organise a vigorous defence against these beasts of prey, who thirsted for the blood of the socialist Republicans. We wanted to throw an obstacle in the way of the sanguinary orgie which these bandits were already enjoying in anticipation.

With this object we proceeded to No. 145, Rue Haxo, at Belleville, the meeting-place of the Engineer Division, where we found some officers assembled. We drew up a plan of the barricades necessary for the defence of La Villette, Belleville, Ménilmontant, and Charonne, the strategical defences of which were very insufficient. From the Place du Château d'Eau to the Porte de Romainville there were scarcely any barricades in the Rue de Paris, Belleville. All the others were open. The military road along the ramparts from Bastion 10, near the Porte de Vincennes, to Bastion 27, by the side of the Ourcq Canal, was not barricaded, so that Belleville and the neighbouring arrondissements were completely at the mercy of a rapid advance of the invading army along the fortifications. They could not only be forced from the front, but turned and taken in the rear; and then the defence of Paris would be at an end. This pressing danger required to be remedied at once. The engineers to whom we had been delegated marked on the ground, in our presence, the barricades agreed upon, according to the plan of Paris; and the auxiliary workmen laboured day and night at them.

In four-and-twenty hours the Place du Château d'Eau, the Boulevard Voltaire, the canal, the Rue de Faubourg du Temple, that of Saint-Maur, the place at the top of this street and at the entrance of the Rue de Paris, the latter itself, the Boulevard Puebla, the Rues de Romainville, Haxo, Saint-Fargeau, and Tourelles, the Place des Trois Communes, and the rampart road of the Portes de Romainville, Pantin, and Vincennes, were covered with enormous barricades as if by magic. Some of them were veritable redoubts, armed with artillery, and guarded by devoted National Guards. Those near the Porte de Romainville, the post-barracks of

Bastion 18, and those at the bottom of the Rue des Lilas, near Bastions 21 and 22, were very strong, and armed with rampart cannons. Above the American quarries, near the Rue des Lilas, was a battery of heavy pieces, commanding the strategical rampart road to the Porte de Pantin, and defending the passage of the canal and La Villette basin, the bridges of which were mined. On the other side, between Bastion 10, at the Porte de Vincennes, and Bastion 19, at the Porte de Romainville, solid barricades, armed with 24-pounders, intercepted the rampart road at the angles of the Rue Saint-Fargeau, in front of the Portes de Ménilmontant, Bagnolet, Montreuil, and Vincennes, in such a manner as to prevent the enemy wheeling round the old suburbs and taking them in rear. These works secured the defenders of La Villette, Belleville, Ménilmontant, Buttes Chaumont, and Père Lachaise against surprise; they protected their rear, and would save them from a general massacre.

Having now given some idea of the means of defence against an attack on the heights of Belleville and their environs, let us hastily follow the sanguinary march of the invading army.

The Ecole Militaire was occupied by the Susbielle Division without the firing of a shot; and a park of two hundred cannons, and enormous depôts of gunpowder, ammunition, and victuals, fell into its hands. Lieutenant-colonel Razoua had been charged with the defence of this important position. The following is the account of the heroic manner in which he fulfilled the commission confided to him, and which he himself published in a letter from Geneva:—" Nominated commander of the Place de l'Ecole Militaire, with the rank of lieutenant-colonel, by Cluseret, the Minister of War, I remained at my post till the 22nd, the day on which the Versaillists entered Paris. At six o'clock in the evening of the same day I evacuated the position with my staff, I being the last, under the fire of the Versaillists, who occupied the Trocadéro and the Champ de Mars. At about seven o'clock I went straight home to No. 6, Rue Dupéré, where, being worn out with fatigue, I rested myself. At eleven I carefully dressed in plain clothes, and visited one of my friends, where I remained, without once going out, till the evening of June 23rd, when I took the express to Geneva, where I arrived safe and sound on the 24th."

This gentleman, it will be seen, remained at his post until the arrival of the enemy, whom he no sooner perceived than, instead of defending the position confided to him, he abandoned it, and saved himself by running home to dress in private clothes; and instead of rejoining his colleagues who were fighting for the Commune, many of whom were killed, Monsieur Razoua betook himself to the railway, and cowardly saved himself by flight to a foreign country. This is the sort of staff-officer who made the entrance of the enemy into Paris so easy, and brought about the massacre of forty thousand National Guards.

During the fall of the Ecole Militaire, the Lian Brigade took the Montparnasse Railway Station. The Second Brigade of the Bruat Division occupied the Ministry of Foreign Affairs and the palace of the Corps Législatif on the same day (May 22nd).

On May 23rd the defenders of the Commune

cannonaded with bomb and shell from the Buttes Montmartre, which were armed with two hundred cannons and commanded the whole of Paris, the enemy's positions at the Champ de Mars, the Trocadéro, &c., in such a style that they were almost untenable. These heights formed the most important, most elevated, and best armed position of the Commune. The efforts of the invaders were, therefore, early on the morning of the 23rd, principally directed against them.

At all the principal approaches to Montmartre, especially the Places de Clichy, Blanche, and Pigalle, and the entrances of the Rue de Clignancourt and the Boulevard Ornano, formidable barricades had been constructed. All of them had been armed with mitrailleuses and cannons from the Buttes Montmartre, where more than a hundred remained, which cannonaded the south and southeast positions of the enemy. But notwithstanding its armament, Montmartre was a very defective and weak point. At the walls of the enceinte it was almost entirely undefended, and consequently easy to attack. The officers and the Committee of War charged with its defence had erroneously believed that it could not be attacked from the rear, and had neglected to fortify that point. This was a terrible mistake. The Versaillist generals perceived this. In his report Mac-Mahon expresses himself on this subject in the following manner:—

"The barricades and batteries of the heights of Montmartre being directed against the south and interior of Paris, the best plan of attack was to wheel round these defences, and gain the same elevation on the opposite side. General Ladmirault was to attack on the north-east, and General Clinchant on the west.

"At four o'clock in the morning the attacking party began moving. The Grénier Division, marching along the fortifications, dislodged the enemy from the bastions, and with the greatest spirit overthrew all obstacles. Arrived at the top of the Rue Mercadet, the Abbatucci Brigade pursued its march to the Boulevards Bessières and Ney, took the barricades of the Porte de Clignancourt and the Northern Railway bridge, and gained the goods station, when it wheeled to the right in order to reach the Buttes by the Rues des Poissonniers and Lubat. On arriving at the Rue Mercadet, it found itself arrested in its course in a quarter bristling with barricades, between the railway and the Boulevard Ornano.

"The Pradié Brigade, which had followed the Rue Mercadet, advanced slowly under a strong fire from the heights and cemetery of Montmartre, which it only entered after the greatest efforts.

"The Laveaucoupet Division marched along the fortifications, and reached the Rues des Senelles and Mont Cenis, by which it tried to arrive at the heights of Montmartre.

"The Fifth Corps, that of Clinchant, following the Boulevard des Batignolles and the streets running parallel with it, took the mairie of the Seventeenth Arrondissement and the great barricade at the Place Clichy, and marching along the foot of the heights, overcame all obstacles and penetrated into the cemetery by the south, at the same moment as the First Corps entered on the north.

x

"At that moment the heights of Montmartre were surrounded on the north and west by the troops of the First and Fifth Corps, and a general attack was made through all the streets running parallel with the slope.

"The Clinchant Corps, advancing through the Rue Lepic, took the mairie of the Eighteenth Arrondissement.

"The Pradié Brigade of the First Corps, at the head of which were the volunteers of the Seine, arrived first at the battery of Moulin de la Galette; and soon afterwards a company of the 10th battalion of chasseurs, supported by a vigorous attack from General Wolff, hoisted the tricolour on the Solférino Tower. It was one o'clock.

"We were masters of the great fortress of the Commune, the heart of the insurrection—a formidable position, from which the insurgents could cover all Paris with their fire. More than a hundred cannons with considerable stores of arms and ammunition fell into our hands."

The barricades of the Barrière Clichy were defended with much courage, and the Versaillists only made themselves masters of them after the most murderous engagements. That of the Place Blanche stood its ground for four hours. The next, in the Place Pigalle, did not resist quite as long; while the other, in the Rue de Clignancourt, might have offered a long resistance, had it not been turned by the taking of the Buttes Montmartre.

Summary executions, domiciliary visits, and arrests immediately commenced. All National Guards found with arms in their possession were massacred. The prisoners were marched to Château-Rouge, or to No. 6, Rue des Rosiers, into the same garden in which, two months before, Generals Lecomte and Clément Thomas were shot. As soon as they were masters of the Buttes Montmartre, the Versaillists erected several batteries; among others, one with eight marine pieces of heavy calibre, with which Paris, the Buttes Chaumont, Belleville, and Père Lachaise had been terribly bombarded.

General Dombrowski was killed on the same day at the Ornano barricade.

On May 23rd, the goods station of the Northern Railway, the Place Saint-Georges, Notre-Dame de Lorette, the Collége Rollin, the mairie of the Ninth Arrondissement, the Grand Opéra, and the Madeleine on the right bank fell into the power of the enemy.

On the left, the Barrière du Maine, the Observatory, Montparnasse Cemetery, the Place d'Enfer, the horse-market, Bois Abbey, and the Babylon Barracks were taken. The Place Saint-Pierre was turned on the rampart side, and attacked in front; and the defenders of this enormous barricade, armed with eight cannons, were obliged to abandon it.

The crossway of the Croix-Rouge was vigorously defended, and was not taken until late at night. The same was the case with the barricades in the Rues Martignac and Belle Chasse, where the National Guards sustained heavy losses. The Rue de Grenelle Saint-Germain, the Ministries of War and Public Works, and the Telegraph Office were also occupied by the enemy.

The barricades at the top of the Rue de Rennes,

and those of the Boulevard Montparnasse, at the angle of the Rue Vavin, having been taken, General Levassor-Sorval advanced his attacking party to the Luxembourg.

We experienced a heavy bombardment from the Versaillist batteries during the night of the 23rd to the 24th, which we passed at the national printing-office superintending the publication of the *Officiel*. It was principally from those of Montmartre, which poured volleys on the Quartier du Temple and the Hôtel-de-Ville. Several shells fell in our office and in the yard. On going to the Hôtel-de-Ville in the morning, we had to crouch on the ground and seek shelter behind barricades in order to avoid the bursting bombs. The Hôtel-de-Ville and the Place de Grève were struck by numerous projectiles.

At the Committee of Public Safety we found only citizens Eudes and Arnaud. They told us that the Place Vendôme was taken at two in the morning, and that the Tuileries and the Palais-Royal were set on fire by the enemy's bombs, and had fallen into their hands. The attack continued furiously, and fresh fires broke out in the Rue de Rivoli. Soon the Hôtel-de-Ville was bombarded by all the Versaillist batteries, and a heavy fire was opened on the surrounding barricades. Their defenders resisted courageously. The Théâtres Lyrique and Châtelet caught fire. The bombardment on the left bank was quite as severe. The Palais de Justice, the Prefecture of Police, the Conciergerie, the Rues du Bac and Lille, the crossway of Croix-Rouge, the Rues Vavin, Bréa, Notre-Dame des Champs, &c., became the prey of the flames.

Notwithstanding a vigorous resistance, the Luxembourg and Panthéon, bombarded by order of General de Cissey, fell into the hands of the enemy at four o'clock. All their defenders who were unable to escape were piteously massacred. The garden of the Luxembourg, covered with dead bodies, was metamorphosed into a slaughter-house and a cemetery. There the prisoners were shot, and their graves dug at their side. The steps of the Panthéon resembled a charnel-house; they were covered with blood and corpses.

It was near the garden of the Luxembourg that the unfortunate Raoul Rigault was shot. Poor Rigault, so devoted, so intelligent, so courageous, and so young! His assassins have charged his memory with the blackest calumnies; they have depicted him as a monster; and yet never was there a man who possessed a finer sense of justice than he. We shall never forget his words at the debate on the hostage law: "I should much rather prefer to let all the guilty escape than to execute one innocent man." And yet this is the man who has been described as a cruel monster!

After having assassinated the son, the executioners of Versailles arrested the father, a very respectable old man, who had never taken any part in politics. By dint of numerous proceedings he was at length liberated, and his son's body ordered to be given up to him. He had it disinterred from the garden of the Luxembourg.

On the same day (the 24th) the Versailles army took the Bank, the Bourse, the Conservatory of Music, the Exchange, the Porte Saint-Denis, Montholon Square, Saint-Vincent de Paul, and the stations of the Northern and Strasbourg Railways. At nine in the evening the Hôtel-de-Ville fell into the hands of the enemy. But it was all on fire : a gunboat at the Quai de Grève had literally riddled it with shells. After having bombarded Paris with the utmost severity, and riddled its monuments with bomb and shell, those infamous calumniating journals, the organs of the Versaillists, carried their baseness so far as to accuse their victims of all the detestable acts of which they knew themselves to be guilty. Not content with firing anywhere and everywhere, the savage invaders shed rivers of blood and massacred *en masse*.

The old mayors, on reoccupying their mairies, instituted permanent courts-martial. The officers held their sittings surrounded by National Guards, defenders of order, and sentenced to death all the unfortunate suspected individuals who were brought before them. Terror and massacre were everywhere systematically organised on a gigantic scale. Blood ran in streams. All National Guards who had defended the Commune were shot. Soldiers penetrated into the houses and massacred everybody; even the women and children were not spared.

The barracks at the Place Lobau and the Châtelet were turned into slaughter-houses, where thousands of victims were sacrificed to the bloodthirsty tigers of Versailles. In these dens of crime, miserable officers, metamorphosed into executioners, sent the unfortunate victims made prisoners by Bashi-Bazouks drunk with wine and blood to execution. Not one found favour from these feeders of the courts-martial. All—men, women, and children—were pitilessly sent to death. Though blood flowed in streams, the executioners did not proceed fast enough for the gold-laced monsters. By the end of the day the massacre became so horrible, so atrocious and disgusting, that one of the paid assassin-colonels felt ashamed of his work, and, disgusted with his infamous *rôle*, refused any longer to continue sullying himself with the shedding of innocent blood, and demanded to be replaced, threatening to resign his commission. Another executioner, ambitious of donning the lace, stepped in to perform the execrable work. In the square near the Tour de Saint-Jacques a large ditch was dug, into which were thrown the still warm and quivering bodies of the victims, many of whom were yet alive. The living were buried with the dead. All night the neighbours heard agonising sobs, lamentations, and desperate appeals for help and pity. Fierce, half-tipsy sentinels, accomplices of assassins, without a spark of human feeling in them, mounted guard, and with a ferocious mien threatened with death any passer-by who dared to make the least appeal to their pity. Wives, daughters, and mothers weeping and imploring pity for husbands, fathers, and sons massacred and buried alive, were pitilessly and brutally beaten with bayonets and butt-ends of muskets. Ten thousand children were murdered.

Similar unheard-of cruelties were likewise committed on the Boulevard Rochechouart. The *Indépendance Belge*, a paper exceedingly hostile to the partisans of the Commune, and which no one can accuse of sympathising with them, or of exaggerating the cruelties of their enemies, says on this subject:—

"It is probable that the number of insurgents killed in Paris will never be known. The executions of the Communists continued during the whole of Saturday afternoon in the barracks near the Hôtel-de-Ville. The hospital waggons were filled with corpses after each musketry charge.

"More than twenty thousand persons were arrested on Saturday.

"The wounded were thrown alive into holes, at the angle of the Rue du Boulevard Rochechouart, near the Café du Delta. Horrible cries were heard in these quarters all night. It is already feared that the great numbers of dead and wounded accumulated in Paris will bring on epidemics, the consequences of which would be horrible."

Such were the deeds of the assassins, bravoes, brigands, and defenders of that most horrible Government, the Government of Versailles. The wounded were buried alive. To the cries and sobs of their victims they were as insensible as to their death-rattle. They left them all night yelling, crying, and mixed up with corpses, without coming to their help. They left them to die a prey to the greatest tortures. It is a duty to hold up to public hatred and execration the wretches who were guilty of such infamy. It is a duty to denounce and stigmatise these abominable executioners in the face of the whole world, in order that all who possess a spark of human feeling may abhor them. It has been said that the greatest horror ever invented by the most abominable tyrant was that of interring the living with the dead. But no tyrant ever thought of such a refinement of cruelty as to bury wounded enemies pell-mell with the dead. The infamous torturers of Versailles were the originators of this ferocious idea. Their perversity, cruelty, and baseness exceeded all limits. These banditti plunged into an infinity of crime— a boundless atrocity.

On the evening of May 24th, which witnessed the shedding of so much blood and the kindling of so many conflagrations by the criminal and barbarous invaders of Paris, we beheld, from the top of the Belleville heights, the most imposing, terrific, and horrible spectacle that can possibly be imagined. A long line of fire lighted up Paris as if it were broad day, the Seine separating and cutting it in two. The flames seemed to reach the clouds and lick the heavens. They were as intense and brilliant as the rays of the sun. The hearths from which they arose were more white-red, more incandescent than the hottest furnace. In comparison with them the electric light grew pale. Some, with fiercer nuclei in their midst than the rest, displayed a brilliancy beyond all description. From time to time terrific explosions were heard, while immense sheaves of flame and balls of fire and sparks rose above the rest to the heavens, piercing the clouds. They were like enormous bouquets of fireworks. Never had we beheld such terrifying sublimity. And all the time we were witnessing this imposing and fearful spectacle the Versaillist batteries poured forth bomb and shell, whose sinister flashes, curves, globes, and cylinders of fire, leaving as it were their trails on the night, we followed with the eye. Their fiery lines crossed each other high over the burning Paris. It was magical, sublime, terrible. It seemed as though, in a world of fire, we were attending a pyrotechnical exhibition, a lightning-play of invisible giants juggling with fire-balls. The conflagrations sprang up under the effect of bomb and shell as if by magic. Wherever any shells burst, they seemed to burn weakly at first, but rapidly increased in intensity, and rising like giants, illuminated the horizon. It is no exaggeration to say that they multiplied with the rapidity of lightning. It was a sight of terror to behold the spontaneous bursting of these multitudes of brilliant ovens. The fires in Paris increased in a most fearful manner. The city presented the aspect of a parterre of fire, with conflagrations instead of roses.

We were petrified and astonished, not being able to understand the incendiary madness which prompted the invaders to burn their finest quarters and the palaces which were their own appanages; and we were then far from believing that they would dare to defy all evidence, and accuse the defenders of the Commune with having fired the capital, when one had only to open his eyes in order to see the Versaillist bombs from the Trocadéro, the Arc de Triomphe de l'Etoile, the Champ de Mars, the Invalides, the Luxembourg, the bastions, Montrouge, the Palais Législatif, the great boulevards, Montparnasse, the Madeleine, the Place Wagram, Montmartre, the Northern and Western Railway Stations, and the gunboats on the Seine, pouring forth fire, in the truest sense of the word, on Paris, kindling immense conflagrations which reduced it to ashes. This any one might have seen; and he must needs be notoriously dishonest who will not acknowledge it. Undoubtedly the defenders' projectiles caused some disasters—we should be the last to deny it; but they were on a much smaller scale, because, for every shot of the National Guards, the Versaillists fired ten. But nevertheless the victors of Paris, who burnt and massacred, and covered it with fire and blood, are called saviours, and its defenders, who protected it against the excesses of the Versaillist hordes, are accused of murder and arson. Those who had the good fortune to escape the flames and the shooting are called brigands, and their incendiary executioners honest men. The victims were arraigned before murderers transformed into judges. In Paris, as in Berlin, St. Petersburg, Constantinople, Pekin, and everywhere else, might oppresses right, and the lot of its defenders is calumny and massacre.

While all these crimes and massacres were being accomplished in the interior of Paris, Forts Issy and Vanves had already fallen into the hands of the enemy; and on the 25th those of Montrouge, Bicêtre, and Ivry, and the redoubts of Hautes Bruyères and Villejuif, were taken. Most of their defenders were massacred, only a few saving themselves in the vaults.

The Barrière d'Italie, the Butte aux Cailles, the station of the Orleans Railway, the Jardin des Plantes, and the Halle aux Vins, on the left bank; the station of the Lyons Railway, Mazas, the Grenier d'Abondance, the national printing-office, the Place du Château d'Eau, Prince Eugène Barracks, and the Arts and Métiers Square, on the right bank, were occupied.

On the evening of the 25th the whole of the left bank was lost to the Commune, and the Versaillists advanced by the right bank to Bastion 33, near the Porte de la Chapelle. The Bastille, the Place du Trône, and the Villette Rotonda were in jeopardy.

Next day, the 26th, the Place de la Bastille was turned on the east, and all the avenues, boulevards, and streets abutting on it were taken possession of by the enemy. Surrounded and attacked in this way on all sides, it was soon taken. A little later the same tactics led to a similar result with the Place du Trône and that of the Villette Rotunda; and simultaneously the victorious troops advanced, by way of the fortifications, along the ramparts, as far as the Saint-Denis Canal.

CHAPTER VI.

THE LAST ACT.

THE last defenders of the Commune were shut up between the Porte de Pantin and the Ourcq Canal, on the north-east; the Saint-Martin Canal and the Boulevard Richard Lenoir, on the west; the Place du Trône and the Porte de Vincennes, on the south; and by the line of fortifications between Bastion 10, near the Porte de Vincennes, and Bastion 26, close to that of Pantin. This line of fortifications ran on the other side along a neutral zone, outside of which the Prussians were encamped. It was within this comparatively small space, which did not comprise a fifth part of Paris, that the last battle between the Versaillists and the Commune was about to be fought.

The tactics of Mac-Mahon were very simple. They consisted in turning all the positions and barricades defended by the National Guards. When the latter were thus cut off from behind, and surrounded on the right and left, they could in most cases do nothing else but abandon their positions, since, if they persisted in defending them, they would speedily be overpowered and massacred.

Had not care been taken to prevent it, the Versaillists would have turned Belleville and Ménilmontant, the last important points of defence, in a similar manner.

The Buttes Chaumont and Père Lachaise had within the last four days been converted into strong places, protected by formidable artillery; but the defences in their rear had been neglected. The rampart road between the Porte de Vincennes and that of Pantin, near the Ourcq Canal, had not been barricaded. This was an unpardonable oversight, and had it not at once been repaired, the Versaillists might have advanced right and left along the fortifications, parting at Bastion 10, near the Porte de Vincennes, and Bastion 27, adjoining the Ourcq Canal, so as to rejoin each other at the Portes de Ménilmontant and Romainville. All the fortifications and gates would then have been in their power; and the remnant of the defenders of the Commune, surrounded by an army of a hundred thousand men, between the eastern ramparts, the Saint-Martin Canal, the Boulevard Richard Lenoir, and the Avenue d'Auménil, could have done nothing but "surrender or die," as Mac-Mahon said in his report.

From the 22nd of May, Mac-Mahon's plan was clear to every intelligent person.

In order to oppose this dangerous plan we constructed and armed numerous barricades at the ramparts, and between the Portes de Vincennes and Pantin; and, in addition, barricaded all the great thoroughfares leading from the centre of Paris to the ramparts, so as to secure the rear of La Petite Villette, Ménilmontant, Belleville, and Charonne. Strong batteries on the heights opposite Bastions 19, 20, and 21, near the Portes de Ménilmontant,

Prés Saint-Gervais, and Romainville, swept the rampart road up to the Portes de Pantin and Vincennes.

At four o'clock in the morning of the 27th, from the battery on the heights between the Rue de Belleville and the Rue des Lilas, opposite Bastion 21, we observed the flashes and heard the whistling of bombs from new batteries erected during the night by the Versaillists in the metal-road in front of the cattle-market, near the Ourcq Canal and Bastions 26 and 27. The projectiles speedily reached the Rue des Lilas, in which some burst with a frightful crash, demolishing and firing the houses, the inhabitants of which hastily fled.

The fire from these batteries was a certain proof to us that the turning movement, and the attack against our positions from the rear of Ménilmontant and Belleville, had commenced. We at once took our dispositions accordingly. Our batteries in position on the heights in front of the Rue des Lilas and at the Place des Prés Saint-Gervais opened a well-sustained fire on the positions of the enemy on the banks of the Ourcq Canal and the Villette Basin. The hail of projectiles that fell on the Versaillist batteries soon silenced them, while the firing from Belleville also ceased.

At the same time that the besiegers' batteries opened fire against the positions of the Portes des Romainville and Prés Saint-Gervais, the left wing of the Ladmirault Division, commanded by General Pradié, advanced along the fortifications, and took shelter behind the railway, near the slaughter-house of La Villette. But we had foreseen this manœuvre, and no sooner had the column cleared the Ourcq Canal than a lively cannonade from the battery in the Rue des Lilas forced it to halt and turn back.

This vigorous attack and unexpected resistance caused considerable hesitation in the movements of the enemy, and induced him to modify his plan. Renouncing for the moment his turning movement along the ramparts, he decided on attacking the Buttes Chaumont in front. He commenced action against the barricades in the Rue de Flandre, the mairie of the Nineteenth Arrondissement, and the church of Saint-Jacques. In the meantime the Dumont Brigade turned the Villette Basin, cleared the Place de la Rotonde, took the barricade in the Rue d'Allemagne, and established itself in the market of the Rue de Meaux.

The Lefebvre Brigade, on the right wing, concentrated itself in the streets of the Buttes Chaumont and Terrage, cleared the canal under a hail of bullets, took the large barricade at the circus and that in the Rue des Ecluses Saint-Martin, and reached the Boulevard de la Villette by the Rues Grange aux Belles, Vicq d'Azis, and Chopinette. But only with the greatest sacrifices, the most frightful combats and massacres, was this movement, which we have thus described in a few lines, executed. It was a terrible struggle. The houses of the Boulevard de la Villette were riddled from top to bottom by ball and shell. At La Villette, as in the whole of Paris, the Versaillists bombarded the houses in a furious manner, without the least care for the immense ruination of property and destruction of innocent human life which they occasioned. They reserved to themselves the power of accusing their enemies of being the authors of all the frightful disasters of which they well knew themselves to be guilty.

In these quarters the conflict lasted three days and three nights, the 25th, 26th, and 27th of May. At the barricade in the Rue de Puebla alone sixty of the defenders were killed. The heroic martyrs well knew that they fought for the most just and most honourable of causes—the emancipation of the working classes, to which for a long time they had sacrificed their all, and for which they gloried in shedding their blood. Such were the noble and generous sentiments which inspired them, and which sufficiently explain their heroic resistance. They were no ordinary combatants, but sublime heroes, who shed their blood for a cause the most humane—the abolition of the prolétariat, pauperism, and misery.

The slaughter-houses, docks, and warehouses of La Villette on the bank of the canal, and the great saw-mill of M. Falck, were fired and totally destroyed by the Versaillist batteries erected along the canal, on the Boulevard de la Chapelle, behind the barricades of the Rue Lafayette, which the enemy had taken, on the Boulevards Ney and Macdonald, and on the goods stations of the Northern and Montmartre Railways. From all these positions the Versaillists bombarded the National Guards, who occupied the triangle between the Rue de Flandre and the Rue d'Allemagne, of which the circus of the Rotunda is the apex, and Bastions 27 and 28 the base. The slaughter-houses, docks, and custom-houses, as we said before, were reduced to ashes by the besiegers. Their loss has been estimated at twenty millions of francs. Two months afterwards, when the rubbish was cleared out, they were still smoking.

On the 27th, at six in the morning, the Dumont and Abbatucci Brigades advanced to the foot of the heights, where they drew up in a semicircle. The attack was sounded, and the assault began. The heights and surrounding positions were taken by storm, and the ferocious victors rendered themselves guilty of the most cruel executions, massacring the soldiers of the Commune to the very last man. The park was strewn with dead bodies. The spectacle was so horrible that the inhabitants vowed they would one day be avenged on these soldier-assassins. They were obliged to burn the bodies of the massacred National Guards in great numbers, in order to prevent infection by their putrefying. After the work of carnage the assassins transformed themselves into buccaneers. Strong railings were fitted up at regular distances on the green lawns amidst beds of roses, fires of coke and pit-coal lighted, and their victims calcined. They took the precaution of carefully closing the park gates, in order that there might be no spectators of their infernal work. They did not dare to confront the public gaze, and hoped to obliterate every trace of their crime; but the odour of burning flesh and the dense smoke arising on all sides to the heights betrayed the calciners of human flesh, who reduced the remains of their victims to ashes. From Sunday to Monday night, with the assistance of petroleum, more than a thousand corpses were burnt. *La Liberté* advised the pulverising of the dead bodies of the defenders of Paris with quicklime, so as to prevent future revolutionists from rendering honour to their bones. These miserable men imagined they could stifle the noble feeling of veneration for the dead. What infamous wretches! But let us leave the remains of the martyrs in the hands of these infernal executioners, and resume the narrative of the battle.

In arresting the turning movement of General Ladmirault's left along the rampart road, it was impossible to save the heights, they being open in front and flank, and opposed to vastly superior forces; but at all events the effort of the enemy to advance along the fortifications to the Porte de Romainville, so as to join the reserve under Vinoy, the object of which was to enclose the remnant of the Commune within a circle of iron and fire, had been paralysed. Had the armies of Ladmirault and Vinoy been able to unite at the heights of Belleville, they would have marched from the west on the positions of the defenders of the Commune, forced them back, and beaten them up like game against the corps of Douay and Clinchant, which were firmly established on the banks of the Saint-Martin Canal and the Boulevard Richard Lenoir, so as to take them between two fires and exterminate them to the last man. The Roquette Prison, the Place Voltaire, and the mairie of the Eleventh Arrondissement, the last points of defence, would then have been lost.

After having partially defeated the plan against the Buttes Chaumont, efforts were made to prevent the execution of a similar design against the cemetery of Père Lachaise. Unfortunately there was no battery on that side high enough to command the rampart roads from Bastion 10 to Bastion 18. It was only defended by a row of barricades, which could be successively taken, and thus a passage opened up for the enemy. It would even suffice to take the one nearest the Porte de Vincennes for all the rest to be doomed.

The Lamariouse Brigade was arrested in its march along the fortifications by a vigorous fire from the barricade at the Porte de Montreuil. The reserve corps under General Derroja was stationed at the Cours de Vincennes, while the Bernard de Seigneurens Brigade advanced through the Rue de Puebla, and, after a terrible struggle, took numerous barricades.

A battalion of the 1st regiment of marines, supported by two battalions and a regiment of the Faron Division, attacked the cemetery of Père Lachaise, which, from the 24th of May, had been fortified and defended by two batteries. One, consisting of six guns and a mitrailleuse, on the platform of the cemetery chapel, commanded the Rue de la Roquette and the entire side of the Bastille; the other, of two 24-pounders, on the elevated position of the small esplanade in front of the Morny Chapel, was intended to reply to the cannons of Montmartre. The Versaillist troops were received with a lively fire, and encountered an energetic resistance.

The enemy commenced the assault from the large terraces commanding the exterior boulevards. The defenders, sheltered by the tomb-stones, drove them back until reinforcements of artillery arrived from the Bastille. The newly-erected batteries bombarded and smashed the large gate of the cemetery. Behind the gate an enormous barricade, protected by twelve-pounders, was taken before its defenders, who were unaccustomed to handle cannon, had time to fire. The besiegers advanced through the breach, while other columns climbed the steep declivity on the north and Charonne sides. The terrible battle at this asylum of the dead lasted half an hour. The besieged, forced back on all sides, retreated skirmishing, sheltering themselves behind the tomb-stones; but the troops, advancing through the avenues, soon reached the high grounds of the cemetery, where, at the foot of the Demidoff monument, the most dangerous batteries had been erected. It was not until after a most desperate fight, the massacre of the gunners at their pieces, and the shooting down of the National Guards, that the cemetery was taken. More than six thousand dead bodies strewed the avenues and tombs. Many were murdered in the graves where they had sought shelter, and dyed the coffins with their blood. The massacre was frightful.

About the same time the mairie of the Twentieth Arrondissement fell into the hands of General Lamariouse. The Douay Corps, and those of Generals Faron and Clinchant, erected batteries to enfilade the principal outlets by which they feared the National Guards might break through their line of battle, and cannonaded the Place Voltaire, the mairie of the Eleventh Arrondissement, and the church of Saint-Ambroise.

Thus, on May 27th, the Buttes Chaumont, Père Lachaise, the mairie of Belleville, and the Boulevard Puebla fell into the hands of the enemy, with a vast quantity of *matériel* and several thousand prisoners, after a most horrible massacre, which lasted till the following day.

After the loss of these three important positions no hope remained. It was, in fact, impossible to continue the resistance much longer, after the loss of the three principal strategical points, the Buttes Chaumont, Père Lachaise, and the Boulevard Puebla. The left wing of the enemy's First Army Corps advanced on Bastion 22, which was defended by an enormous barricade armed with cannon, and protected by another battery on the height opposite Bastion 21. The right wing of Vinoy's reserve corps, commanded by General Lamariouse, took some barricades on the rampart road between the Portes de Vincennes and Bagnolet, which had been abandoned by their defenders after the loss of the cemetery of Père Lachaise, who feared they would be cut off and massacred. Soon afterwards the Porte de Bagnolet was taken.

In the evening of May 27th the defenders were enclosed within the space of a few hundred mètres in width, and the distance from Bastion 15 to 21 in length, forming a segment of a circle. Supported by the fortifications, they were protected on the right by a strong barricade at Bastion 21, and by the Place des Fêtes, which was very strongly barricaded and heroically defended; on the left by the barricades of the Place des Trois Communes, the Rue des Tourelles, and the Porte Ménilmontant. On the east the line of barricades extended to the Rues des Prés Saint-Gervais, Calais, and Bois. They were shut up within a triangle, the periphery of which was half a kilomètre, and in this confined space the battle lasted twenty-four hours.

The last defenders of the Commune expected the fall of their barricades every instant, and with them the loss of their only remaining position. They lost all hope of seeing the following day. A magnificent light illumined the night, and rose with the brilliant splendour of an aurora borealis in north and south. Never had we beheld so intense a light. Rays and floods of sparks rose high over the Villette Basin. Intermingled with the curving and whistling of the projectiles falling and bursting near us, we heard tremendous explosions from the docks and custom-houses of La Villette, set on fire by Clinchant's batteries, and blazing in a grand and sinister manner.

To the south-west another hearth of fire illuminated the banks of the Seine. An enormous column of flame and smoke, shining with phosphorescent brightness, shot up to the clouds. It seemed as though immense tongues of fire were licking the heavens. We have since been told that this extraordinary flame was caused by the burning of the dead bodies of the unfortunate defenders of Paris, which had been accumulated on the Champ de Mars, and burnt with petroleum by the ferocious Versaillists. Possibly such was the case; for we should not be at all astonished to find that those who have so falsely accused the Commune of having set Paris on fire with petroleum were the first to use this mighty weapon of destruction, not only for the burning of the corpses of their enemies, but also for incendiary purposes, in the form of petroleum bombs, as was proved by Assi and his advocate at the third court-martial of Versailles.

A little more to the south, on the right bank of the Seine, another fire lighted up the heavens. It was the Grenier d'Abondance, the damage to which amounted to ten or fifteen millions of francs, and which had been set on fire by the batteries of the Faron Division and the gunboats, which likewise riddled with shell and bomb the Boulevard Bourdon, the Quai de la Rapée, and the neighbourhood of the Bastille.

The fires multiplied in many other parts of the capital; and what was incomprehensible and inexplicable to us was the uselessness of bombardment in the midst of such disasters.

During all these calamities, and while Paris was in flames, unheard-of scenes of carnage were being enacted at the cemetery of Père Lachaise, the Buttes Chaumont, the Boulevard Puebla, and the mairie and streets of Belleville. Terrible fusillades, frightful platoon fires, intermingled with the crackling noise of mitrailleuses, plainly told of the wholesale massacre of our unfortunate companions who had been taken prisoners. On hearing these dreadful sounds we were filled with indignation, and broken-hearted. We redoubled our activity and vigilance in order that our position might not be turned, and so the last defenders of the Commune fall into the hands of those brigands who would have ruthlessly murdered all of them.

The daylight, which we no longer hoped to see again, came at last. The dawn witnessed a more intense battle. Newly-erected batteries poured forth a surging sea of lead and fire, the fusillade approaching nearer and nearer, with a din of iron and the roar of a metallic wave, crushing everything in its passage of destruction. The billows of rattling grape made one shiver. We waited anxiously for the *dénoucment* of this horrible struggle. Our cannons, which had been silent during the night in order to conceal our positions, now replied vigorously, and retarded the progress of the surging sea which was advancing and encircling us closer and closer with fire and iron. Relatively speaking, however, we lost little ground and but few men.

The Langourian Brigade advanced to the Avenue Philippe-Auguste, and at five in the morning took Roquette Prison. Here a fearful massacre was enacted, not one of its defenders being spared. A friend of ours, who saw this theatre of carnage a few days afterwards, told us that it was impossible to imagine a more horrible sight.

The same brigade then descended the Rue de la Roquette, and attacked the Place Voltaire, which Vinoy at the same time also bombarded from the Places du Trône and Bastille. Citizen Delescluze then repaired to the third barricade, which stood the shock of the 2nd provisional regiment of tirailleurs, and, in conjunction with Colonel Brunet, attempted to prevent the abandonment of this important position. At the expiration of about twenty minutes Colonel Brunet declared that it was impossible to hold it any longer. The Delegate of War protested against this, and ordered the continuance of the struggle; but the fire became so murderous that it was abandoned, notwithstanding this order. Brunet tried several times to draw citizen Delescluze away; but he resisted, and remained alone behind this heap of paving-stones, which shook beneath the bullets and shells. The Delegate of War fell, struck by two bullets from the foremost soldiers. Wounded in the right temple, he was killed as if by a thunder-stroke.

The houses near this barricade were levelled to the ground by bombs. The old Republican sank beneath a burning beam, and the skin of his forehead was almost entirely burnt off. His body was found among those of eighteen other defenders of the barricade, being recognised by the card of the Commune. In his pocket was found a letter addressed to his colleague Vésinier, asking for reinforcements. He still possessed his gold watch, but no money; and his gold-headed walking-stick was picked up near him. He was attired, as invariably, in civilian clothes, consisting of the everlasting brown great-coat with deep pockets, black trousers, cravat of the same colour, and a black silk hat. Citizen Delescluze detested the military uniform; and he was the only man among his brilliant, much-gilded, and belaced general staff who wore neither insignia nor decoration of any sort. For the last few days he had been continually armed with a revolver, which he always held in his hand while walking with his usual gait straight on, under the hail of shell and bomb, without moving a muscle or ever looking back. He was a man of great courage and coolness, having for a long period sacrificed his all to the Republican cause, in which he fell a martyr. Delescluze died as he had lived, simple, honest, and heroic. He was a man of the antique mould, stoical, disinterested, and incorruptible. Like another Cato, he did not wish to survive the Republic. He would not and could not become the victim or plaything of the victorious reaction: after so many defeats he " could not bear another," as he wrote in a touching letter to his much-beloved sister.

The last head-quarters of the defenders of the Commune, the mairie of the Eleventh Arrondissement, fell into the power of the soldiers of Versailles. All the National Guards who were taken prisoners by these infuriated madmen were killed. In one room on the ground-floor lay seventy-five dreadfully mutilated corpses. Those who have seen towns taken by storm, and know from experience the horrors of war, could never imagine a more disorderly, frightful, and sanguinary spectacle than that presented by the municipality of the Eleventh Arrondissement. The mixture of blood, dirt, weapons, fragments of uniforms, and corpses was a sight loathsome to behold, and made one shudder. It seemed as though a herd of jaguars, tigers, hyænas, or jackals had passed by, and glutted their thirst for blood and carnage. On looking at this charnel-house it was difficult to believe that men, fellow-citizens, could be guilty of such atrocious, unheard-of deeds; and yet such was the work of the Versaillist murderers.

In all Paris nothing remained but the small corner between the Portes de Bagnolet and Prés Saint-Gervais. A few thousand National Guards and some cannons still defended this weak position at the ramparts, on which now alone floated the red flag of the Commune.

The Derroja Brigade advanced by the Boulevard de Charonne towards Père Lachaise, which since the day before had been in the possession of the enemy, and took the barricades in the Rues des Amandiers, Tlemsen, Cendrier, and Ménilmontant. At the same moment another column attacked the market-place, which was bristling with barricades, and defended with great courage. After a desperate and murderous conflict it was taken. The space occupied by the Commune now became still more contracted, and Bastions 18, 19, 20, and 21 alone remained in its possession.

On the right General Grenier advanced from the Porte des Prés Saint-Gervais, and took the great barricade at the rampart road near Bastion 22 and the Rue des Mignottes. The Place des Fêtes, solidly barricaded and armed with two well-served cannons, commanding the Rues de Crimée, Solitaires, and Compans, opposed a most vigorous resistance, and for a long time arrested the onward march of the enemy; but the barricades were at length taken, as well as those at the angle of the Rues des Bois and Prés Saint-Gervais.

On the left the Lamariouse Brigade advanced, by the Boulevard Mortier, against the Porte de Romainville, and took the barricades of the Porte de Ménilmontant and the Rue Saint-Fargeau.

In the centre the Faron and Derroja Divisions advanced by the Rues des Prés Saint-Gervais, Romainville, Négro, Paris-Belleville, and Borrégo, and, after a lively engagement, the barricades at the junction of the four last-named streets, with that of the Rue Haxo, were taken. A great number of the defenders were killed, and two thousand taken prisoners. Once master of the Rue Haxo, the enemy advanced like an irresistible sea of fire.

On the left the barricades at the Place des Trois Communes, and on the right those at the angle of the Rues des Bois and Haxo and the Boulevard Serrurier, were now the only ones which still held out; but they, in their turn, were speedily attacked. They were defended by fifteen hundred men, the last remnant of the National Guards. But longer resistance against the sixty thousand men who took part in the attack on Belleville was impossible. If taken, they would have been shot to the very last man: the Versaillists gave no quarter. Only one way of saving themselves from certain death remained—to clear the fortifications and seek refuge in the neutral zone. This was at once decided upon and executed. The drawbridge at Romainville was lowered, the flags floating on Bastions 19 and 20 taken down, and the last defenders of the Commune marched across the rampart ditch. Unwilling to give up their arms either to the Versaillists or the Prussians, they broke them in pieces, and buried them in the ditch as they passed over it.

On arriving without arms in the village of Romainville, they found themselves in front of the Prussian outposts, who prevented their passage.

Two Freemasons in full insignia advanced, and made us a sign to follow, saying that we, in common with a few friends, might be saved. We, in fact, were conducted to a house in the neighbourhood, where we met with a hospitable reception. A number of National Guards gave themselves up as prisoners to the Prussians, and were conducted to Fort Noisi le Sec; others in private clothes, or only disguised with blouses, remained with the inhabitants or gained the open country; while many took their way along the neutral zone to Vincennes.

No sooner had the National Guards passed through the Porte de Romainville than the Versaillists took the barricades at Bastions 19 and 20, and, without the slightest respect to the neutral territory, fired on the last defenders of the Commune. Their bullets fell in great numbers in the streets of Romainville and in the Prussian lines. The Prussian soldiers left their barricades, and advanced in quick march towards the fortifications of Paris in order to stop the firing, and to prevent the violation of the neutral territory. This was an extremely favourable movement for us and our comrades of the National Guard; for the Prussian lines advanced so far that we found ourselves in their rear, and were enabled to escape across the country.

We still heard some artillery and musketry fire. This was undoubtedly caused by the shooting of the unfortunate prisoners by the Versailles banditti. The noise grew fainter and fainter as we got further away. The struggle soon came to an end. The last defenders of the Commune were either killed, prisoners, or in flight. In depopulated Paris, *order*, massacre, arrests *en masse*, and the wildest and most sanguinary terror reigned supreme. Property, religion, and society were once more saved. With the assistance of an army of vagabonds and brigands enlisted from the most corrupt, vile, base, and cruel elements of France—the sbirri, the convicts, gendarmes, and sergents de ville, and the traitors of Metz, Sedan, and the National Defence—the bourgeoisie had again conquered the prolétariat. The socialist-republican workmen were exterminated or imprisoned *en masse*, pending their transportation to New Caledonia, condemnation to death, or hard labour. Old men, women, and children shared the same fate of sanguinary destruction and general extermination. The victorious bourgeoisie showed neither pity nor mercy. It had sworn to annihilate the revolutionary and socialist prolétariat for ever—to drown it in its own blood. Never had a better occasion presented itself; and it profited by it with ferocious joy. To destroy its enemies was its highest enjoyment. Within six days forty thousand men were massacred, and as many more imprisoned; and even yet its abominable crimes have not come to an end. The Communists, and all suspected of being partisans, were ferreted out and pursued with jealous ferocity, and without the least distinction as to age or sex. Ten thousand women and children were killed, and about the same number imprisoned. Paris is depopulated, commerce and industry annihilated; but that matters little to it, so long as its so-called order is re-established, and provided it reigns and governs, be it over corpses and a lifeless, down-trodden population.

It is contented, happy, and proud. It can now respire and digest freely; and it rejoices at the standstill of progress, fondly imagining it has stifled all reform; secured the reign of misery, pauperism, and ignorance; and perpetuated its domination and the exploitation of the prolétariat. It takes for granted that it has for ever chained the unfortunate working classes to its system of compulsory labour, without profit and without hope.

Yes, the bourgeoisie is implacable in all its reactionary work, and oppresses without limit, mercy, or pity. It will proceed on its path of crime to the end; it will load itself with shame and infamy. It is destitute of decency and heart, deaf and blind, cowardly, cynical, and infamous. The French bourgeoisie is in a fair way of dishonouring itself completely and for ever in the eyes of the whole world—of proving its weakness and its incapacity. We congratulate it on this course. Our epoch was in need of so shameful a spectacle to become disgusted with everybody and everything, and to surround itself with misery, corruption, degradation, and decay.

The bourgeoisie, glorying in its apogee, is approaching its decline and its fall. Its decomposition has already begun, and the prolétariat is near its complete emancipation. The blood of forty thousand martyrs which has been shed, and that which is yet to be spilt—the tears of forty thousand other victims in prison, and of their children and parents suffering in misery—will fertilise the principles of right and justice sown eighty years ago, and to make which germinate was the mission of the Commune.

The prophetic words uttered by citizen Delescluze only a few days before his death will be verified: " Out of each drop of its blood, and of that of all the massacred defenders of the Commune, will six avengers one day arise to establish the reign of justice and right, the triumph of which was only prevented to-day by the want of education."

The prolétariat will be abolished, in the same way as slavery and serfdom have been.

There is no power in this world capable of arresting the onward march of progress. The principles of justice are indestructible, and the persecutions and blood of their defenders will make them germinate and fructify.

The Commune will rise again from the ashes of its martyrs burnt by the executioner-incendiaries of Versailles. The wind has already borne them to the four corners of the heavens, to sow the fields of Revolution, whose final triumph is certain.

THE END.

www.ingramcontent.com/pod-product-compliance
Lightning Source LLC
Chambersburg PA
CBHW030307240426
43673CB00040B/1092